Known for her honesty, integrity and leading authority in the field of dysfluency Stewart, together with highly respected collaborators, weaves this collage of exciting topics into a collection of valuable chapters. The passion, dedication and expertise of each author is reflected in every chapter.

In clear and practical language, the book provides an insight into new approaches *and* offers inspiration and reflection whether you are a student, a clinician or a fluency specialist looking for interesting approaches to spark new ideas. This book is on my bookshelf and should be required reading for anyone interested in fluency disorders. What a wonderful supplementary text to the Dysfluency Resource Book. It is truly a wonderful piece of art!

Dr. Joseph Agius, European Fluency Specialist, University of Malta/ ECSF, author of iOS app 'Fluency Smart Intervention Strategy'

This book covers hot topics that all speech-language therapists need to understand if they want to make a difference in the lives of people who stammer. It contains expert advice written by world-renowned clinicians who provide critical insights about both basic clinical procedures and advanced helping skills for working with people who stammer. With chapters on key aspects of service delivery, counseling methods, and the clinical process, readers will learn new ways of improving their therapy with people who stammer and gain deep insights into the experience of stammering. They will also learn about key skills, such as mindfulness approaches, that can help them in their own lives, as well!

Chapters are clearly written and easily accessible for novice and advanced therapists.

This book should become an indispensable companion for speech-language therapists seeking to help people who stammer.

J. Scott Yaruss, Professor of Communicative Sciences and Disorders at Michigan State University, Fellow of the American Speech-Language-Hearing Association (ASHA)

Stammering Resources for Adults and Teenagers

This comprehensive and practical resource is a second volume to the highly influential *Dysfluency Resource Book* (2010). It brings together the very latest developments in the field of stammering and dysfluency in adults and teenagers and builds upon some of the approaches explored in the *Dysfluency Resource Book*. The book draws on the expert knowledge of contributors from a wide range of fields, such as specialist speech and language therapy, education, psychology and youth work, with a focus on presenting practical guidance for those working in this complex area.

This valuable resource:

- Has chapters exploring the latest clinical developments, such as acceptance and commitment therapy (ACT) and narrative therapy.
- Provides in-depth discussion of some established therapeutic practices, including avoidance-reduction therapy and group work.
- Offers concrete application to theory, both the social and medical models, guiding the reader on how to integrate new evidence into clinical practice.
- Provides a wealth of activities and photocopiable handouts that can be used in practice.

Designed for clinicians and students working with teenagers and adults who stammer, this flexible and practical book embeds an ethos of reflection and adaptation. The detailed overview of therapeutic approaches allows the reader to explore a wide range of techniques, building a strong foundation of knowledge from which to tailor and develop their own practice.

Trudy Stewart is a retired consultant speech and language therapist. She studied in universities in Glasgow, Michigan State (USA) and Leeds. She worked in the UK with children and adults who stammer for nearly 40 years. Her last role was clinical lead of the Stammering Support Centre in Leeds. Trudy has taught undergraduate, graduate and specialist courses for clinicians in the UK, Europe and Sri Lanka, including on the European Clinical Specialisation in Fluency Disorders (ECSF) course. She has carried out research while a clinician, presented her work at international conferences and has written several texts on stammering. Her last book, published in 2016, is *Stammering: A Resource Book for Teachers*.

Stammering Resources for Adults and Teenagers

Integrating New Evidence into Clinical Practice

Edited by
TRUDY STEWART

Routledge
Taylor & Francis Group

LONDON AND NEW YORK

First published 2021
by Routledge
2 Park Square, Milton Park, Abingdon, Oxon OX14 4RN

and by Routledge
52 Vanderbilt Avenue, New York, NY 10017

Routledge is an imprint of the Taylor & Francis Group, an informa business

British Library Cataloguing-in-Publication Data
A catalogue record for this book is available from the British Library

Library of Congress Cataloging-in-Publication Data
Names: Stewart, Trudy, editor, contributor.
Title: Stammering resources for adults and teenagers : integrating new evidence into clinical
   practice / [edited by] Trudy Stewart.
Description: Abingdon, Oxon ; New York, NY : Routledge, 2020. | Includes bibliographical
   references and index.
Identifiers: LCCN 2020010008 (print) | LCCN 2020010009 (ebook) | ISBN 9780367505066
   (hardback) | ISBN 9780367208684 (paperback) | ISBN 9780429263835 (ebook)
Subjects: LCSH: Stuttering—Treatment. | Stuttering in adolescence—Treatment.
Classification: LCC RC424 .S689 2020 (print) | LCC RC424 (ebook) | DDC 616.85/54—dc23
LC record available at https://lccn.loc.gov/2020010008
LC ebook record available at https://lccn.loc.gov/2020010009

ISBN: 978-0-367-50506-6 (hbk)
ISBN: 978-0-367-20868-4 (pbk)
ISBN: 978-0-429-26383-5 (ebk)

Typeset in Frutiger
by Apex CoVantage, LLC

For my sons, Callum and Alastair from whom I have learned much about communication, life and love.

Contents

Figures, Tables and Resources

Acknowledgements

My thanks to my colleagues in the SLT and the academic worlds who offered advice and pointed me to several useful texts, in particular, Sue Clark, Monica Bray and Joseph Agius, and those who reviewed the initial proposal and gave good critical feedback to myself and the publisher: Jo Holmes, Ruth Edwards, Ben Bolton, Kurt Eggers and others.

I would also like to mention those who have reviewed the finished drafts of various chapters and the book as a whole: Ellen-Marie Silverman, Scott Yaruss, Kurt Eggers, Joseph Agius and Clare Bull. All very busy individuals, but each of them found time and energy to read and respond to my request for a review, for which I am very grateful.

In relation to the inclusion of the social model, I must mention Katy Bailey, with whom I had several interesting and lively discussions. Although not featured in the book, her influence is there nonetheless. Also in this regard, my thanks to Sam Simpson and Patrick Campbell, whose workshop at a CEN meeting gave me further food for thought.

My thanks also go to those who have guided my editing process, especially Katrina Hulme-Cross, the senior editor at Routledge, whose calming emails kept me on track.

Finally, my love and thanks to Mark, who has been a source of encouragement and sounding board throughout the whole writing and editing process. His patience and listening ear have enabled this book to reach its conclusion.

Foreword

Known for her honesty, integrity and leading authority in the field of dysfluency, Trudy Stewart never fails to reach for the stars. She dips her brush and, together with highly respected collaborators, weaves this collage of exciting topics into a collection of valuable chapters. The passion, dedication and expertise of each author is reflected in every chapter.

In clear and practical language, the book provides an insight into new approaches such as mindfulness, narrative therapy and acceptance and commitment therapy (ACT). The link between voice and stammering is eloquently described, and I particularly enjoyed Chapter 1 'the art and practice of being a clinician with individuals who stammer'. It is a must for all students and professionals because it highlights the right skills and attitude needed to develop what is considered this most essential 'therapeutic alliance'. It is truly a wonderful piece of art!

For sure, this book offers inspiration and reflection whether you are a student, a clinician or a fluency specialist looking for interesting approaches to spark new ideas. This book is on my bookshelf and should be required reading for anyone interested in fluency disorders. What a wonderful supplementary text to the *Dysfluency Resource Book* (Turnbull and Stewart 2010).

Dr. Joseph Agius,
European Fluency Specialist University of Malta/ECSF
Author of iOS app Fluency Smart Intervention Strategy

Introduction

This book was the result of conversations with the publishers of the *Dysfluency Resource Book* (DRB) (Turnbull and Stewart 2010), who asked me to consider another edition. I was not minded to revise the DRB, as I know many therapists find it useful in its current format, and it continues to be a recommended text for undergraduate students and postgraduate students in the UK and Europe (i.e. ECSF course).

However, I was aware that there were topics which had not been included in the first DRB, such as the links between voice and stammering. In addition, as time has moved on, there are new areas, such as mindfulness, narrative therapy (NT) and acceptance and commitment therapy (ACT), which could have appeared in another edition of the DRB had there been one!

Consequently, I decided to collaborate with specialist clinicians, academics and others in producing this book, which acts as a supplementary text to the DRB; written for speech and language therapists, student therapists and advanced practitioners (i.e. graduates of the ECSF advanced practitioner course) working in the field of dysfluency. It may also prove useful to other professionals wishing to know more about the management of fluency disorders and to some individuals who stammer.

Aims

The aims of this book are to:

- Update professionals working with clients who stammer on current management approaches
- Provide accessible resources for these management approaches for clinicians
- Stimulate reflection and discussion within the SLT (speech and language therapy) community on these different ways of working and their theoretical underpinning.

Style

As an editor I was keen to reflect some key aspects of stammering in the style of the text. Firstly that each person who stammers (PWS) is an individual in his own right. As clinicians meeting a client for the first time it is important that we set aside any assumptions that we may have about stammering, its effect, limitations, implications and so on and just see the person as he is. For that reason I have asked authors to use the singular when referring to the client.

(This has had its challenges, especially for the chapters which described groups, and I want to thank those authors in particular for bearing with me on this point.) The use of 'he', referring to a person who stammers (PWS) across all chapters, reflects the fact that the majority of people who stammer are male. However, with regard to the use of the female pronoun to refer to a speech and language therapist (SLT), I apologise to all male speech and language therapists who will read this book and perhaps be annoyed or feel excluded by the use of this pronoun and the presumption that all therapists are female. I know several male therapists specialising in dysfluency but for the sake of brevity, to avoid the repetition of he/she every time an SLT was referred to, I have opted for the female pronoun.

Authors

The chapters are written by a number of authors, all of whom have proven experience in their area.

- **Alison McLaughlin** is currently Clinical Lead in Voice (East Lancashire Hospitals Trust), an Advanced Practitioner (ECSF), has lectured on dysfluency at The University of Manchester and was Clinical Lead at the Stammering Support Centre, Leeds. During her work in the Centre we had several occasions to discuss the often grey area between difficulties with voice production and stammering which appeared to be initiated at the level of the larynx. In her chapter for this text, she addresses this overlap of issues and helps clinicians work through this difficult area. With her experience of voice applied to stammering, she has been able to share some useful resources for PWS to establish and maintain healthy vocal production.

- The work of the City Lit, an adult education college in London which has become a centre of excellence in adult stammering therapy, is well represented in this book. The SLT department has been offering group therapy for the past 50 years. Over time, different therapeutic approaches have been trialled, evaluated and modified, reflecting and influencing practice worldwide. In the past approaches primarily focused on fluency have at some stage been part of the course offer, and stammering modification (i.e. stammering management/ modification or block modification) have always been on offer alongside other approaches. A few years ago the decision was made to only offer stammering modification, as it aligned most closely with the team's philosophy around stammering. Three authors – **Rachel Everard, Carolyn Cheasman** and **Cathinka Guldberg –** work/have worked at the centre.

- **Rachel** has collaborated with **Cathinka** on a chapter on groups which again extends the more general chapter in DRB by outlining two interesting groups; the City Lit intensive programme and public speaking. This chapter treats what can be quite a complex issue in a way which should enable therapists to feel that it is an option which is appropriate for their clinics.

- **Carolyn's** chapter on mindfulness provides a gentle and thoughtful introduction to the topic and will be especially useful for clinicians thinking about the relevance of this approach for their clients.

- **Rachel** and **Carolyn's** chapter on acceptance and commitment therapy will provide clinicians with an understanding of the approach and an accessible range of ideas to enable them to add ACT to their tools of management of dysfluency.

- **Fiona Ryan** and **Mary O'Dwyer** are also specialist SLTs and ECSF graduates. Together they provide a programme for adults who stammer that has narrative therapy (NT) at its core. They are known for their teaching and research on narrative therapy with PWS. This work stretches over a number of years and has grown in depth and understanding. Their chapter uses client stories to illustrate the process of NT. I was pleased to have them included in this text, as I think NT has much to offer the field of dysfluency.

• **Jonathon Linklater** is a specialist clinician and person who stammers (PWS) working in Ireland. He has extensive experience working with individuals and groups of people who stammer, alongside self-help organisations and not-for-profit agencies. He comes from a background steeped in the Sheehan approaches to stammering, having been to Joseph Sheehan's clinic and met with and seen the work of Vivian Sheehan, Joseph's wife. He has contributed two chapters to the book, one which draws on his experience with the Sheehan clinic and extends the introductory chapter in DRB on avoidance-reduction therapy and the second on service delivery. This commentary on service delivery for PWS provides an overview of the accepted ways of offering therapy but also introduces therapists to some alternative 'distance' learning approaches which may be new to many readers. His review of digital resources is particularly interesting.

• **Hilary Liddle**, a specialist SLT who has worked in Doncaster, at the Stammering Support Centre in Leeds and now works at the Willy Russell centre, Liverpool, has joined forces with **Bob Adams**, a performance coach and a PWS with a reputation for a lively and entertaining approach to self-advocacy for stammering. Bob has facilitated the self-help group for PWS in Doncaster for many years. Their collaboration provides readers with an interesting perspective on the interface between an SLT and a self-help group. There are useful sections on how an SLT can contribute to the setting up of a self-help group, including mentoring a PWS to adopt a leadership role, and maintaining and ending a group.

• **Margaret Leahy** has extensive experience in the area of dysfluency studies, having worked as a lecturer, researcher and clinician at Trinity College, Dublin for many years. She recently retired but continues to contribute to the ECSF. I (**Trudy Stewart**) have written a chapter with Margaret on the clinician who works with PWS. Over the years we have collaborated on many projects, including teaching advanced courses on personal construct psychology and writing research articles. In this chapter we discuss the preferred characteristics of a therapist who works with a PWS, starting from generalist education to guidelines which are more specific to the area of dysfluency. The chapter also considers the clinician's personal traits, the therapeutic relationship and ways of being in this work.

All the chapters have gone through multiple drafts which have reflected the careful, detailed approach the authors have taken to the writing process. My sincere thanks goes to each and every one of them.

Theoretical basis

One aspect that I feel I must mention here relates to the theoretical basis for the text. The social model of disability is a topic which is currently being discussed by many individual SLTs and interest groups and has been referred to by authors of most of the chapters here. The social model, as defined by Oliver (1990) and drawing on the previous work of Hunt (1966), has relevance for the stammering community (Oliver 1993). The model argues that impairments (i.e. temporary or permanent loss or difference in the anatomy, physiology, psychology of a person) may not be disabling. Impairments do not have to automatically lead to a reduction in experience of an individual. Rather the degree of impairment or disablement is dependent on society not taking into account a person's difference, whatever that may be.

For a PWS, the degree of impairment will depend upon the attitudes to and stereotyping of dysfluent speech:

• Held by the society in which he operates,

• Carried and reproduced by his communication partner(s) and

• The extent of his own internalised stigmas associated with stammering.

While individual authors will describe the application of this model to their own topic area, for me it raises important questions about the clinical options open to a client who stammers. On one hand there are fluency-enhancing techniques: those which promote the use of strategies by a PWS to enable them to experience a type of controlled fluency while they are in use but which have no effect on the person's spontaneous speech production. The use of such techniques could be seen as compromising an individual's natural speech pattern and playing a subservient role to society's perceived perception of acceptable levels of fluency. On the other hand, there are strategies which have come to be known as 'stammer more fluently' approaches. These approaches advocate open stammering with some modification to reduce or minimise effort and/or struggle. The use of this therapy may create dissonance for some clients. For example, a person who has developed a covert stammer, characterised by avoidance of open stammering, can achieve self-acceptance and openness. However, while he is accepting of his stammer and openly stammers in day-to-day life, he is likely to encounter a lack of tolerance and acceptance in those to whom he is speaking (St Louis 2015). Consequently the PWS continues to experience the negative attitudes and reactions to his dysfluency that were the original triggers to the development of this more covert type of stammer. For this therapeutic approach to be effective in the longer term, there is a need for both the PWS and those interacting with him to have a corresponding level of acceptance and tolerance of dysfluency. This dilemma challenges the stammering community and the speech and language profession to work together to address negative attitudes and discrimination in society (Stewart 1995).

I hope as you read the various chapters and the different approaches that they espouse, you will consider the social model and the role you might play in promoting a world that is accepting of stammering, in all its individual forms.

References

Hunt, P. (1966). *Stigma: The Experience of Disability*. London: Geoffrey Chapman.

Oliver, M. (1990). *The Politics of Disablement*. London: Macmillan Publishers Limited.

Oliver, M. (1993). Disability and dependency: A creation of industrial societies? In J. Swain, V. Finkelstein, S. French and M. Oliver (eds.), *Disabling Barriers – Enabling Environments* (pp. 49–60). London: Sage.

Stewart, T. (1995). Efficacy of speech and language therapy for fluency disorders: Adults who stammer. *International Journal of Language & Communication Disorders*, 30(S1), 478–483. https://doi.org/10.1111/j.1460-6984.1995.tb01737.x

St. Louis, K.O. (2015). *Stuttering Meets Stereotype, Stigma, and Discrimination: An Overview of Attitude Research*. Morgantown, WV: West Virginia University Press.

Turnbull, J. and Stewart, T. (2010). *The Dysfluency Resource Book* (2nd Edition). London: Routledge.

1 | The art and practice of being a clinician working with individuals who stammer

Trudy Stewart and Margaret Leahy

Introduction: consideration of the clinician choosing to work in dysfluency

We have met and collaborated with many clinicians across several decades. This experience has led to questions regarding the nature of the therapist who finds herself or chooses to work with dysfluent clients. Is there a particular "type" of clinician or an adopted style that works better within the fluency specialism and with individual PWS?

In this chapter the development of clinical skills will be explored, with particular emphasis on interpersonal behaviours. Various professional guidelines will be examined for indicative characteristics considered to be important. The remainder of the chapter is concerned with defining and describing specific attributes and ways of interacting, the nature of the therapeutic relationship and intrapersonal behaviour.

Developing skills

Moving towards graduation: There are many stages along the way to becoming a therapist: some have signposts, written in a language one can read, while others arise in a person's thinking, generated by a sense of altruism, of wanting to make a contribution, and there are those that appear more opportunistically, like a door that opens, inviting entry.

The phases with signposts include undergraduate and post-graduate experiences. The journey towards graduation as a therapist encompasses a growing awareness of an individual's personal attributes, therapeutic interests and qualities.

The development of a clinician-scientist's knowledge, skills and attitudes generally follow a hierarchy, with overlap across the stages:

a   Student clinician as a listener–observer

At this stage, learning to listen is of central importance, with its accompanying responsibility of interpretation, an investigative, questioning approach which is attuned to a client's information.

b   Student clinician as assessor and diagnostician

Here the listener–observer becomes adept in assessment, evaluation and the processes involved in diagnostics: data collection via interviewing, testing, analysis, leading to differential diagnosis and naming of the problem. In dysfluency studies, a student acquires knowledge regarding causative factors and clear descriptions and definitions of non-fluency/developmental dysfluency, stammering/stuttering, cluttering, acquired stammering (idiopathic and neurogenic).

c   Student clinician engaging in the application of science in clinic, with supervision

At this point, experienced, trained supervisors assume the role of supervising a student in applying theory to practice and developing clinical skills to work effectively with clients.

A student interacts with clients, learns to introduce specific topics to build upon client strengths and facilitates the acquisition of skills and strategies for her communication needs.

d   Student as clinician–scientist, becoming an autonomous professional SLT

A therapist who is a clinical scientist has the scientific knowledge and skills that can be applied to evidence-based clinical decision making. The clinical element refers to the art of practice with good communication skills and with informed ethical action and social responsibility. The scientific element presupposes a therapist who critically interprets, reflects upon and contributes toward the evolving theoretical knowledge base in her area of work, often through original research.

Developing a specialism: In developing skills as a clinical scientist working with PWS, Shapiro (1999) suggests a model with a series of phases:

• Early developmental level: in which the clinician has her own view of the client's issues and sees herself as in control of the client's change process. She tends to focus on a limited number of issues and has few problem-solving strategies and limited flexibility to modify the therapeutic direction.

• More advanced clinical development: here the clinician is able to incorporate the client's understanding of his problem into intervention and the change process. She considers stammering as a multidimensional problem, including thoughts, feelings and behaviours, and has several intervention strategies at her disposal. She is also able to reflect upon and modify the process as it proceeds.

Expanding Shapiro's model, we suggest the most advanced clinician is able to hand over control of the change process to the client, enabling him to identify the issues to be changed, the means by which change will occur, reflecting with him on the process and jointly determining what and how modifications should be made. There is a significant shift in attitude, with the client seen as the expert in his problem and in finding his own solution, ultimately being his own therapist.

On "being" a clinician: exploring some characteristics

There are several ways of understanding what is necessary to be the best, most effective clinician working with PWS: using professional guidelines, looking at the research evidence, critically appraising best practice. This section will explore all of these areas in an attempt to understand the nature of the clinician working with PWS.

What professional guidelines suggest

There are documents which specify the competencies, knowledge and understanding required for working clinically with a PWS (e.g. RCSLT Clinical Guidelines 2005). However, often such documents fail to address issues concerning personal characteristics and attributes a clinician brings to the therapeutic process and which can be crucial in achieving desired outcomes. For example, for a clinician in the USA, can refer to the ASHA Special Interest division on Fluency and Fluency Disorders "Guidelines for Practice in Stuttering Treatment" for details of clinician attributes (which is based on the Texas Speech & Hearing Association Fluency Task Force's list of "Personal Clinician Competencies"). This document lists:

Personal Attributes

- Has good problem-solving skills and uses them when things do not go according to plan in evaluation and treatment.
- Is flexible in thinking and planning.

Learned Attributes

- Has an understanding and appreciation of the basic processes of dynamic clinical interaction, such as transference, denial, grief, victimization.
- Can communicate relevant ideas about stuttering to clients and their families.
- Has a general working knowledge of psychopathology.
- Has a general working knowledge of cognitive and behavioral learning theory.

(ASHA 1999)

How should a clinician "be" when working with a PWS?

As valid as these attributes and undergraduate/Shapiro's model of development may be, neither address fundamental questions which a clinician who is starting to work in the field of dysfluency might ask:

- How should I **be** while working with a client who has a stammer? When should I challenge, probe, reflect on what has been said?
- What sort of relationship is effective with this client?
- Is this any different from how I am when I work with any other client?
- Does it make any difference how I am with a client to the therapy process?

One might consider such questions as unnecessary and possibly the result of clinical inexperience. However, they are important, as research clearly shows that how a clinician is with a client does make a difference. In fact, it is considered to be one of, if not the most important factor in determining good therapeutic outcomes, and this is regardless of the management approach being used (Van Riper 1975, Cooper and Cooper 1985, Shapiro 1999).

Emerick (1974) puts this very clearly:

> After laboring with stutterers for over a decade I am convinced that it is not only what I do that helps the person get better but also how I do it and who I am.
> (pp. 92–93)

In the context of psychological change, other researchers have talked recently about the characteristics of an effective clinician. Wampold (2015) discussed the factors that differentiated effective from a less effective therapist. He stated:

> Studies have shown that effective therapists (vis-à-vis less effective therapists) are able to form stronger alliances across a range of patients, have a greater level of facilitative interpersonal skills, express more professional self-doubt, and engage in more time outside of the actual therapy practicing various therapy skills.
> (p. 273)

It seems pertinent, therefore, to delineate the factors that contribute to interpersonal skills for a clinician working with a PWS. In this chapter we will also provide a means of practising these skills outside a therapeutic context.

While we underline the importance of these issues, we would also urge a clinician not to regard them as part of "the recipe" for successful intervention. There is not one single set of techniques or strategies that should be applied to each and every therapeutic encounter. A therapist should engage with each client individually, adopting a flexible and responsive approach. Owen and Hilsenroth (2014) found evidence that a rigid adherence to a particular protocol caused issues with the therapeutic alliance and increased resistance to the treatment. They concluded that a more flexible approach related to better outcomes for the client.

Returning to our questions of how a clinician might be when working with dysfluent clients: In order to consider the multitude of significant factors in a therapeutic exchange we propose subdividing this section into those shown in Table 1.1.

While there may be overlap between these categories, some sub-categorisation is necessary to aid understanding.

Table 1.1 Chapter summary

Topic area	Issues covered
• Clinician attributes and ways of interacting	The role of counselling: • Listening • Genuineness • Acceptance and positive regard • Self-awareness • Empathy • Affirmations and validations • Summarising • Humour • Silence

Topic area	Issues covered
• Therapeutic relationship	• Openness • Asymmetry • Rapport • Negotiation
• Intrapersonal behaviours	Asking questions using: • Personal construct psychology (PCP) in therapy • Socratic questioning • Solution-focused brief therapy (SF) • Motivational interviewing • Using reflective skills

Clinician attributes and ways of interacting

The role of counselling

In an interesting publication Stein-Rubin and Adler (2012) discuss how a clinician's role has evolved to include a counselling component. The authors differentiate between adopted and adapted counselling:

> To summarize, there have been two basic schools of thought in the counselling arena. One is the results-oriented directive approach that is based on content; to inform and to advise. The other, a nondirective approach, is based on deep listening; to validate and to connect. It is process oriented, with the focus on the relationship rather than on the goal. The non-directive or person-centered approach has its roots in Carl Rogers's branch of humanistic psychology.
> (p. 11)

Both approaches have a part to play when working with PWS, depending on the context and needs of the client.

In his seminal work *On Becoming a Person* (1967), Rogers discusses the key components of a counselling relationship. It is valuable to be reminded of these components:

Listening

Rogers states that listening is "the most effective agent we know for altering the basic personality structure of an individual and improving his relationships and communication with others" (p. 332). Goldman (2012) reiterates this view:

> The singular most important thing (and for most of us a very difficult thing) a clinician can do is to listen. . . . Listening is paramount because it sets the stage for empowering our clients to help themselves. . . . When Reik (1948) called for clinicians to "listen with their third ear," he may not have solely been providing aid to the practice of psychoanalysis. Perhaps all health professionals can be mindful of the suggestion. In effect, providing direction in a therapeutic journey that will result in your client's desired behavioural changes is dependent often on good timing from a clinician who is listening.
> (p. 4)

Luterman (2011) also discusses the importance of listening:

> Listening for client affect and reflecting it back enables the client to identify their feelings and express them in a safe relationship; this attenuates client isolation and validates their feelings. Listening deeply to our clients is a great gift we can give them.
> (p. 5)

Personal experience of listening to oneself express a problem would suggest that the very act of hearing one's problem being articulated openly can lead to feelings of relief and begin the process of resolution.

Genuineness

Rogers states: "In my relationships with persons I have found that it does not help, in the long run to act as though I were something I am not" (p. 16). Although he does not call this "genuineness", it has become known as such. This is further elaborated in, what he calls, a learning point: "I find I am more effective when I can listen acceptantly to myself, and can be myself" (p. 17).

Acceptance and positive regard

Rogers emphasises the need for a person to be accepting of, and open to another: "I have found it of enormous value when I can permit myself to understand another person" (p. 18).

Self-awareness

Rogers goes on to talk about the need to be aware of his own sense of self and the powerful effect this can have on relationships:

> As I try to listen to myself and the experiencing going on in me, and the more I try to extend that same listening attitude to another person. . . . So I become less and less inclined to hurry in to fix things, to set goals, to mold people, to manipulate and push them in the way that I would like them to go. I am much more content simply to be myself and to let another person be himself.
> (p. 21)

Empathy

Rogers regards this attribute as having powerful healing properties, which enables a person to realise his humanity: "It is one of the most potent aspects of therapy, because it releases, it confirms, it brings even the most frightened client into the human race". Brown (2018) describes qualifications for becoming empathic:

> Empathy is not connecting to an experience, it's connecting to the emotions that underpin an experience. . . . If you've ever felt grief, disappointment, shame, fear, loneliness, or anger, you're qualified.
> (p. 140)

Brown suggests five major elements of empathy, described as skills, that can be learned:

1 To see the world as another sees it, or perspective taking

2 To be non-judgemental

3 To understand another person's feelings

4 To communicate your understanding of that person's feelings

5 To be mindful, or pay attention.

Empathy begins with "active listening" (Goldman 2012), being in alignment with the client, which is supported by affiliation, and as we will discuss later, can be accompanied by gentle humour. Manning (2009) also discusses the importance of empathy; he regards it as a way of understanding the client and refers to Egan's work of (2001), which found that clients rate this as most helpful during counselling.

Affirmations and validations

Affirmations have become a popular idea in the area of self-help. The use of self-affirming thoughts has been found to promote self-confidence and self-esteem, especially when linked with specific goal setting. While this could be a strategy used in therapy for PWS, what this section is concerned with is the use by a clinician of statements which positively underline the success or achievement of the client.

The use of affirmations also links with the personal construct psychology (Kelly 1955) notion of validation. Here the client's hypothesis about a particular issue is proved to be correct, and his pre-emptions or predictions are found to be justified.

Affirmations can be used at many points in a clinical encounter. They can help build rapport when used at the outset of a clinical encounter (e.g. "It can be difficult to get here at this time of the morning. The traffic is often quite bad. Thank you for managing to get here on time").

Obviously affirmations can punctuate progress when specific targets have been met ("I know how hard you have worked on this, and we can see how your efforts are getting results"), and/or when difficult disclosures have been made in conversation: (e.g. "I think its better to have said that than to keep it bottled up. Well done").

They also create an acknowledgement that therapy is moving in the desired direction.

In addition to this, affirmations may draw attention to and underline areas about which the client is unaware. He may not have acknowledged his skills and abilities in certain areas, and by affirming achievements in these "blind spots" the clinician is able to reveal these undiscovered and unused strengths to him (e.g. "Have you noticed how you were able to initiate that conversation and keep it going despite feeling very anxious? That's quite something to do under those circumstances. How were you able to do that?").

Summarising
Summarising is defined as a comment in which the clinician draws together two or more of the client's thoughts, feelings or behaviours. It is often used to help the PWS see connections which he may miss. An example might be: "So you are saying that you have tried to reduce your word avoidance but notice that you are stammering more". Here the therapist makes the link between open stammering and reduced avoidance.

Leahy and Watanabe (1997) demonstrate how the therapist's use of the client's words in summarising produces a kind of power-sharing effect: the client's expertise or opinion is acknowledged and is not evaluated but repeated. The effect of this repetition is to give added value. In addition, Goffman (1981) describes how a person expressing her social role, or "principal" identity (e.g. that of partner, therapist), is also adopting the role of "talking machine" by selecting the words chosen and the sentiments expressed. In summarising, the therapist acts as animator and principal but not author. The author is the client, whose sentiments and words, used by the therapist, clearly acknowledge his contribution.

Humour
Humour is the sense of fun or amusement, and when shared, it creates the possibility of laughter or smiles. For many people, humour serves to reduce tension and to lighten serious subjects or situations. An individual is aware of feeling at ease when he laughs with others, and this encourages him to enjoy company and relationships.

Humour indicates an appreciation of a creative side of language use that can encourage solidarity and understanding and may be used to "lubricate the therapy process" (Agius 2018). It has been noted as an important aspect of therapy interaction to:

- Strengthen rapport
- Facilitate cooperation (Simmons-Mackie and Schultz 2003)

- Increase the client's coping skills (Agius 2018) and
- Be an alternative means of viewing situations for a client (Manning 2009, Walsh and Kovarsky 2011).

Self-deprecating humour can be used to take some responsibility for client discomfort, minimising social distance and aligning more closely with the client, as demonstrated by Van Riper (Leahy 2009). Manning (2009) provides an extensive review of humour in stammering therapy and how it can impact therapeutic change. Agius (2018) discusses how humour can influence changes in feelings, beliefs and attitudes, especially those of a PWS. He has studied humour and developed a programme for children who stammer (CWS) – the smart intervention strategy (SIS) – that uses humour and creativity as major therapy tools. The SIS includes practical means for a child to appreciate and develop humour to facilitate change in his feelings and beliefs.

> Humour and creativity can provide a new insight about a problem and allow for a wider degree of objectivity. In creativity we say "ah-ha" while in humour we use "ha-ha". The therapeutic (creativity and humour) "ha-ah-ha" techniques include activities leading to shifting perceptions and activating the "real" smile.
> (p. 2)

A reader interested in developing skills in the use of humour for herself or for a client is directed to the 7 Humor Habit Program in McGhee's book *Humor as Survival Training for a Stressed Out World* (2010).

Silence

A therapist's use of silence as an activity in therapy can signify paradoxical elements, including power and weakness, control and yielding control, initiating and avoidance. For the inexperienced therapist, silence may be difficult. It may convey uncertainty or weakness in terms of not knowing how to proceed or avoidance of a sensitive topic. Silence draws attention to itself, as exchanges in therapy tend to be continuous. It can feel uncomfortable, as it signals an open space that needs to be filled. Silence is probably best explored by an experienced therapist who has been working with a supervisor and with familiar clients, where an understanding trust has been established between them. A therapist can explain the use of silence as reducing her questions to leave time and space open for a client to contribute unspoken aspects of his story in problem situations and expression of feelings. In a study regarding experienced therapists' perspectives on why they used silence, Ladany et al. (2006) found that therapists' appropriate use of silence can convey empathy and facilitate reflection as well as challenge a client to take responsibility and to express feelings. These authors reported that therapists typically believed they did not use silence with some clients who were highly anxious, angry or psychotic.

It can be useful for a clinician to ask a client whether he needs time to think and reflect at key moments in an exchange, perhaps where new issues have been uncovered or when the topic is complex or difficult. In this way the silence is negotiated not imposed by the therapist.

Therapeutic relationship: What makes a relationship therapeutic?

It is vital for the clinician and the client to establish a trusting working relationship, a "social bond" (Wampold 2015), that encompasses mutual respect, so that they can understand each other, negotiate the goals of therapy and work effectively together. This process is complex, with multiple contributing aspects, some of which are clear and many that are not well defined or understood. We discuss here the clear elements that can be described, practised and learned as skills.

Openness

The therapeutic relationship ultimately depends upon degrees of openness of both parties to engage in exchanging aspects of personal and professional information. The personal characteristics of warmth, empathy and genuineness, with unconditional positive regard as discussed previously (Rogers 1967), are the primary responsibility of the therapist in establishing an open relationship.

Self-disclosure is part of personal presentation, including, for example, style of clothes and hair, non-verbal behaviour, emotional communications, and in facial and body expressions. In addition, verbal language reveals a considerable degree of personal attributes, via accent, vocabulary and in daily communication, a person discloses information about himself routinely regarding his feelings and thoughts.

In the professional relationship, the therapist uses personal questions to engage the client and discover the problem, its impact and how it has been managed. In responding, the client will disclose a great deal of information, some of which may not have been disclosed previously (Bailey 1993). As part of showing empathy or perhaps to normalise the client's behaviour and/ or thoughts, the therapist will draw on personal experiences and may disclose some details of these to the client. However, it is vitally important that any details disclosed do not draw the client's undue attention to the therapist's experiences and divert the focus from the client's problems.

Bailey (1993) describes self-disclosure as a specific skill and suggests that therapist self-disclosure can be used "as a powerful therapeutic ally" that can empower a client to change "through the appreciation of other people's experiences" (p. 45). He adds the caveat that excessive self-disclosure "is as unhelpful to clients as too little" (p. 46).

Asymmetry

Some asymmetry is natural in clinical conversations, as the therapist-helper's responsibility is to focus on the needs of the client, ensuring that conversations are goal oriented in order to move toward problem resolution.

At the outset, the relationship is asymmetrical in nature. Participants do not have equal resources and will have different levels and kinds of expertise. Mutuality or sharing of common interests in the relationship at the early stages is limited, as the client and his problems are the main focus, and both parties share a common goal of facilitating the client's desired change. The client should not have any concern (or, at best, limited, cursory concern) regarding the therapist or her problems, and the therapist has ethical responsibilities that include not discussing her own problems with the client.

Asymmetry is particularly noted in clinical discourse. Prutting et al. (1978) were among the first to study SLT interaction where therapist/client roles can be differentiated. They noted the dominant (powerful) therapist as the one who initiates conversations, usually by asking questions, giving information, making requests of the client and using specific discourse markers (e.g. "now, okay, let's try . . . good, well done, good talking") that a client will rarely use. They also described the request-response-evaluation (RRE) as the dominant, asymmetric exchange. Here the therapist requests the client to respond, the client responds and the therapist comments with evaluation. The client rarely initiates the interaction and never evaluates or comments upon the therapist's speech, thus emphasising the asymmetry. The RRE routine occurs in many other therapy and teaching interactions, where the powerful, dominant lead role is that of the therapist (or teacher), and the client (learner) role is passive.

However, this style of discourse may only be applicable to more directive therapy. In many instances when working to empower a PWS, greater symmetry in therapy interaction is desirable.

Rapport

Rapport can be described in terms of product and process. Walsh and Felson Duchan (2011), suggest that a traditional view of rapport is a product created by a clinician, that encompasses clinician traits such as "empathy, genuineness, serenity, and an inspiring attitude" (pp. 55–56). These professional characteristics are important for a clinician to nurture, as they can help instil confidence in a client. However, there can be no rapport without directly involving the client; rapport is co-created by clinician and client and co-experienced over time. In this process, rapport has to be maintained and refreshed, generating a trusting warmth between the therapist and the client. Such sharing of responsibilities or mutuality (Walsh and Felson Duchan 2011) may need to be discussed openly so that the client becomes aware of the "right to contribute" (Bunning 2004, p. 55).

Establishing rapport is facilitated by "small talk" (Walsh 2007, Leahy and Walsh 2008, Walsh and Felson Duchan 2011). Clinical visit initial exchanges often include greetings, checking about preferred names, seating arrangements, chatting about the weather and the journey to the clinic. This enables the therapist and client to become acquainted and to help put the client at ease in introducing him to the clinical setting. When a therapist invites a client to consider preferences (e.g. in seating or regarding timing of appointments etc.) elements of flexibility and concern to accommodate the client are demonstrated. A client who is able to express an opinion, ask a question and/or disagree is indicating his confidence and showing that he is able to be on equal terms with the clinician in the interaction.

These exchanges can create opportunities to encourage ease in the social contact between client and therapist, aiming to share sociability. Walsh (2007) refers to small talk as "relational", observing how it serves as a bridge into telling troubles and more task-oriented talk, where a client's problems and therapy-related tasks are discussed.

Walsh and Felson Duchan (2011), referring to Leahy (2004), demonstrate how social "small talk" serves to strengthen the engagement between clinician and client as task-related focus is suspended for a brief exchange. Entitled "Are You Getting Your Son That Dog He Wants?", this exchange is led by a 13-year-old client with dysfluency who refers the therapist to an earlier personal exchange (social small talk) with her regarding pets. The clinician listens, accepts the new topic and responds with a laugh, showing alignment with the client, along with affiliation and a willingness to be distracted by small talk:

C = Client (13-year-old girl)

T = Therapist (specialist therapist)

1 C: *Are you getting your son that dog he wants?*

2 T: *(laughs) He's still talking about it. ooh (laughs).*

3 C: *Don't you want one then?*

4 T: *Yeah I think so. It's just, we would need to . . .*

5 C: *Quite hard work*

6 C: What breed do you think he'll be?

7 T: Slightly slower

8 C: Wha:t breed do you think he'll be?

9 T: I don't know. What do you reckon?[1]

Both parties observe and listen, taking account of the myriad of interaction perspectives that are part of this encounter between the professional helper and the person seeking help. The clinician is a guide along the way, sometimes offering the lead in the journey but always acknowledging that the trip has to be made by the client. The process of taking that journey with a knowledgeable and sensitive partner is the therapeutic process.

Negotiation

Negotiation involves consultation between people who disagree about an issue in order to arrive at a common understanding of how to resolve a problem. In the context of working with a client where dysfluency is under discussion, the kinds of disagreement or divergence of opinion may be myriad. For example, lack of agreement regarding the definition of stammering, its causes, the goals of therapy, best therapy approaches etc. When working with a person from a different ethnic background, it is particularly important that there is clarity regarding the best means to cooperate in the therapy process.

As a prerequisite to negotiation, both parties need to realise and agree on its objective: that it meets the interests of both parties; that it should improve the working relationship and resolve conflicting interests fairly and, finally, agree that each person's view will be respected/valued equally. The therapist's perspective has to be clearly presented to the client and the client's perspective relayed to the clinician to ensure effective communication. Drawing on principled negotiation ideas from Fisher, Ury and Patton (1991), it is important to focus on the following four elements to facilitate the process:

• People: Separate the people from the problem

• Interests: Focus on interests, not positions

• Options: Generate a variety of possibilities before decisions

• Criteria: Try to base the result on some objective standard, independent of the will of either side.

Leahy and Wright (1995) provide examples of working through each element.

One example from "objective criteria" is how a family understanding of providing almonds for their dysfluent child is helpful in reducing the dysfluency. The family belief is that almonds are a good source of vitamins and minerals that will help the child to become more fluent. The therapist, on the other hand, recommends that helping the child reduce her speech rate would be the best course of action. Both parties agree to accept their individual understandings on the basis that the therapist does not have objective criteria about almonds and the client does not know about slower speech rate. So they agree to experiment with both solutions, perhaps by alternating the procedures: two days eating almonds, without a focus on speech; followed by two days slowing the rate of speech, in coordinated practice, for eight days, and review progress.

Intrapersonal behaviours

Many clinicians who specialise in working with adults who stammer, certainly in the UK, have been influenced by the work of George Kelly and his personal construct psychology (PCP). There is not the space to discuss this approach in depth, but readers are referred to Hayhow and Levy

1989, Stewart and Birdsall 2001, Hayhow and Stewart 2006 for discussion of PCP's application to the field of stammering.

There are, however, a number of principles which are key:

- Constructs about stammering: In his theory, Kelly talks about "personal constructs", which are ways of individual understanding or knowing. These constructs are organised into a hierarchical system which allows a person to anticipate events. In therapeutic change a client will be encouraged to alter or "loosen" his system of constructs by exploring and experimenting with alternative ways of construing.

  However, construing and changes in construing are not the sole prerogative of the client. The clinician will also have her own set of constructs and her own way of organising them in a way which is meaningful to her. The nature of the clinician's constructs about stammering, clients who stammer and the change process would all be important to consider, as they are likely to have a direct impact on the clinician's intrapersonal behaviours. Let us explore some examples:

- Construing stammering: Perhaps a clinician thinks that fluency is the best option or the preferred outcome for a PWS. If this is the case, then she is more likely to advocate fluency management programmes than other approaches such as self-acceptance or avoidance-reduction. Another clinician may negatively construe certain types of stammering behaviours, such as rapid, multiple repetitions or blocks with facial tension. Consequently she will find she is less tolerant of these behaviours than others. In this scenario she is more likely to direct the client's attention to these repetitions or blocks, whether consciously or not, and seek to engage him in changing these aspects of his stammer.

  Thus, it is important for a clinician working with a PWS to consider how she views stammering, what her responses are to different presentations of stammering and always examine her motivations if she finds herself directing a client toward one therapeutic option in particular rather than having him make an informed choice of his own.

- Construing loosely and the change process: Kelly described how a person's construct system would "loosen" during a change process. Firstly, the individual establishes a hypothesis, which he sets out to test. For example, a client may decide to test out his view that people react negatively to his stammer. He will experiment with more open stammering, perhaps stammering while asking for an item in a shop or in a conversation with a work colleague. In these situations his focus will be on observing reactions rather than on his internal experience of stammering. Given a scenario in which he observes little or no reaction from others, the individual is able to loosen his construing about the need to hide his stammer in certain situations. In PCP, this loosening process is dependent upon a period of experimentation or trial and error and key to the occurrence of change. During loosening, the alignment and linkages of the constructs in the person's system are reconfigured before a tightening process which ends the period of change.

  How does this apply to a clinician? Simply, in exactly the same way. A clinician learning a new skill, engaging with a new client, trying out a new approach will be involved in the same process. She will establish a hypothesis to be tested, such as: "This approach is not relevant to the clients who come to my clinic". She will then experiment by using the approach, perhaps role-playing with colleagues or trialling it with a small number of clients before using it more widely. In that experiment she can loosen her constructs and make new links and alignments. Her observations may led her to see the approach's value with clients experiencing certain feelings or behaviours, see its relevance to a group setting, or she could reject it and confirm her original hypothesis.

In clinic a therapist should be aware of being open or loose to a range of possibilities or options, especially when seeing a client for the first time. These possibilities will be in relation to his narrative and in relation to the change process ahead. In many cases, her constructs will be more loose than the client himself in this regard. She should be able to have a vision which extends his own view of himself beyond his current situation. She will need to show him the vision she has of him and ways in which he could achieve this should he choose to do so.

Asking questions
Aside from the use of open-ended questions, there are other questioning techniques which are useful when working with a PWS.

Socratic questioning

- This type of discovery sits well as a means of exploring and critically examining ideas. It can be used to help a client establish his hypothesis, as discussed in the previous section. Socratic questioning differs from general questioning in that it is systematic and focused on a particular issue or problem. Examples in a clinical context are:

- Clarification and exploration of thinking

  e.g. Can you say a bit more about that? Why do you think that?

- Challenge

  e.g. Have you always thought that? When did you think differently? Are there any exceptions to that?

- Asking for evidence

  e.g. What makes you think that is true? What evidence do you have for that?

- Exploring alternatives

  e.g. Do you know anyone with an alternative viewpoint? What did they say?

- Examining the implications and consequences

  e.g. If x happened what do you think would be the result? How would it affect you/other significant people in your life?

Solution-focused (SF) questioning

- Based on the work of Steve De Shazer (1985, 1988, 1994, 2012), SF therapy carries the assumption that the client already knows the solution to his difficulty and is already doing some thing of it. It is the therapist's role to help him become aware of this.

  SF therapy sessions start with a period of problem-free talk where the client and clinician engage in a conversation without discussion of the problem at hand. The clinician will then move to determine if there have been any changes in the client prior to their meeting (if it is the first visit) or between sessions. Elaborating the nature of this change will indicate to the client his potential for change and has echoes with the "loosening" process referred to in a previous section on personal construct psychology.

  SF therapy also poses the "Miracle Question", which helps the client to envisage a time without the problem – his desired outcome.

The Miracle Question: I'm going to ask you a kind of strange question now.

> Suppose [pause] you go to bed and go to sleep tonight as usual [pause]
>
> and while you are asleep a miracle happens [pause] and the problem that brought you here today is solved
>
> [pause].
>
> But you are asleep and don't know that it has been solved [pause].
>
> What will be the first small signs that this miracle has happened and that the problem is solved?

An alternative to the Miracle Question is a series of questions relating to the outcome or goal of therapy.

Goal setting

- What will it be like when the problem is solved? What will you be doing instead?
- When that happens, what difference will it make? How will other people know that things are better? Who will notice first? And then who?
- What else will be different? What else? What else?

The "What else?" question, which can be repeated throughout a SF session, is one which allows the client to elaborate and add meaning to his ideas and when used in a goal setting (or Miracle Question) context will help him determine what his outcome looks like ultimately in behavioural terms.

A SF approach also helps the client explore times when the problem is not apparent, or exceptions, to help identify components which may be helpful to him in achieving his goal.

Exceptions: key questions

- What about times when the problem is not happening? Or when it is less?
- You mentioned earlier that some days/times are better. What is it like at these times?
- What are you doing instead at these times?
- Who notices when things are better for you? Anyone else?
- What do they notice at these times? What else?

Scaling is used throughout the process, both to assess where the client is in relation to his desired goal and in relation to smaller issues or aspects of change.

Scaling: key questions
Please think of a scale from 0 to 10, with 10 being the best. Nought is how you felt when things were at their worst. Ten is as good as things can be in relation to this problem.

- Where are you now on that scale right now? Give it a number.
- If 10 is as good as it can be, what number would you settle for?
- If x is where you are right now what needs to happen to move you a point up toward your goal?
- What will you be doing/saying/thinking that will tell you you are at that point?
- What else will be different when you are one point further up? Who will notice?

Motivational interviewing

Summerson, Carr and Smith (2014) discuss the poetics of therapeutic practice in the counselling approach of motivational interviewing (MI), directing attention to aspects of cultivating 'stylistic elements' in clinical discourse. This approach can be useful to support and motivate personal change within the clinician's interaction style. We therefore echo their use of the acronym OARS, referring to four basic speech acts:

• Open-ended questions

• Reflections

• Affirmations

• Summaries.

An activity is included at the end of this section specifically for clinicians to practise these aspects of interaction.

However, it is important to emphasise that we include examples here not as a technical manual or recipe book from which a clinician selects. A specialist clinician is far from a technician and will employ these approaches in a timely and considered way, not just because these techniques are known and available to her but being led by her knowledge and understanding of the client and what would fit best to move him in his change process in her dialogue with him.

Being an effective reflector

There is no doubt that it takes courage to engage in regular, structured reflection. There is much risk taking in opening up one's practice to self- and/or peer evaluation. The greatest risk, of course, is to be found wanting, falling short of expectations. But there is also much to be gained, and a clinician can make great strides in development and extending her practice by engaging in a genuine reflective process.

Reflective practice has been influenced by the work of Schon (1983, 1987). He differentiated between the process of reflection on action and reflection in action. Reflection in action, as its name indicates, is much more in the moment of the clinical interaction. This is much more difficult to carry out and may, to some extent, be dependent on good, regular clinical supervision. Meeting with a supervisor enables the clinician to reflect on the interaction of herself and the client, which then can be carried into future therapeutic encounters.

Other strategies for developing reflection in action include the use of reflective questions. Examples were suggested by Burnham (2005) when describing relational or self-reflexivity, which he defined as:

> the intention, desire, processes and practices through which therapists and clients explicitly engage one another in coordinating their resources so as to create a relationship with therapeutic potential. This would involve initiating . . . responding to . . . and developing, opportunities to consider, explore, experiment with and elaborate the ways in which they relate.
> (p. 6)

For example, by asking a client questions about the questions a clinician might ask him, such as "What question might I ask you now which would be most helpful in moving you forward?", the client is empowered to co-construct a conversation with great power and potential. The client is, in effect, telling the clinician what will work! Simultaneously, the clinician can reflect on what she is being told and use that information to inform subsequent interaction and increase the effectiveness of the dialogue.

Questions, which Burnham describes as "warming the context", can be asked:

• At the beginning

• Setting the scene for the conversation

• During a dialogue – possible at points where direction or guidance is needed

• At the end, to reflect on what has been of little of most use.

Examples can be found in the Resources section at the end of the chapter.

Reflection on action is an opportunity to consider past clinical events and experiences and review them in line with knowledge and understanding available to one's peer group. This process is chiefly carried out in formal clinical supervision.

A clinician's reflections on clinical supervision

CH is a specialist clinician working for several years with PWS. She has had clinical supervision from the start of her specialist career and is aware of its value, the impact it has had on her personal and professional growth as a clinician and her practice with clients. The following excerpt (Handsley 2019) is from her reflections on her years of experience of clinical supervision from a number of different supervisors:

> Supervision is fundamental to my existence as a Speech and Language Therapist, perhaps even as a person. It is something I would never be without, certainly for my working life.
>
> Specialist clinical supervision has seen me on a repeated cycle of growth from a complete and utter novice to developing expertise – no sooner is something achieved, a step made, a decision taken, than an awareness of another area to explore emerges. It is both exciting and reassuring, regular yet responsive, varied yet familiar.
>
> I came to supervision after a career break of eleven years. I had just been appointed to a new one day a week specialist post for adults who stammer. I initially came with practical questions about how to deliver a service to adults who stammer, numbers, frequency of appointments, etc. But as caseload demands grew I was able to glean so much information and insight from my supervisor and my clinical skills and understandings continue to be honed. Without specialist clinical supervision I would not have grown as a stammering therapist but would rather have floundered, often felt inadequate, lost enjoyment and failed to see success and development in my work. I believe I have learnt to learn from my working experiences; successes and failures, encouraged to develop skills to be able to find my own solutions. Supervision has enabled me to have skills and confidence to advocate for people who stammer, to consider suitable service deliveries for people who stammer and look creatively beyond prescriptive approaches.
>
> Every new challenge can be explored in a supportive, confidential environment where I, as a Speech and Language Therapist supporting people who stammer, have been able to expect my needs, queries, and deliberations to be the focus of attention with no external demands from management.
>
> Development has been through discussion, role modelling, direct advice, guidance, challenge and reflection. I have particularly appreciated solution focused questioning. The reflective nature of supervision has been vital to my growth. My ability to use reflective practice has developed considerably over the years.
>
> I will always use the principles of supervision with which I started as I find them so useful. I review my previous supervision, consider the issues I wish to raise, make notes

of an "agenda", and share them with my supervisor beforehand. This process can be really enlightening in itself.

What is particularly valuable to me is the process of reflection with which I engage after each session and which I document and share with my supervisor.

I will always seek supervision from a therapist with specialist clinical skills but have also found supervision from non-specialists with good supervision skills to be of value too. I believe it is partly my commitment to supervision that is a significant factor in the success of the process as well as the skills of the supervisor.

Final remarks

This chapter has focused on, firstly, the particular attributes and ways of interacting that a clinician working with an adolescent and/or adult who stammers might demonstrate. Secondly we discussed the nature of the therapeutic relationship and finally the intrapersonal behaviours often seen in a clinical context.

The key factor in determining when and where any or all of these are used in a session is, of course, the client himself. The clinician must always be attuned and sensitive to the needs of the client and allow those sensibilities to guide her in the use of specific behaviours, ways of interacting etc.

We know that when a clinician is tuned into the client's needs in the moment and successfully uses a particular attribute, a special connection is created. This connection is one in which the client feels known and understood by the therapist, and this has powerful implications for change for both the client and the therapist.

Listening exercise
(adapted from Rogers 1967, p. 332)

The next time you get into an argument with your partner, colleague or friend or with a small group of friends, stop the discussion for a moment and for an experiment institute this rule:

> Each person can speak up for himself only *after* he has first restated the ideas and feelings of the previous speaker accurately and to that speaker's satisfaction.

Reflect on the effect this has on the interaction.

What are the implications for your clinical practice?

Thoughtful listening
(based on Egan 2002, pp. 26–27)

- Narrate a problematic situation or scenario from your own life in as much detail as possible with a work colleague.

- When you have finished both you and your colleague should each write what you consider to be the three key factors from the story.

- Repeat the exercise, this time with your colleague narrating his/her scenario.

- Compare what you both recorded from each story.

  - In your colleague's opinion, how well did you summarise the key elements of his/her story?

  - How did you determine what the key factors were?

  - Did you have any problems determining what the key factors were?

  - What have you both learned about your thoughtful listening skills?

Observing and scaling

This exercise can be used with each of the clinical skills discussed in this chapter, e.g. rapport, empathy, listening, asymmetry, etc.

It is suggested that a clinician selects one of the skills she wishes to develop and use the exercise as described.

Example: empathy

Observe your empathy during a conversation with a friend or colleague.

Look for an example of a truly empathetic response.

Rate on a scale of 1 to 10 how empathetic you think the response was.

Evaluate the components of your response.

Consider moving the response up the scale (i.e. increased by 1 point or .5 more).

What would have to happen? What would you be doing differently?

Example: humour

Find examples of how you use humour during a day at work.

Look for an example of a humorous response.

Rate on a scale of 1 to 10 how humorous you think the response was.

Evaluate the components of your response.

Consider moving the response up the scale (i.e. 1 point or .5).

What would have to happen? What would you be doing differently?

Questions on attending
(based on Egan 2002)

Record a clinical session with a client. When reviewing the recording consider the following questions on attending:

• What are my attitudes toward this client?

• How do I show this in my non-verbal and verbal behaviour?

• How would I rate the quality of my presence to this client?

• To what degree does my non-verbal behaviour indicate a willingness to work with this client?

• What attitudes am I expressing in my non-verbal behaviour?

• To what degree does the client experience me as effectively present and working with him/ her?

• To what degree does my non-verbal behaviour reinforce my internal attitudes?

• In what ways am I distracted from giving my full attention to this client?

• What am I doing to handle these distractions?

• How might I be more effectively present to this person?

Use of empathy

Review your skills in relation to one or several clinical sessions.

- List how you are being empathetic.

- Observe your attending: how are you physically and psychologically present?

- Are you able to summarise the client's point of view? Is there evidence in a session that you use this understanding effectively?

- Do any of your own personal biases, attitudes or opinions interfere with your empathy for the client? If so, how do you manage this?

- Observe your responses to the client's story; how often are you making a response? What is the nature of your responses?

- How do you use empathy to maintain the client's focus on significant issues?

- How do you explore sensitive and emotionally charged areas of concern for the client?

- Observe how your empathetic responses are received by the client. Which responses are most helpful?

- How does the client show signs of stress, and how do you manage these events?

- How can you best improve your use of empathy?

© Trudy Stewart (2020). *Stammering Resources for Adults and Teenagers: Integrating New Evidence into Clinical Practice.* **Routledge.**

Self-reflection/evaluating process

Review your skills during one or several clinical sessions.

General issues:

- What problems do I avoid?
- What opportunities do I waste?
- What am I likely to overlook?
- What do I avoid doing?
- What assumptions do I make?
- What do I do least?
- What do I do most?
- What areas should I challenge myself to change?
- What honest critical feedback would others give me if I were to ask them?

How effective am I in:

- Establishing a therapeutic alliance with the client?
- Helping the client tell his/her story?
- Evaluating and re-evaluating a client's issues during therapy?
- Helping a client move through the change process?
- Jointly evaluating the process with the client?

© Trudy Stewart (2020). *Stammering Resources for Adults and Teenagers: Integrating New Evidence into Clinical Practice.* **Routledge.**

Activity to develop OARS

Write examples of:

- Open questions,
- Affirmation statements,
- Reflections (reflecting to speaker what you are hearing) and
- Summarising.

Begin using each element of OARS in personal interactions with family and friends.

Role-play: in groups of three, with therapist role, client role and observer role.

Therapist interviews client with observer making notes on the therapist's use of each OARS element and the associated client responses.

Observer and client feed back to therapist at the end of the interview on the appropriateness of her use of the elements.

Switch roles and repeat.

© Trudy Stewart (2020). *Stammering Resources for Adults and Teenagers: Integrating New Evidence into Clinical Practice.* **Routledge.**

The iceberg

The iceberg analogy is often used in assessment to differentiate between overt and covert aspects of stammering or cluttering. However, it can be used by a clinician when reflecting on a therapy session to develop the following:

• A greater awareness of her own visible emotions (above water level) e.g. frowning, smiling

• Internal/external experiences (above the water level) e.g. annoyance, loss of concentration

• The feelings that are hidden (below the surface) e.g. lack of empathy

• Thoughts or cognitions experienced in moments of the therapy session (below the surface) e.g. those unrelated to the present moment.

The therapist could record a therapy session and then use the iceberg as a means of exploring the visible and unseen aspects of her behaviour, thoughts and feelings.

Supervision exercise: which aspects of stammering do you relate to most?

Summary: The exercise is designed to facilitate the exploration of participants' relationships with different aspects of stammering. It consists of mapping influences of different aspects of stammering and how some aspects come to be more significant than others for clinicians. It is proposed that the exercise is used in the context of a supervision group, where the supervisees and supervisor share their personal experiences and beliefs related to stammering. (It can also be carried out in a dyfluency interest, mentoring group or an individual supervision context.) Team members' reflection offers a further opportunity for learning.

Mapping of influences

Using the questions listed, each group member writes down ideas individually, including the supervisor.

Part 1

• Which aspects of stammering do you relate to most and why? Focus on the two most influential ones, but feel free to comment on other related aspects.

• Which aspects of stammering mean more to you? Which ones are more important to you?

• Which do you think about most?

• Which influence your development as a clinician working with individuals who stammer and your practice most?

• How did these influences develop? Think about significant experiences (for example, client and/personal stories) in your practice/other relationship contexts which influenced you.

• How do you think different aspects of stammering relate to each other?

Part 2

• Which aspects of stammering do you find more difficult to relate to and why?

• Which ones mean less to you? Which ones are less important to you?

• Which ones influenced your development/your practice least?

• How do they relate to your beliefs/prejudices/values about working with a PWS?

• How do these influences relate to your strengths, weaknesses and blind spots?

• How do they impact on your practice? How do they help/hinder your practice?

Part 3. Interviews and reflection (allow minimum 30 minutes for each member)

One team member interviews another (20 minutes). The rest of the team reflects on the conversation (5 minutes).

Reflection questions

• What struck you most?

• What are the similarities and differences between you and your colleague?

• What did you learn from the conversation?

The interviewee reflects on the reflection (5 minutes).

All team members, including the supervisor, should be interviewed.

Whole-group discussion and feedback.

The supervisor may wish to facilitate discussion on the following issues:

• What learning needs did this exercise highlight for you?

• What support/help would you like from the team and the supervisor?

• Which aspects of stammering featured more/less in the interviews?

• What implications might this have on our practice?

Part 4. Supervision exercise: the follow-up interview

• When you look back on the exercise, what stood out for you?

• Did the exercise have an impact on your practice and your thoughts about stammering in any way? If so, how? Do you have examples of situations or cases in which it helped you in any way? What do you think your supervisor and the team may have seen you do more or less?

• Have your relationships with different aspects of stammering changed? If so, how? If you were asked now which ones you relate to more/less what would you say?

© Trudy Stewart (2020). *Stammering Resources for Adults and Teenagers: Integrating New Evidence into Clinical Practice.* Routledge.

Questions about questions

Experiment with using these questions at different points in your clinical sessions:

Questions to co-organise sessions

(These kinds of questions could be asked in the early stages of therapy to actively and openly include a client in the construction of the therapeutic relationship and orient the therapist towards the client's preferred way of working.)

As a therapist I can ask you questions that:

• Help you think of your own ideas about what to do

• Tell you about what other people have done in your circumstances

• Give you advice from my own experiences as a person.

Which do you think would:

• Fit with how you usually go about your life?

• Be most useful to you at this stage in your life/therapy?

• Make this therapy relationship different from other therapies that you might have experienced?

General questions used to guide therapy

   • Of all the questions I ask you, do you experience those relating to:
      a Behaviour
      b Explanation
      c Emotion
   • Of all the questions I ask you which are the most difficult to answer?
   • Of all the questions I ask you which are the most useful to you?

To which ones do you have a "ready answer"?

Which ones do you need to think about before you answer?

• When you came for therapy did you expect me to ask more questions and/or make more comments?
   Do you prefer me to ask you questions or to make comments?
   When is it more useful to you for me to make comments/ask questions?

• When I ask you (x particular kind of questions e.g. "what does that feel like?") what do you imagine that I am thinking about? What do you think my intentions are?

• When I ask you x do you imagine that I am more interested in my ideas or your ideas?

• When I ask you x do you imagine that I am more interested in finding out about how things are for you now or more interested in how things might be different or more interested in pushing you in a particular direction?

• Supposing I were to ask you y kind of questions; how might you respond and what do you imagine might be the effect for you?

• What kind of questions might I ask you that would help you create a new experience, have different thoughts etc.?

• If your friend/partner/significant other were advising me about the session what kind of questions might he/she suggest I ask or don't ask you?

Differentiating the clinical relationship

The professional relationship is built upon a "friendly" basis, but it is not a friendship.

Write a list of all the elements you consider to be components of a friendship.

Option: Compare and discuss with a colleague or in a supervision group.

Write a second list of elements you consider to represent components of a client–clinician relationship.

Option: Compare and discuss with a colleague or in a supervision group.

Compare the two lists. Explore areas of difference. Explore in more detail areas of similarity and overlap.

Reflect on your own practice and consider whether your boundaries between friendship and client relationship are clear.

Exploration of clinical skills

List four ways in which you use:

• Affiliation

• Negotiation

• Symmetry/asymmetry

• Humour

• Silence.

Compare your list with a colleague or in a supervision group.

Consider additional ways in which you could demonstrate these skills/strategies.

Note

1 Transcription conventions for discourse extract (following Tannen and Wallat 1993) are as follows:

: prolonged or elongated vowel sound

. falling intonation

? rising intonation

.. brief pause < .5 seconds

. . . longer pause – > 1 second

CAPITALS. emphatic stress

/?/. inaudible or unintelligible utterance

[Linking two lines show overlapping utterances

(+t) stuttering block with tension

References

Agius, J. (2018). Shifting perceptions: Using creativity and humor in fluency intervention. *Forum Logopedyczne*, 26, 49–61.

ASHA, (1999). Guidelines for practice in stuttering treatment: Special interest division on fluency and fluency disorders. In D. Shapiro (ed.), *Stuttering Intervention: A Collaborative Journey To Fluency Freedom*. Austin, TX: Pro-Ed.

Bailey, R. (1993). *Practical Counselling Skills*. Oxon: Winslow Press.

Brown, B. (2018). *Dare to Lead*. London: Penguin Random House.

Bunning, K. (2004). *Speech & Language Therapy Interventions: Frameworks and Processes*. London: Whurr.

Burnham, J. (1992). Approach – method – technique: Making distinctions and creating connections. *Human Systems,* 3, 3–27.

Burnham, J. (2005). Relational reflexivity: A tool for socially constructing therapeutic relationships. In C. Flaskas, B. Mason and A. Perlesz (eds.), *The Space between: Experience, Context, and Process in the Therapeutic Relationship*. London: Karnac.

Burnham, J. (2012). Developments in Social GRRRAAACCEEESSS: Visible – invisible and voiced – unvoiced. In I.B. Krause (ed.), *Culture and Reflexivity in Systemic Psychotherapy: Mutual Perspectives*. London: Karnac.

Cooper, E.B. and Cooper, C.S (1985). The effective clinician. In E.B Cooper and C.S. Cooper (eds.), *Personalized Fluency Control Therapy* – Revised (handbook). Allen, TX: DLM.

De Shazer, S. (1985). *The Keys to Solution in Brief Therapy*. London: W.W. Norton Co.

De Shazer, S. (1988). *Clues: Investigating Solutions in Brief Therapy*. London: W.W. Norton Co.

De Shazer, S. (1994). *Words Were Originally Magic*. London: W.W. Norton Co.

De Shazer, S. (2012). *More Than Miracles: The State of the Art of Solution-focused Brief Therapy*. Abingdon, Oxon: Routledge.

Egan, G. (2001). *The Skilled Helper: A Problem-management Approach to Helping*. Pacific Grove, CA: Brooks Cole Publishing Co.

Egan, G. (2002). *Exercises in Helping Skills*. UK: Brooks Cole Publishing Co.

Emerick, L. (1974). Stuttering therapy: Dimensions of interpersonal sensitivity. In L.L. Emerick and S.B. Hood (eds.), *The Client-clinician Relationship: Essays on Interpersonal Sensitivity in the Therapeutic Transaction*. Springfield, IL: Charles C. Thomas.

Fisher, R., Ury, W. and Patton, B. (1991). *Getting to Yes: Negotiating Agreement without Giving in* (2nd Edition). New York: Penguin.

Goffman, E. (1981). *Forms of Talk*. Philadelphia: University of Pennsylvania Press.

Goldman, C. (2012). An introduction to assessment: A diagnostic philosophy in speech-language pathology. In C. Stein-Rubin and R. Fabus (eds.), *A Guide to Clinical Assessment and Professional Report Writing in Speech-Language Pathology*. Clifton Park, NY: Delmar-Cengage Learning.

Handsley, C. (2019). *Reflections on Supervision*. Personal Communication.

Hayhow, R. and Levy, C. (1989). *Working with Stuttering*. Bicester, Oxon: Winslow Press.

Hayhow, R. and Stewart, T. (2006). Introduction to qualitative research and its application to stuttering. *International Journal of Language & Communication Disorders*, 41(5), 475–493.

Kelly, G.A. (1955). *The Psychology of Personal Constructs: Vol 1 and 2*. New York: W.W. Norton Co.

Ladany, N., Hill, C., Thompson, B. and Karen, M. (2006). Therapist perspectives on using silence in therapy: A qualitative study. *Counselling & Psychotherapy Research*, 4, 80–89.

Leahy, M.M. (2004). Therapy talk: Analyzing therapeutic discourse. *Language, Speech and Hearing Services in Schools*, 35, 70–81.

Leahy, M.M. (2009). Multiple voices in Charles Van Riper's desensitization therapy. *International Journal of Language & Communication Disorders*, 43, 69–80.

Leahy, M.M. and Walsh, I. (2008). Talk in interaction in the speech-language pathology clinic: Bringing theory to practice through discourse. *Topics in Language Disorders*, 28(3), 229–241.

Leahy, M.M. and Watanabe, Y.C. (1997). Discourse in group therapy for stuttering. In C.E. Healey and H.M.F. Peters (eds.), *Proceedings of the 2nd World Congress on Fluency Disorders*. Nijmegen, The Netherlands: Nijmegen University Press.

Leahy, M. and Wright, L. (1995). Therapy for Stuttering: Facilitating working with people from different ethnic backgrounds. *Proceedings of 1st World Congress on Fluency Disorders*, 2, 355–360.

Luterman, D. (2011). Ruminations of an old man. In R. Fourie (ed.), *Therapeutic Processes In Communication Disorders*. Hove Essex: Psychology Press.

Manning, W.H. (2009). *Clinical Decision Making in Fluency Disorders*. Canada: Singular Thompson Learning.

McGhee, P. (2010). *Humor as Survival Training for a Stressed Out World: The 7 Humor Habit Program*. Bloomington, IN: AuthorHouse.

Owen, J. and Hilsenroth, M.J. (2014). Treatment adherence: The importance of therapist flexibility in relation to therapy outcomes. *Journal Counselling Psychology,* 61, 280–288.

Prutting, C.A., Bagshaw, N., Goldstein, H., Justowitz, S. and Umen, I. (1978). Clinician-child discourse: Some preliminary questions. *Journal of Speech & Hearing Disorders*, 43, 123–129.

Rogers, C.R. (1967). *On Becoming a Person: A Therapists View of Psychotherapy*. London: Constable & Constable Ltd.

Roper-Hall, A. (1998). Working systemically with older people and their families who have 'come to grief '. In P. Sutcliffe, G. Tufnell and U. Cornish (eds.), *Working with the Dying and Bereaved: Systemic Approaches to Therapeutic Work*. London: Macmillan.

Royal College of Speech and Language Therapists (2005). *Clinical Guidelines*. Oxon: Speechmark Publishing Ltd.

Schon, D.A. (1983). *The Reflective Practitioner: How Professionals Think in Action*. New York: Basic Books.

Schon, D.A. (1987). *Educating the Reflective Practitioner: Toward a New Design*. San Francisco: Jossey-Bass.

Shapiro, D.A. (1999). *Stuttering Intervention: A Collaborative Journey to Fluency Freedom*. Austin, TX: Pro-Ed.

Simmons-Mackie, N. and Schultz, M. (2003). The role of humour in therapy for aphasia. *Aphasiology*, 17(8), 751–766.

Stein-Rubin, C. and Adler, B.T. (2012). Counseling and the diagnostic interview for the speech-language pathologist. In C. Stein-Rubin and F. Fabus (ed.), *A Guide to Clinical Assessment and Report Writing in Speech Pathology*. Hampshire, UK: Cengage Learning.

Stewart, T. and Birdsall, M. (2001). A review of the contribution of personal construct psychology to stammering therapy. *Journal of Constructivist Psychology*, 14, 215–226.

Summerson Carr, E. and Smith, Y. (2014). The poetics of therapeutic practice: Motivational interviewing and the powers of pause. *Culture Medicine and Psychiatry,* 38(1), 83–114.

Tannen, D. and Wallat, C. (1993). Interactive frames and knowledge schemas in interaction: Examples from a medical examination/interview. In D. Tannen (ed.), *Framing in Discourse*. Oxford: Oxford University Press.

Totsuka, Y. (2014). Which aspects of social GGRRAAACCEEESSS grab you most?' The social GGRRAAACCEEESSS exercise for a supervision group to promote therapists' self-reflexivity. *Journal of Family Therapy*, 36(1).

Van Riper, C. (1975). The stutterer's clinician. In J. Eisenson (ed.), *Stuttering, a Second Symposium*. New York: Harper & Row,

Walsh, I.P. (2007). Small talk is "big talk" in clinical discourse. *Topics in Language Disorders*, 27(1), 24–36.

Walsh, I.P. and Felson Duchan, J. (2011). Product and process depictions of rapport between clients and their speech-language pathologists during clinical interactions. In R. Fourie (ed.), *Therapeutic Processes for Communication Disorders*. Hove: Psychology Press.

Walsh, I.P. and Kovarsky, D. (2011). Establishing relationships in speech-language therapy when working alongside people with mental health disorders. In R. J Fourie (ed.), *Therapeutic Processes for Communication Disorders*. Hove: Psychology Press.

Wampold, B.E. (2015). How important are the common factors in psychotherapy? An update. *World Psychiatry,* 14(3), 270–277.

2 | Service delivery

Jonathon Linklater

This chapter will provide the reader with an overview of different service delivery models that may be used with clients who stammer. Current literature will be considered, reflected upon and related to other chapters in this text.

Sheehan (1970) suggested that stammering was a disorder of social presentation of the self. Stammering should be treated within a social milieu; group therapy allows for this, and using his psychotherapy background, Sheehan was keen to utilise this setting. While clinicians work on a one-to-one basis with a client, many do not have the option to run groups. However, a client can be encouraged to interact with those who stammer and to tell his friends, family and the wider public about his stammering. Later in the chapter, the option of telehealth and non-clinical resources that can assist the therapeutic journey will be explored.

The client's issues

- Personal preference. Each individual will have his own preferred way of receiving therapy. Not every client wants to attend group therapy, while another may prefer this format. One person can feel daunted by a group meeting, while for another, meeting those in similar circumstances and reducing the sense of isolation will be a major motivator to attending a group session.

- Rate of change. There are different rates of therapeutic change. Some evidence suggests slower rates of change lead to better long-term maintenance (Stewart 1996a, 1996b). At what point a client falls on the overt–covert continuum can affect how quickly he may be able to change. A person who is more covert and appears highly fluent is likely to find it difficult to undo such patterns in a short period of time. Conversely, someone who presents with more overt stammering may be more likely to adopt fluency-increasing strategies.

- Frequency of sessions. This relates to the number of sessions over a given time frame that the client feels is right for him i.e. weekly or fortnightly sessions in blocks of 6/8/10 sessions. Therapy should not be interminable, but a client may prefer to return on (for example) a six-monthly or annual basis to check in and set new goals.

- Personal circumstances. Perhaps a client can only attend once a month for financial or practical reasons. He may work away or have home commitments which limit attendance. In addition he may not feel able to devote enough time and energy to practice between sessions.

- The demands of work can also be a significant factor here. Some jobs may be less flexible and an employer less understanding than others. However, in my experience, employers can be supportive towards a person who is working to change his stammering.

- Motivating factors. An individual may not feel very motivated if, for example, he has been asked to attend therapy by his employer or by family members who have put pressure on him. Also a client with a young family may not be able to give therapy the priority it needs to make the changes he wishes for.

- Openness. It can be valuable to disclose stammering and details of therapy to friends, family and colleagues. In this process the client may learn that there are less negative perceptions about stammering than he supposed.

- Venue. Does it matter to a client whether therapy is in a community clinic or an educational institution? For some individuals it can be a factor. It may be easier for a client to discuss going to 'evening classes' to work on issues around stammering rather than attending a community clinic at the same time as the baby/dental/chiropody clinics are being held.

The clinician's issues

- Client–clinician relationship. (See chapter 1 by Stewart and Leahy in this text.) There is more to a therapeutic approach than the therapy itself; the interplay between the client and the clinician and their working relationship; and the competence displayed by the clinician are highly significant factors (Wampold 2001). It is crucial that adequate time is given to establish a good working relationship, irrespective of therapy option or the mode of service delivery.

- Blocks of therapy. A clinician may work as part of a funded health or education system and therefore, a fixed number of sessions may be stipulated for each client per block of therapy. Conversely, the client may pay for his sessions (personally or via health insurance). As a result, the number of blocks of therapy or sessions he can attend may be limited by finances or the constraints imposed by an insurance policy. Unfortunately, time and healthcare needs are finite; consequently there are implications for a clinician.

  How many sessions is enough for the client and clinician to achieve any agreed goals? How many sessions would be too few? How can this be calculated at the start of the therapy process? These are some of the more difficult questions facing a clinician.

  However, some assumptions can be made based on how a client presents. For example:

- Where is he starting from?

- Is this his first experience of therapy?

- What does he need to know/not know/undo?

- Where there is a finite number of sessions available how can a clinician fit this 'time versus need' puzzle together? What can be achieved in four or six sessions in relation to the client's expressed goals?

- Establishing joint goals. Can a therapist agree a structure of therapy with her client at the start of a care plan? I begin each initial consultation with (friendly) questions to my client: 'What do you want?' and 'What has brought you here?' Having established this as a starting point, I am then open and honest as to whether I believe it is a goal that can be achieved together. Does a clinician always work off the same plan, or is there flexibility within a framework? Someone who has been for therapy previously may require a different approach to one who has never attended before. While a PWS may often place the clinician in the expert role, it is important that the clinician does not make assumptions about the client's experience.

- Importance of maintenance. Intensive therapy can make a huge impact. The literature is littered with reports of therapy programmes with only short-term data, but as much as therapy gains can come quickly, they may disappear just as quickly. Therefore, it is more prudent that maintenance is built into whatever therapy is offered. Maintenance and follow-up should not be seen as optional. They should be seen as integral to the long-term success of the intervention, however success may be defined.

- Client as therapist. Discouraging dependency should not be the first thing a clinician works on with a client, but it needs to be an underlying part of the process. A client should aspire to become his own therapist in time. However, as a clinician benefits from supervision and peer support, so might a client. There are advantages for a client in having the option to check in and return to therapy when appropriate, perhaps for a one-off appointment to "touch base', ask for advice or just discuss his progress with a therapist. Troubleshooting can also be a valuable support. Once a client has finished therapy, the maintenance stage can be on-going. A person may benefit from a phone call with his therapist before an interview to practise techniques. A text or email can be a boost and a reminder of progress. Do not underestimate the value of a supportive clinician as an ally for the PWS.

- As discussed in chapter 3 on stammering and voice by McLaughlin, sometimes onwards referrals to other professionals will be appropriate. As a rule of thumb, if the issue relates to the stammering, then it is in the realm of the SLT's expertise. However, if there is a problem which is bigger than stammering then the SLT may not be equipped and/or qualified to manage it.

   A therapist needs to be aware of the relevant professionals to refer to and liaise with. It is useful to keep a list of appropriate individuals, both local contacts and nationally recognised experts, and their contact details.

Overview of service delivery types

Different service delivery types are documented in the literature. Individual case studies appear, and group therapy data are presented by various authors. Some therapies are pure in their approach, while integrated therapies mix and match ideas and strategies. An SLT often wants to know which therapy she should use, but different approaches suit different personalities for both clients and clinicians. For example, Sheehan worked with groups, while Van Riper seemed to prefer individual client work.

Individual therapy may be the more prominent therapy in health centres and clinics around the UK, Ireland and further afield. Such a model of 1:1 intervention can allow more client-specific goals to be set as well as more time to be dedicated to the client, allowing for adaptable and directed therapy. In such settings, the client will also be more comfortable to disclose information. Less positively, there can be less of a social element, in that a client does not meet other people who stammer. Consequently, it can be more difficult to desensitise a person.

Group therapy is more difficult to arrange in terms of numbers of clients presenting and willing to attend therapy. When a number of clients do present at the right time there are many positives to this approach. There is a social aspect to therapy whereby a client can meet others who are like and unlike him – but they all stammer (Stewart and Richardson 2004).

Desensitisation can take place by watching and listening to other people's stammering and hear about other's experience of communication challenges. Depending on the group therapy it can be fluency shaping focused (De Nil and Kroll 1995, Onslow et al. 2004), stammering modification (Georgieva 2015, Blomgren et al. 2005) or more of an integrated approach (Irani et al. 2012, Langevin et al. 2006, Stewart and Richardson 2004).

A former client might be invited to these therapy groups as a model to show a new client what may (and may not) be achieved through therapy. Sheehan's work stressed the importance of 'auxiliary clinicians' and can be seen in video documentaries of his work. A person might be challenged to consider what he believes by different views held by others. Thus, he may grow through vicarious experience and gain confidence (Prins 1984). He can also learn from others and be motivated by his peers' progress and successes. Yaruss, Quesal, Reeves et al. (2002) and Stewart and Richardson (2004) reported on participant experiences of therapy; clients reflected on the positive effect of the group dynamic reducing aloneness and isolation as well as showing others with similar difficulties how they are able to be more positive, with a lasting effect on changing attitudes. The group may bond and be able to encourage/offer peer support to continue in challenging times. A group member can experiment with taking different roles in the group; by leading and supporting or being the wisdom on certain topics. Irani et al. (2012) suggested that clients drew a more positive perception of the effect of treatment when they felt part of a group undergoing therapy.

While group therapy has many positive aspects, some drawbacks appear in any group. Overarching themes of therapy perhaps will not address specific individual needs, and as a consequence, there may be less time to focus on an individual who requires more input. This can be addressed by specific 1:1 sessions outside of a group. Therapy may also be quite structured and unable to explore different options for different people. A clinician is tested and challenged in these environments to be effective and show creativity and ingenuity in problem solving as a group evolves. A clinician who is running groups would often benefit from investigating group facilitation skills or training. However, there is no substitute for experience, and we all have to start somewhere!

The frequency of therapy can be variable too, in both group and individual formats. Should therapy be delivered intensively in a short dose, or is it better to spread sessions out over a longer period of time e.g. on a weekly basis? Intensive therapy should allow a client to achieve gains within a condensed time frame. However, these gains may be more difficult to maintain without regular follow-up. While intensive therapy can show quick gains, weekly therapy may take longer for a client to show progress, and changes are often not as dramatic. It can also be time and schedule consuming for both client and clinician. Commitment is required by both parties.

Therapy approaches can be delivered beyond a clinic in residential settings (Evesham 1987). Dublin Adult Stuttering (DAS) operated two methods of service delivery during its lifetime. WASSP (Wright and Ayre 2000) is a useful self report outcome measure that can be used with adults who stammer. When the WASSP was used in DAS no significant difference in scores between residential and non-residential group data was found at 12 months post-therapy, i.e. each method of service delivery had a similar outcome (Linklater 2017).

Programmed online therapy is also available for a PWS. Therapy is often more structured for the client e.g. CBT (Helgadóttir et al. 2014, Menzies et al. 2008). There may be less time or possibility for clients to question and engage with a clinician in these more structured methods of service delivery.

Stewart reported on her clients (Stewart and Richardson 2004) who stated their on-going need for support. She reflected on the challenge for the clinician to provide a dynamic long-term service within modern health structures, where costs of intervention are often required by purchasers prior to therapy. There are many aspects to balance as therapy is planned and delivered.

Telehealth

This method of service delivery enables a client who is geographically remote, physically or economically disadvantaged to attend for therapy where he might be unable to attend were this option unavailable.

A systematic review of speech and language therapy delivered via telehealth found that 85% of 103 studies showed some advantages (Regina Molini-Avejonas et al. 2015). While more robust evidence will be required over time, early indications suggest that there is no evidence of significant negative impact on outcomes using remote therapy. Telehealth has a variety of operating systems, from phones (landlines and mobiles) and household computers to "highly expensive, fully immersive virtual reality systems with haptic interfaces" (Theodoros and Russell 2008, p. 131).

Teletherapy has been used in the UK with adults who stammer by the Airedale NHS Foundation Trust and the British Stammering Association. Therapeutic focus in this case was "achieving the individual's personal goals and equipping them with the skills and strategies needed to effectively live with their stammer"(Burgess 2019, p. 1). Data from pre- and post-outcome measures showed the negative impact of stammering was reduced for the 29 out of 64 who completed the treatment process.

Teletherapy can be time efficient for both client and clinician schedules. However, high levels of attrition were noted in the Airedale project. Initially IT/technical difficulties were apparent but a new system was introduced which improved the situation. While there may be initial reticence in a clinician who feels it can be difficult to build rapport in teletherapy, this is not always borne out by the data. Clients themselves had mixed views about the therapy initially but reported "being comfortable using telemedicine". Additionally many "preferred learning in their own home rather than in a clinical environment".

So what are the practicalities when considering setting up a telehealth service?

Basic overview

- A clinician will require relevant licencing to work in specific jurisdictions, and insurance must provide adequate cover. Different licencing and insurance laws will be applicable in different places, such as between countries and state boundaries.

- Both clinician and client are required to have hardware and software which is up to date and ensure that network connection speeds are acceptable.

- Software should be updated well in advance of each session. Applications must not be updated minutes before a scheduled appointment.

- Best practice would be to use a secure or encrypted-connection video link.

- Online systems need to be established without distractions and interruptions (as far as possible).

- A clinician may wish to establish a contract with an individual to agree how telehealth sessions will work. This may differ from face-to-face therapy. For example:

  o Agree exercises and activities with a client

  o Agree any arrangement for summarising sessions

    ○ Agree the procedure for sharing resources with a client

    ○ Agree a timeline for therapy and follow-up

    ○ Agree when information will be shared with a client, i.e. are handouts sent to a client before, during or after a session? Or can screenshots be safely and professionally shared with a client?

• Regular note taking schedule and best clinical storage practice still apply i.e. a clinician still needs to keep contemporaneous notes on client progress and maintain these in her usual manner. An SLT should be aware of how her jurisdiction handles personal data (e.g. territorial scope of GDPR).

• The SLT must consult her professional body and obtain details of telepractice guidelines. In absence of guidelines from the professional body, there are others available. For example, the American Speech-Language Hearing Association (ASHA) guidelines www.asha.org/Practice-Portal/Professional-Issues/Telepractice/.

Mixing options

• Individual assessment followed by telehealth. In terms of the practicalities of teletherapy, Chmela (2013) suggests that meeting the client in person is her preferred way to start therapy. This may not always be possible for a client where, for example, distance is an issue. Chmela suggests a practical solution could involve another SLT, local to the client, who could carry out the initial assessment She would then liaise with the 'telehealth' clinician, who would continue with the therapy sessions.

• Hybrid option. An alternative involves starting off with teletherapy and mixing this with face-to-face meetings over time depending on client preference, convenience and what issues are being worked on.

The limitations of telehealth

• The observable. Practically teletherapy does have its limitations for stammering. A clinician may not be able to observe certain overt aspects of stammering behaviour. For example a client may move his foot as part of his stammering, and this could be out of sight of the clinician watching on screen. Of course, a clinician can ask an individual if he has extra movements, but a client may not always be aware or could be sensitive when asked direct questions early in the process.

• The 'betweening'. Communication is more than merely the words and gestures which can be observed. Certain less tenuous energies and sensitivities occur when individuals interact when in the same space. These factors impact the communication process, but this will be different in tele-health. The absence of these factors needs further exploration to determine whether or not it has an impact on therapy effectiveness.

• Furthermore, glitches in technology or an unsuitable setting can impact on communication. This may be due to variable internet service provision, unreliable WiFi and/or poor acoustics. All of which can make a session more difficult. In these instances do not be afraid to ask the client for repetition and clarification being clear about the reason for the breakdown in communication.

Beyond service delivery

A client can engage in activities outside clinic contact with a therapist which can have great value from a therapeutic perspective.

A range of resources and activities are available to a PWS and those who work with him. We must bear in mind an important point of order: not everything is for everyone. Adults I have worked with have tried public-speaking groups and organisations such as Toastmasters International or drama groups. Another programme, Speaking Circles®, was developed by Lee Glickstein as a way to become a more comfortable and engaging speaker. These may be more suitable once a client has made some progress in therapy and wants to become a more engaging communicator.

Sometimes a PWS will have a preference on what he wants to take part in, read or listen to. A therapist will be respectful of this but can challenge the client's choices where appropriate. A client should be encouraged to explore the reasons for his reluctance; i.e. is it because he doesn't want to do something because it isn't to his taste, or is it more related to avoidance of stammering?

Resources include:

• Websites/newsletters etc. of national and international stammering associations. Furthermore, they may have accessible events that a PWS could attend. Many of my clients have reported the benefit of attending such events as part of their journey in stammering to become more informed and more comfortable about their own stammering.

• Attending national/international events on stammering. A clinician can encourage a client to attend events, such as the national conferences of stammering organisations. Associations typically have open days that are open to members of the public. As a coordinator of National Stammering Awareness Day (in Ireland) we have held an annual event since 2007, offering a range of speakers including people who stammer, professionals who work with people who stammer and also other speakers of interest. Attending an event can be a significant moment for a PWS to realise that he is not alone.

• Support groups or self-help groups can also be an additional support for a PWS. (See chapter 9 by Liddle and Adams in this book.) Again, there is a chance to meet other people who stammer and potentially work on areas to improve stammering and associated attitudes. Support groups, however, are difficult to maintain with variable attendance and varying needs. Not all PWS who take part will be attending for the same reasons, which fuels the challenge of managing and cultivating a group. More social events can also take place such as quizzes or 'walk and talk' events. While these are not therapeutic in their aim or in a classic sense of service delivery, the importance of meeting other people who stammer cannot be underestimated. For a young person who stammers to meet a potential role model will have a significantly positive impact on his future outlook and aspirations; it enables him to see that people who stammer can live fulfilling lives.

• It is also useful to consider recommending other more academic conferences such as the UK's Oxford Dysfluency Conference or the European Symposium on Fluency Disorders hosted in Belgium. A long-term goal for a client could be to attend a World Congress. For example, the International Fluency Association, International Stammering Association and International Cluttering Association recent congress in Japan (2018) hosted many PWS.

Before we dive into the world of online resources, I predict that offline resources, such as this book, will continue to be accessible to many. Writers have been writing about stammering since writing began. For example, there are hieroglyphic symbols for stammering and a reference in the Bible. In the more modern era we have seen more people who stammer appear in the role of author. Wendell Johnson's *Because I Stutter* or Marty Jezer's *A Life Bound Up in Words* (available on archive.org) were earlier books to be recognised in this genre. More recently, Nina G's *Stutterer Interrupted: The Comedian Who Almost Didn't Happen* looks at stammering, disability and activism from a different angle.

Technology and online resources

Directing a client to an online resource is part of developing his responsibility to become more informed about stammering and to adopt a more expert and advocate role. This particular change in role is an important part of therapy; rather than feeling that stammering happens to the person, he can move towards a position of knowledge and understanding of stammering that can be shared and explored with others.

At time of writing, the following are considered the most useful fixed resources for a client to use:

• The stuttering homepage – www.stutteringhomepage – has been an important part of my therapy recommendations for a client and for individual session plans. It has been in existence since the mid to late 1990s and is a vast collection of essays, reflections and creative pieces written by individuals who stammer, those who know them and professionals who work with them.

• Whether or not an SLT and her client agree with all of the suggested resources is not of concern. However, the pieces that are recommended reading and/or discussion points in therapy should provoke thought, debate and critical thinking. My main intention for directing my clients to particular resources is to inspire them to action and change.

Deep inside the Stuttering Homepage is one of the most valuable resources. Voices: past and present: www.mnsu.edu/comdis/voices/voices.html.

This is an amazing resource with clinical and personal experiences of stammering shared from the 1950s up to the 2010s. Many of the talks contain humour and candid reflections on the mix of tragedy and comedy that comprise stammering.

• ISAD. The Stuttering Homepage also links to International Stuttering Awareness Day (ISAD) conferences, which are archived here from 1998. There are 20 years of ISAD conferences currently hosted, and each year contains a number of articles, features, shared experiences and audio and video clips available to be explored. These can be used as discussion points with a client and topics to discuss and review in a therapy group setting. The diversity of materials ensures that there will be something of relevance to each individual client at various stages of his therapy. Furthermore, as an active exercise, each October clients and clinicians are encouraged to take part in an annual online ISAD conference prior to the day itself on October 22.

Using technology/the internet as 'therapy'

The positives: While some contemporary commentators suggest that technology is designed to distract, it can be used in ways which are beneficial. Alarms, phone reminders and pop-ups remind a person to use a strategy, a particular technique, to initiate a conversation, to work a feared word into a sentence for that meeting/situation/day. Conversely, a sticky note can be used for the same objective.

While social media currently has its proponents and detractors, it has had an impact on how a PWS engages with others, those who stammer and those who are more fluent. It can be embraced for desensitisation and increasing approach behaviour (see chapter 5 by Linklater on avoidance-reduction therapy in this book). As with other disorders and disabilities, the internet has enabled connections to be made between individuals who would otherwise have remained isolated. Specific platforms have come and gone, and the current platforms have different uses. A client may use these to connect with others who stammer and to become more informed about a range of topics on stammering and management options.

In addition, the act of 'liking' an organisation dedicated to supporting people who stammer can be viewed as an active advertisement and proactive statement that a person is doing something about his speech. A PWS is often highly self-conscious of how his stammering is perceived. Therefore, a simple like, retweet or share (an 'engagement') is an active step in becoming more comfortable with stammering on a social level. Thus, while actively having a presence on social media may not be the same as carrying out an introduction to strangers on the street, it can allow for acceptance and encouragement from a variety of other sources and people, many of whom would be very unlikely to walk down the same street!

The negatives: A note of caution is included here on how best to engage with any online presence or platform. For example, beware the use of electronic communication as a tool for a person to avoid speaking! Sometimes email and messaging are the more efficient ways to connect with another person, but social media and electronic communication do often reduce the opportunity for conversation. A client may adopt the approach of "I'll just send a message rather than talk to that person", and this is not likely to reduce the impact of stammering. This is avoidance. Thus, moderation and balance are called for. Make some calls, send some emails; but be sure a client challenges himself.

Social media does of course come with a health warning regarding possible negative responses a person might receive. Thus, any engagement should be treated with caution. A client should be encouraged to challenge misperceptions where possible and educate others on the nature of stammering. However, some 'hard-of-thinking' individuals operate in this medium, and a client should be advised to treat such people with equanimity or, when necessary, ignore misdemeanours and trolling.

Virtual Reality (VR) resources

Scenari-Aid is an online virtual reality system which allows a person to experience situations without directly being in them. Developed by Grant Meredith (Meredith and Achterbosch 2014, Swift et al. 2015), it is a more realistic version of role-play in which a PWS can experience everyday interactions such as ordering in a shop/over a counter, taking part in a job interview or booking accommodation for a holiday. While there is no substitute for real-life experience, sometimes it is too great a leap for a client to go from the safety of the clinic setting to the outside world. Scenari-Aid provides that bridge. A clinician can watch a video with her client and talk through these scenarios, planning and responding to possible outcomes, essentially troubleshooting in advance. This will give a client confidence that he can handle a situation and several of the possible outcomes. While every eventuality cannot be anticipated, success breeds success in speaking situations. Success does not necessarily mean fluency but achieving the outcome a client desires. Thousands of people have registered with the website, and future updates are in process, with platforms for children due for release (Personal communication Meredith, 2019).

Videos

Sometimes, an SLT can use alternative means to promote her message. Having worked with both groups and individuals, I know that sometimes a PWS will benefit from seeing other people outside of his immediate situation. Such people may not necessarily look and sound the same as the client but they do also stammer; stammering can be normalised through seeing a different person stammer, whatever his background.

The video will likely back up the message a therapist is espousing in therapy, but even if there are areas of disagreement between a client and his clinician, this is a good way to develop critical thinking and adds variety to therapeutic interactions.

With the nature of the internet, videos come and go, I would expect that the following videos would remain online for the foreseeable future or at least be archived for public access. Many videos will also continue to be available on loan or for purchase through different countries' national stammering associations:

- The Stuttering Foundation of America has a wide range of videos including *Adult Stuttering Therapy With Clinician Dr Charles Van Riper*.
- Documentaries about Dr Joseph Sheehan and Vivian Sheehan are available from www. stutterstutter.com.
- The UCLA 1968 feature with Sheehan, *The Iceberg of Stuttering*, is archived at: https://archive.org/details/theicebergofstuttering.
- *Transcending Stuttering*, a documentary featuring Dr Philip Schneider and clients, provides realism and uplifting messages about the experience of stammering.

Podcasts

Similar to videos, some podcasts give strength to the message that a therapist and the client are working on in therapy. This would not be the first thing I suggest to a PWS when he comes to therapy. However, after a few visits, a client sometimes asks for different things to be working on between sessions. Podcasts are a way to keep a PWS focussed on working on stammering in an indirect way. A client can become more desensitised by listening to others who stammer as part of his daily routines, for example, on his commute to work or while exercising. Therefore, listening to people talking about stammering and changing attitudes is a positive start to the working day, on a day off, or while washing dishes. The beauty of a podcast is that it can be listened to when and where the person wants. From one perspective it gives a client an option to choose what he listens to and starts increasing his choices about what he thinks about stammering and what he agrees and disagrees with.

There are currently several podcasts in existence pertaining to stammering. A quick online search will bring up options of how to access these via a computer, smartphone or other device. There will be other podcasts that an individual can access not mentioned here. Either they appear to be dormant or they are have not been launched at time of writing.

Noteworthy current example of stammering podcasts are:

- Stuttertalk (http://stuttertalk.com/) is a not-for-profit organisation that has been around since 2007 and has produced hundreds of podcasts talking about stammering. These are freely available online and feature people who stammer and professionals who work with stammering.
- The Stutteringiscool (http://stutteringiscool.com/) podcast by Daniele Rossi has also been established for more than 10 years. He has used the internet as a way to become more comfortable with stammering. As well as podcasting, Daniele has published comics and books about stammering.
- Pamela Mertz interviews women who stammer in her podcast hosted on her website; 'Make Room for the Stuttering' (https://stutterrockstar.com/). Due to the gender ratio in

stammering it can be more difficult for a woman to meet and engage with other women who stammer. Therefore the 'Women Who Stutter Podcast' is an ideal and accessible resource for a therapist to share with her female clients. (For the male readers, Pam does also interview men now and again!)

Podcasts need not necessarily be about stammering. At time of writing a recent range of critically acclaimed podcasts have been produced by BBC Radio 4 (UK) titled "Don't Tell Me the Score". The programme looks at sporting achievements and interviews a range of athletes, competitors and coaches. Hosted by journalist Simon Mundie, the aim is to find out "what sport can teach us about life". In these podcasts, practical everyday challenges and strategies are illustrated and discussed for self-development. Resilience, perseverance, vulnerability and self-acceptance are fundamental qualities that can support changes that a PWS can make with regard to stammering. A client may not win a gold medal at the Olympics for stammering but he can apply some of the life lessons learned by these athletes directly to his stammering (www.bbc.co.uk/programmes/p06qbt0y).

Articles promoting growth and positive self-change beyond stammering might provide a useful direction once the initial stages of therapy are completed. For example, Oliver Burkeman's writing in *The Guardian* newspaper (UK) can be found online ("This Column Will Change Your Life") and in his books. Burkeman (2011) writes short articles about effective change, acceptance and how to remember to keep up positive habits, all of which can be used to open up a discussion with a client. Burkeman (2008) delves into 'the art of acceptance', which a client can read and reflect on where his stammering might fit in and how he might start to change his attitudes towards his stammering. The benefit of such articles is that it makes stammering part of everyday life. It is easy to work on changing stammering and its associated attitudes in a clinic room. It's far more difficult when a PWS is in a meeting, in an interview or in a shop with someone who is asking questions while he is trying to work on his eye contact.

As with anything, an SLT and her client may not like or agree on everything in these podcasts or the content of the articles. However, there is a range of options which can be presented to a client from which he can choose .

Beyond stammering-specific podcasts, there will be instances of people who stammer who are interviewed not talking about stammering. This is important too. An individual who stammers doesn't always want to talk about stammering. He may want to talk about other things in his life. It is useful for a therapist to encourage a client to seek out people who stammer, perhaps those who have had some successes in aspects of their lives which do not relate to stammering. Clients have reported that it is useful to hear about famous people who stammer, but it's also important to hear about less famous people who stammer. For example, the teacher, the lawyer, the homemaker, the bus driver, the person who works in the call centre talking on the phone all day, all of whom are getting on in the world and stammering as they go about their lives.

Apps

An app is an application that can be installed on a computer, tablet or smartphone. Since the recent ubiquity of the smartphone, many apps that have particular focus on stammering have been in and out of development. They come and go, and some have even been renamed since I started to write this chapter. However, it would be remiss not to acknowledge their presence.

Most apps appear to be in the realm of offering delayed auditory feedback and fluency counters to work out percentage syllables stammered (%SS) and occasionally how a person feels about stammering. There are, however, some apps that are linked to stammering programmes typically with more of a fluency-shaping therapeutic leaning. Some apps are more generic than being directed at stammering. Some apps may give a clinician access to a person's data (related to stammering) for analysis and therapeutic planning reasons. Some apps will also offer online support either through chat or through a voice call. There may be charges for such services. These apps may or may not be run by qualified professionals.

At time of writing, some national organisations have pages where they outline the apps that they are aware of. It is important to note that these are apps that they may or may not endorse. This neatly brings us to the final thoughts of this chapter.

Developing critical thinking

A quick search with Dr Google will reveal some questionable magic cures, quick fixes and outright quackery in the internet repository. However, there is an ample range of resources to support a client's progress. It is beyond the remit of this chapter to be prescriptive about developing critical thinking, but it must be addressed. How should critical thinking for a client and his clinician be developed? When exploring the internet options, how can a quality product be identified? What questions should be asked to help separate the useful from the misleading?

When reading information from the internet, it is likely that each person will come to different understandings and opinions of the same piece. Individuals appreciate articles about stammering in different ways, in the same way as people differ in their culinary tastes. However, a client should be encouraged to read and listen with more critical eyes and ears. Having some guidance in interpretation is useful for both a client and his therapist. Here are a list of questions to start this process:

• Who is writing the piece?

• What is his background?

• Is he a person who stammers?

• Is he a professional working with people who stammer?

• Is he a person running independent services for PWS?

• What is his experience? Is it apparent that he has a 'good' experience of working with stammering?

• Is he a quack promising a quick cure or unrealistic results?

• Does he refer to knowledge from the stammering world? Does he reference peer-reviewed journal articles and published books? Is he mainly referring to unverified internet sources?

• Does it sound like he is trying to sell something?

Can we trust Dr Speakfree PhD from The Speakfree Institute For People Who Want To Talk Good In Three Easy Steps? Or do you want to buy a light therapy app that will control and reduce your stammering for £50? Variants of such an app may also 'work' to solve a number of other conditions such as autism, numerous disabilities, insomnia and even general life dissatisfaction. Looking at the developer or author and research background of an app may give a clinician more confidence in the product. *Caveat emptor*; let the buyer beware. I will let the reader decide.

The internet is content driven, and it is very easy to publish anything today. This is different from the early/mid-2000s, when blogging was more of a niche activity, and most of today's social media was not available. Therefore a therapist should bear this in mind when reading online features.

It should be considered that just because a person, outlook or treatment approach appears in the media or at an event, it does not always mean that the editor, producers or organisers endorse and agree with all points being promoted. Sometimes, features are extremely valuable and can promote increased awareness of stammering or an event that is coming up. However, various media forms have increased in recent years, and there is not always critical judgement of context. Therefore, be critical and cautious. Typically, if something appears too good to be true, it is too good to be true. While I encourage people who stammer to be hopeful and open to the possibilities of change, I do ask my clients to be critical of the content they come across and to scrutinise it.

A clinician should encourage discussion and debate about stammering with both her clients and colleagues. Talking about stammering with others can only increase knowledge and understanding and ultimately develop the ability to evaluate and identify what is fair and worthy of further consideration.

Looking ahead

In writing this chapter I have been considering the question of how the overarching themes of therapy can be met within the various parameters of service delivery. I am conscious of the need for therapy to evolve, whether as the result of findings from clinical research or more organically. Therapy needs to reflect our changing society; changes in the workplace, leisure pursuits and the way people interact. It needs to adapt in the present as much as it adapted in the 1970s and 1980s, and it needs to adapt to be relevant to the reader of this book in 2040.

In some circles there is a very simplistic view of therapy. This is reflected in the beliefs of a client who says "Give me more speech therapy and I'll get better". (See an online article by Eckhardt (2012) entitled "If I Practiced More, I Would Stutter Less". The article questions this opinion and explores the alternative of becoming more accepting of glitches that occur in stammering.)

It is important that the therapy delivered by a therapist is not restricted by the way she delivers it. If the service within which she operates specifies a certain number of sessions per client, then she should not limit the choices offered to a client so they fit that service parameter. Therapy is complex and needs time. Moreover, the methodology of the therapy used must be tailored to the needs of the client and continually adapted for and by him.

The clinic must be a safe place to learn and experiment with new ways of managing stammering, but at some point the client has to apply them in his everyday life. The client has to be engaged in this process and ultimately take responsibility for that change. While he is doing that a clinician may support him in a more advisory and coaching role. This may necessitate being less clinic based and engaging in situations with the client. Service delivery should, therefore, encompass the need to move out of the clinic with the client as he progresses. Ultimately the service a clinician delivers is about sharing in the many opportunities available to her client to reduce the impact of stammering and increase his opportunities in everyday settings.

In some ways, as much as this chapter is for the clinician, it is for clients too. Service delivery is more than about service. A PWS doesn't stop stammering at 5 p.m. when the clinics close, he stammers at different times and at different levels throughout his life. The message to each PWS is to keep maintaining and keep moving forward; watch a video, listen to a podcast, talk to someone, write a reminder on a Post-it note. He needs to do that each day as long as he feels he needs to.

Acknowledgement

Dr Speakfree PhD (quack) was dreamed up by speech and language therapists Stephanie O'Connor and Dr Jonathon Linklater several years ago.

References

Blomgren, M., Roy, N., Callister, T. and Merrill, R.M. (2005). Intensive stuttering modification therapy: A multidimensional assessment of treatment outcomes. *Journal of Speech, Language, and Hearing Research*, 48, 509–523. http://doi.org/10.1044/1092-4388(2005/035)

Burgess, S. (2019). www.health.org.uk/improvement-projects/delivering-speech-and-language-therapy-through-telemedicine-to-adults-who-stammer

Burkeman, O. (2008). This column will change your life. *Guardian*, newspaper (UK). Retrieved November 2019. www.theguardian.com/lifeandstyle/2008/aug/23/healthandwellbeing1.

Burkeman, O. (2011). *Help! How to become Slightly Happier and Get a Bit More Done.* Edinburgh, UK: Canongate.

Chmela, K. (2013). What makes for effective online treatment? *American Speech & Hearing Association Leader*, 18(1), 12–13. https://doi.org/10.1044/leader.OV.18012013.12

De Nil, L.F. and Kroll, R.M. (1995). The relationship between locus of control and long-term stuttering treatment outcome in adult stutterers. *Journal of Fluency Disorders*, 20(4), 345–364. http://doi.org/10.1016/0094-730X(95)00024-2

Eckhardt, J. (2012). *If I Practiced More, I Would Stutter Less.* Retrieved November 2019. www.mnsu.edu/comdis/isad16/papers/therapy16/eckardt16

Evesham, M. (1987). Residential courses for stutterers combining technique and personal construct psychology. In C. Levy (ed.), *Stuttering Therapies: Practical Approaches* (pp. 61–70). London, UK: Croom Helm.

Georgieva, D. (2015). Intensive non-avoidance group therapy with adult stutterers: Follow up data. *Procedia – Social and Behavioral Sciences*, 193, 108–114. http://doi.org/10.1016/j.sbspro.2015.03.249

Helgadóttir, F.D., Menzies, R.G., Onslow, M., Packman, A. and O'Brian, S. (2014). A standalone Internet cognitive behavior therapy treatment for social anxiety in adults who stutter: CBTpsych. *Journal of Fluency Disorders*, 41(C), 47–54. http://doi.org/10.1016/j.jfludis.2014.04.001

Irani, F., Gabel, R.M., Daniels, D. and Hughes, S. (2012). The long term effectiveness of intensive stuttering therapy: A mixed methods study. *Journal of Fluency Disorders*, 37(3), 164–178. http://doi.org/10.1016/j.jfludis.2012.04.002

Jezer, M. (1997). *A Life Bound Up in Words*. New York: Basic Books.

Johnson, W. (1930). *Because I Stutter*. New York: D. Appleton & Co.

Langevin, M., Huinck, W.J., Kully, D., Peters, H.F.M., Lomheim, H. and Tellers, M. (2006). A cross-cultural, long-term outcome evaluation of the ISTAR Comprehensive Stuttering Program across Dutch and Canadian adults who stutter. *Journal of Fluency Disorders*, 31(4), 229–256. http://doi.org/10.1016/j.jfludis.2006.06.001

Linklater, J.P. (2017). *Effectiveness of Avoidance-reduction Therapy for Adults Who Stutter*. (Doctoral thesis). University of Limerick.

Menzies, R.G., O'Brian, S., Onslow, M., Packman, A., St Clare, T. and Block, S. (2008). An experimental clinical trial of a cognitive-behavior therapy package for chronic stuttering. *Journal of Speech, Language, and Hearing Research*, 51(6), 1451–1464. http://doi.org/10.1044/1092-4388(2008/07-0070)

Meredith, G. and Achterbosch, L. (2014). The perceived benefits of video-based simulation for people who stutter. Presented at the *10th Oxford Dysfluency Conference*, 16–10 July.

Nina, G. (2019). *Stutterer Interrupted: The Comedian Who Almost didn't Happen*. Berkley, CA: She Writes Press.

Onslow, M., O'Brian, S., Packman, A. and Rousseau, I. (2004). Long-term follow up of speech outcomes for a prolonged-speech treatment for stuttering: The effects of paradox on stuttering treatment research. In A.K. Bothe (ed.), *Evidence-based Treatment of Stuttering: Empirical Issues and Clinical Implications* (pp. 231–244). Mahwah, NJ: Lawrence Erlbaum.

Prins, D. (1984). Treatment of adults: Managing stuttering. In R.F. Curlee and W.H. Perkins (eds.), *Nature and Treatment of Stuttering: New Directions* (pp. 397–424). London: Taylor & Francis.

Regina Molini-Avejonas, D., Rondon-Melo, S., de La Higuera Amato, C.A. and Samelli, A.G. (2015). A systematic review of the use of telehealth in speech, language and hearing sciences. *Journal of Telemedicine and Telecare*, 21(7), 367–376. https://doi.org/10.1177/1357633X15583215

Sheehan, J.G. (1970). *Stuttering: Research and Therapy*. New York: Harper & Row.

Stewart, T. (1996a). A further application of the Fishbein and Ajzen model to therapy for adult stammerers. *European Journal of Disorders of Communication,* 31(4), 445–464.

Stewart, T. (1996b) Good maintainers and poor maintainers: A personal construct approach to an old problem. *Journal of Fluency Disorders,* 21(1), 33–48.

Stewart, T. and Richardson, G. (2004). A qualitative study of therapeutic effect from a user's perspective. *Journal of Fluency Disorders,* 29(2), 95–108.

Swift, M.C., Meredith, G. McCulloch, J. and Turville, C. (2015). Use of Scenari-Aid to aid maintenance of stuttering therapy outcomes. *Procedia – Social and Behavioral Sciences,* 193, 253–260.

Theodoros, D. and Russell, T. (2008). Telerehabilitation: Current perspectives. *Studies in Health Technology and Informatics,* 131, 191–209.

Wampold, Bruce E. (2001). *The Great Psychotherapy Debate: Models, Methods, and Findings*. Mahwah, NJ: L. Erlbaum Associates.

Wright, L. and Ayre, A. (2000). *WASSP: The Wright & Ayre Stuttering Self-rating Profile.* Bicester: Speechmark.

Yaruss, J.S., Quesal, R.W., Reeves, L., Molt, L.F., Kluetz, B., Caruso, A.J. and Lewis, F. (2002). Speech treatment and support group experiences of people who participate in the National Stuttering Association. *Journal of Fluency Disorders*, 27(2), 115–134. http://doi.org/10.1016/S0094-730X(02)00114-6

Video references

Schneider, P. (2005). *"Transcending stuttering: The Inside Story."*

Sheehan, J.G., Amick, R. and Holzman, A. (1987). *Joseph G. Sheehan's Message to a Stutterer*. Los Angeles: Amick/Holzman Co.

Sheehan, J.G., Amick, R., Holzman, A. and Amick/Holzman Company (1988). *"No Words To Say"* Los Angeles: Amick/Holzman Co. (via www.stutterstutter.com)

Van Riper, C., and Guitar, B. (2005). *Adult Stuttering Therapy*. Western Michigan University Television & Stuttering Foundation of America.

Van Riper, C., Spink, M. and Bosze, S. (1992). *Adult stuttering therapy*. Western Michigan University & Stuttering Foundation of America.

Van Riper, C. *Adult Stuttering Therapy*. **The Stuttering Foundation DVD No. 1080.**

Podcast links

Stuttertalk – http://stuttertalk.com/

Stutteringiscool – http://stutteringiscool.com/

Women Who Stutter Podcast – https://stutterrockstar.com/

Don't Tell Me the Score – www.bbc.co.uk/programmes/p06qbt0y

3 | Stammering and voice

Alison McLaughlin

In my experience as an SLT working with both those who stammer and those with voice disorders, therapy can experiment with and draw from several areas. Some of these areas do not necessarily set out to work with the dysfluency itself but can, nevertheless, effect positive change. While working with voice and its disorders I have found the following useful for a PWS:

- Understanding the anatomy and physiology of voice and its power source as a prerequisite to introducing direct speech work

- Encouraging a healthy voice and how to maintain this

- Focusing on relaxation with specific targeting of the extrinsic and intrinsic muscle groups of the head and neck

- Emphasising the value of warming up and warming down the voice for everyday speaking and not just for 'performance'.

This chapter will encourage the reader to ask the question – should a therapist working with a PWS consider voice as one of the important parameters of his communication?

Voice change and challenge can happen to anyone at any time. Knowledge and understanding of voice, how it is used and how an individual can take care of it can be valuable preparation for direct speech work. For the PWS raising awareness and learning about what supports and what can affect his voice performance compliments the maintenance process and 'toolbox' ethos fostered throughout the *Dysfluency Resource Book* (Turnbull and Stewart 2010).

A PWS can experience co-occurring conditions independent of and as a consequence of stammering e.g. higher levels of social anxiety and depression (Craig and Tran 2006, Erickson and Block 2013). There is little research on the incidence or the potential risk factors for dysphonia in the stammering population. What we do know is that in the moment of stammering the functioning of the larynx and the whole speech system are affected.

For example, stammering may involve:

- Muscle tension not only in the larynx, head and neck but whole body

- Excessive phonatory effort to initiate voice

- Incoordination of respiration and phonation

- Variation of speech volume and effort.

All of these features are often compounded by secondary behaviours when a person attempts to gain control of his speech. A person's emotional and physical anticipation of stammering and his emotional and physical response following the moment of stammering are all crucial in changing the impact of stammering (Guitar 2013). These same behaviours can lead to hyperfunctional voice disorders, characterised by excessive phonatory effort, commonly referred to as *muscle tension dysphonias* (Boone and McFarlane 2014).

If a total-communication approach to stammering therapy is taken it is important to have explored voice and know how to take care of it. When working with a PWS I have seen voice change occur for several reasons. The therapist working in the area of fluency disorders may encounter:

- A PWS with no concerns about his voice
- A PWS who develops voice change during direct speech variation and speech modification work/stammering therapy
- A PWS who presents for stammering therapy with a diagnosed voice disorder e.g. vocal cord nodules; this could be related or unrelated to the stammering behaviour
- A PWS who either presents or develops voice change that is unrelated to the stammering behaviour or stammering therapy.

This chapter aims to focus on the first two types of presentations. Included in the chapter is a section called 'Onward referral', which delineates when and how to signpost a person presenting with voice change that persists or show signs and symptoms that are more concerning. (It should be noted that at no point in this chapter am I advocating that the reader assume the role of the voice therapist.)

How to describe voice

A voice disorder occurs when voice quality, pitch, tone and loudness differ or are inappropriate for an individual's age, gender, cultural background or geographic location (Boone et al. 2014, Stemple, Glaze and Klaben 2010). Each voice is individual to that person, and there is no universally accepted way of identifying and categorising voice. Following ear, nose and throat (ENT) evaluation a voice therapist would typically obtain:

- A detailed case history with a combination of perceptual and instrumental voice analysis
- Formal and informal assessments for voice[1]
- The client's self-report to determine the impact of voice change on quality of life
- Environmental and family/significant others perspective of both vocal demand and performance
- Observation analysis of breathing and posture and
- Palpation of the larynx.

For the purpose of this chapter, the therapist's ear and her ability to understand and appreciate the client's experience are sufficient to determine the necessity for attention to the voice of the PWS. To understand any speech and language disorder, key questions need to be considered when taking a case history.

---

[1] Sue Jones provides an excellent summary of standardised and non-standardised assessments for voice in chapter 1 of her book Laryngeal Endoscopy & Voice Therapy: A Clinical Guide (2016) as does chapter 13 of Leslie Mathieson's The Voice and Its Disorders (2001).

Resource 3.1: Questions to Ask a Client about Voice has been designed to support the SLT in gathering key information about voice. It can help both SLT and the PWS work logically through a list of key questions to gain an understanding as to how voice change may have come about.

It is worth noting that to simply describe voice quality and the client's experience of voice in his own words goes beyond predefined descriptors and checklists. It is meaningful for the client, and it allows the therapist to connect with that person's experience, thoughts and feelings about his voice. Personal descriptors can give an indication of what and where the breakdown in the vocal system may be. Table 3.1 is not exhaustive but is an example of some of the descriptors that a PWS may experience.

Table 3.1 Exploring personal descriptors for voice

Client's experience	Client's personal descriptor	Potential drivers
Feels	Strangled	• Muscle tension
	Tight	• Laryngeal constriction
	Aching	• Pushing and forcing voice
	Dry	• Poor vocal hygiene
		• Dehydration
		• Medication
		• Inhalers
		• Underlying medical condition e.g. thyroid
	Itchy	• Allergy
		• Hay fever
		• Reflux
	Lump in throat	• Muscle tension
		• Emotion
Sounds	Quiet	• Poor breath support
	Harsh	• Too much effort when voicing
		• Changes to the vocal fold mucosa e.g. nodules/oedema/ fluid filled (smoking)
	Full	• Congestion
		• Allergy
		• Structural changes to the vocal tract and or the larynx

How is voice produced?

Understanding how voice is produced and how the voice systems can be affected when a person stammers can be both empowering and practically useful in terms of control (emotion and fluency) when working directly on speech. Voice relies on the interaction of the lungs, the vocal folds and vocal tract. The terms 'power', 'source' and 'filter' have been borrowed from voice theory and practice and will be used here to help the PWS understand how voice is produced and how his own voice process may be affected.[2]

Let's consider voice as being made up of three systems:

• Power

• Source

• Filter.

A simple line drawing (Figure 3.1) is sufficient to support a PWS in understanding where anatomically each system is located. This can be quickly drawn 'live' in a session using an outline like the one here if the SLT does not have access to a larynx model or voice literature in the clinic setting.

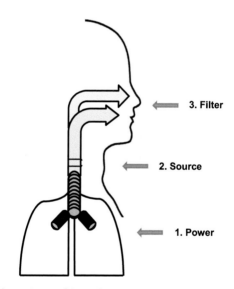

Figure 3.1 Simple line drawing of head, neck and lungs

Power – the respiratory system (lungs)

When sound is created there are number of necessary processes before speech is created:

• Good breath support will ensure that pressure below the glottis is sufficient to bring the vocal cords together

• A breath is taken in (inspiration), and the vocal cords are brought together, momentarily, until the pressure subsides and the air is allowed to move through the glottis

• Followed by fine muscle control resulting in closure of the cords and correction to the tension and length to enable the desired pitch and range to be achieved.

---

[2] I have found the work of Jo Estill, a singer and voice researcher in the fields of vocal physiology, acoustics and perception of voice quality influential in my work as a voice therapist. Her work is an extension of the useful analytical model of how speech sounds are produced, the source filter model (Rosen and Howell, 2010). Estill's view of systems that make up speech and voice is a useful framework for clinician and client in understanding how voice is produced.

Source – the larynx (voice box)

This aerodynamic tracheal pressure from the lungs sets the vocal cords into vibration and produces sound. The cords move in a wavelike motion. The larynx is a mobile structure, and it can be moved consciously by the speaker. This ability to change the position of the larynx, breath support and the shape of the vocal tract allows for variation in sound (see Filter). Sound production requires that several mechanical properties are met. Once these conditions are met, sound is generated from the vocal cord vibration. The conditions are:

• Adequate breath support to produce sufficient subglottic pressure

• Adequate control of the laryngeal musculature to produce not only glottic closure but also the proper length and tension of the vocal cords

• Favourable pliability and vibratory capacity of the tissues of the vocal cords.

Filter – resonance (vocal tract)

The structures of the vocal tract include:

• Pharynx

• Oropharynx

• Nasopharynx.

Vibratory sound waves that are created by vocal cord vibration move within these structures, and this is known as *resonance*.

The articulators include:

• Velum

• Hard palate

• Tongue

• Teeth

• Lips.

These structures help to shape and create distinct sounds that are recognised as speech.

It is also worth considering the three systems as a succinct way of observing how a PWS uses his voice when talking. ***Resource 3.2: Observation: Power, Source and Filter*** can be used to organise observations but also identify where a breakdown in his system may occur. Observing voice and speech production in this way adds an extra dimension to the identification process – a crucial part in stammering therapy and preparation for change.

Laryngeal health and how the larynx functions will influence quality of voice production. We have explored the importance of good breath support. A compromised respiratory (power) system will decrease the vocal cord vibration i.e. range, volume and quality of sound produced. Equally any change in the shape or size of vocal tract (filter) will affect resonance i.e. too much constriction will make a sound thin, tight and high. For a PWS it may be assumed that there is an increased risk for the development of a voice problem as a result of how the systems of voice behave in the moment of stammering. Stammering behaviours such as blocking, prolongation, increased volume and hard attack could be viewed as 'hyperfunctional patterns of phonation' (Mathieson 2001). If left unmanaged or improved patterns of phonation are not established this could cause significant deterioration in the voice (source), as reported by Salihovic et al. (2009):

> Abnormal functioning of the larynx (pws) may include excessive muscular tension and variable subglottal pressure, which could be caused by muscle incoordination of

the respiratory tract. Weaker laryngeal neuromuscular control and disturbances in respiratory and laryngeal control may also lead to voice problems.
(p. 73)

Drivers for voice change

Understanding the drivers for any voice change is essential when thinking about how to support it. Most voice disorders will have contributions from more than one etiologic factor (Stemple, Roy and Klaben 2014). Drivers for voice change include:

• Emotional

• Medical

• Mechanical

• Environmental.

Each driver and their relationship with each other should be explored if there has been voice change. This process can be helpful in formulation or when creating a picture to help the therapist and the client understand why voice change happened. I have found exploring potential 'drivers' with a PWS can be useful as an awareness-raising activity and a prevention tool. Perhaps, more importantly, it also allows an SLT to see which drivers can and cannot be changed. Let's now look at each driver and the stance that could be adopted by the clinician working with a PWS.

Emotional: How a voice sounds and performs reflects how a person is feeling. The intrinsic and extrinsic musculature of the larynx works in balance and contributes to how emotion is expressed in voice. This in turn provides a 'psychological impact' that conveys meaning to the listener (Rubin and Greenberg 2002). Discrete and obvious changes to pitch, effort, volume and the flow of voice quality reflect particular emotional states e.g. an excited person will use a high pitched voice with loud volume.

Role of the SLT: Observe a client who presents with a high level of emotion before, during and after the moment of stammering. Tension along the vocal tract is likely to a greater or lesser degree for this person. Emotional voice use could potentially result in a muscle tension dysphonia that is secondary to the stammering behaviour.

Explore the emotional well-being of the client. In particular note any diagnosed mental health issues such as anxiety and depression. Bereavement, financial worries and work stress are also examples of emotional factors that can manifest themselves in voice change.

Medical: Co-occurring medical issues may contribute to voice change e.g. reflux (indigestion), heart conditions, thyroid, asthma and allergies. Previous surgeries, particularly those requiring intubation, can cause laryngeal trauma. Also, some medications tend to dry the laryngeal mucosa and the protective mucosal layer covering the vocal cords themselves.

Role of the dysfluency SLT: Consider the use of a general case history/interview format that includes questions pertaining to voice use and care (see **Resource 3.1: Questions to Ask a Client about Voice**). Include questions around potential medical drivers for voice change such as:

• Current medications and existing conditions such as asthma and allergies

• Presence of reflux; check that this has been discussed with his GP and is being managed appropriately

- Previous surgeries that required intubation (potential laryngeal trauma)

- Any previous ENT history if there is one

- Liaise with voice therapist if there is a diagnosed voice disorder for advice and support

- Concerns should **always** be signposted to GP for assessment and referral on if appropriate (see **'**Onward referral' at the end of this chapter for further information).

Mechanical: Pushing, forcing, hard attack are all examples of 'abuse' behaviours that can cause laryngeal trauma and muscle tension dysphonia's. Dryness, 'tickling' sensation or a feeling of a lump in the throat (globus) can contribute to coughing or throat-clearing behaviour. Persistent and repetitive behaviours such as these can lead to the development of vocal cord nodules. Poor posture for speaking, smoking and alcohol intake can also be considered as mechanical behaviours that impact voice performance and laryngeal health.

Role of the dysfluency SLT: Observe how the client uses his voice. Notice points of tension at each level of voice production i.e. power, source and filter. Check via palpation (touching the throat) for the position of the larynx and hyoid bone. A tight and high larynx due to increased tone in thyrohyoid and tongue base muscles can be visible in the neck and palpated. The PWS may describe physical discomfort in or after the moment of speaking.

Abuse behaviours such as throat clearing, shouting, screaming, loud volume and speaking with tension should be identified and listed.

Signpost to GP or local services for smoking cessation, alcohol and drug dependency or misuse.

Environmental: Working with chemicals or in environments that are dusty or dry can impact vocal health. Loud environments or places where there is significant background noise may mean a client needs to raise his voice e.g. nightclubs, factories and outdoor work. Smoke inhalation, either direct or passive, is a significant irritant to the larynx.

Role of the dysfluency SLT: Explore each environment that a client is in i.e. work, home and social. Troubleshoot with him where possible changes could be made to reduce or change and environmental drivers identified.

Resource 3.3: Drivers for Voice Changeand ***Resource 3.4: Drivers for Voice Change – Identification Grid*** are designed to provide the PWS with a summary of the key drivers that are known to affect voice. Encouraging him to take home this information and spend some time identifying his own emotional, medical, mechanical and environmental factors can be really valuable. Looking together at the identification grid at a subsequent session can inform how much further voice performance and voice care should be explored in the context of stammering therapy or if further assessment and onward referral is needed (i.e. to GP/ENT/ Voice SLT).

Experimenting with voice

I am a great believer in establishing good vocal hygiene, targeted head and neck relaxation and vocal warm-up as a prerequisite for a client that engages in voice therapy. Once a clinician has explored the power, source and filter level of voice production for the PWS alongside the identification of potential drivers for voice change what then? It is hoped that the following subsections and complimentary resources will be helpful for the dysfluency SLT before, during or as part of the maintenance phase of stammering therapy.

Vocal tract care and vocal hygiene

Adequate hydration and the elimination of laryngeal irritants should always be the first steps to optimising laryngeal health. It is important to maintain a healthy larynx especially if a person is working on creating and maintaining new vocal behaviours. Well-hydrated vocal folds are less likely to get injured and more likely to recover from any damage that is caused by effortful voice use (Verdolini-Marston, Sandage and Titze 1994). Education on how to do this can be given by providing the person who stammers with information and advice on voice care. **Resource 3.5: Top Tips for Voice** and **Resource 3.6: Taking Care of Your Voice** have been specifically designed to support direct fluency work where focus is on reducing:

• Vocal loudness

• Effort for speech

• Hard glottal attack

• Speech rate.

Muscle tension

When observing a PWS, the following features may be apparent:

• Muscle tension before, during and after the moment of stammering

• High position of the larynx when voicing

• Jaw tension

• Lip tension

• Tongue tension

• Tension at the level of the vocal folds (laryngeal level)

• Reported tenderness in the thyrohyoid and cricothyroid area following stammering behaviours such as blocking or prolongation

• Prominent and tense extrinsic muscles of the neck such as the sternocleidomastoid

• High and tight shoulders.

Targeted relaxation can help when the muscles of the larynx and the head and neck are overused during vocalisation. Head and neck relaxation is a helpful prerequisite to voice therapy. It can also be a useful tool in stammering therapy, particularly if tension points are observable in the jaw, neck, shoulders and chest. Being able to identify and 'reset' tension can be helpful before, during or after speaking for a PWS.

Resource 3.7: Reflecting on Posture for Speech and **Resource 3.8: Relaxation and Re-setting the Larynx** are designed to facilitate reflection on posture and identify points of tension. It is important to check before carrying out any head and neck stretches that an individual does not have any existing neck or back issues. If any discomfort or strain is reported whilst carrying out any direct stretching and re-setting exercises it is important to stop.

Breathing and phonation

There is much debate in research about the relevance of breathing in therapy for both voice disorders and stammering (Harris 2017). Clinical experience shows that gaining a holistic understanding of breath and voice and a freedom of breath flow i.e. breathing without tension, has a positive impact on voice sound and experience. Breathing is of course automatic, and it is not necessary to overthink it. However, taking time to look at simple breath flow patterns as preparatory work for vocal exercises may help the client identify how breathing can be different. It can also be useful for the clinician to observe breath flow in different activities and watch how it is shifted from automatic/reflexive to a conscious adjustment to suit different tasks – see **Resource 3.9: Attending to the Breath**.

Learning to breathe freely can be liberating, and understanding that breath flow can reduce tension may then enhance fluency. It also has advantages in balancing the parasympathetic and sympathetic systems when speech anxiety occurs (Russo, Santarelli and O'Rourke 2017). Coordinating breath and voice onset is not new to stammering therapy e.g. easy onset (Cooper 1979). Co-ordinating breath and voice draws from Estill's 'breath before tone' (2005) and the concept of 'flow phonation' (Sundberg 1987). This is particularly useful when a client who stammers presents with hard attack or blocking behaviour and may well be experiencing complete glottic constriction, similar to that seen in spasmodic dysphonia.

Vocal warm-up

A short vocal warm-up can help prevent vocal injury. It keeps the voice healthy and mobile, freeing the voice and improving the quality of sound a speaker makes. The idea of warming up the voice is often associated with performance i.e. singers or actors. **Resource 3.10: Vocal Warm-Up** and **Resource 3.11: Exercises to Brighten Up a Tired Voice** have been designed to help the client see that warming up the voice for a speaking situation can have benefits. I have combined exercises and techniques which are useful in releasing laryngeal tension, brightening and lightening the voice. I have found they not only support direct fluency work but can help with confidence and preparation for public speaking or using the telephone.

Remember, these activities are very simple versions of established approaches in voice therapy. They should be useful for freeing up tension and encouraging forward flow for speech. They complement and add to the chapters dedicated to relaxation, breathing and easy onset in the *Dysfluency Resource Book* (Turnbull and Stewart 2010). They can be used as part of the preparation phase for fluency-enhancing techniques or contribute to the long-term-maintenance and meaningful-change phases of stammering therapy.

Onward referral

An SLT working with a PWS should always seek medical opinion if voice change is persistent, lasting more than 2–3 weeks, according to the latest guidance from Cancer Research UK. Though unlikely, laryngeal cancer should always be considered as a possible reason for voice change. Early detection of laryngeal cancer is essential for the best chance of survival, response to treatment and quality of life after cancer (Mathieson 2001). Other 'red flags' to be aware of include:

• Difficulty swallowing

• Weight loss

- A cough that doesn't go away
- Shortness of breath.[3]

A clinician should not assume that the pushing or forcing behaviours associated with a stammer are the cause of a presenting hoarseness or vocal fatigue. Benign lesions such as vocal cord nodules need accurate diagnosis, as they will need specific voice therapy techniques, conservative treatment with a 'watch and wait' approach or possibly surgery to correct (Awad et al. 2019). As with all practice it is essential that the SLT does not work outside her level of competency

Final remarks

This chapter has discussed voice production, including the three systems involved, vocal issues and the drivers for change and finally vocal hygiene useful for a PWS. The intention of this chapter is to enhance the direct or indirect fluency work being carried out with a client who stammers. It is for guidance purposes only and is in no way intended to replace the specialist assessment and advice of an ear, nose and throat (ENT) doctor or an SLT specialising in voice. I wholeheartedly encourage the reader to collaborate with colleagues who specialise in the area of voice for advice and to seek their expert evaluation and opinion regarding the voice quality of the PWS. Such collaboration can be beneficial to all parties, therapists and client alike.

[3] For a comprehensive list of signs and symptoms of head and neck cancer, refer to a text such as Ward and van As-Brooks (2014).

Questions to ask a client about voice

Aim:

- To support the SLT in gathering key information about voice.

Table 3.2 Questions to ask a client about voice

Key information			Questions to consider	SLT notes
Onset of voice change			Sudden?	
			Gradual?	
Presentation			Variable?	
			Getting worse?	
			Improving?	
Factors that affect voice			Explore drivers for voice change e.g.	
			What helps?	
			What makes it worse?	
			What has been tried e.g. over-the-counter remedies/voice rest?	
			What are the stammering behaviours that could impact voice?	
			Link to *Resource3.3: Drivers for Voice Change* and *Resource 3.4: Drivers for Voice Change – Identification Grid*.	
Voice use			Work?	
			Home?	
			Social?	
			Performance?	
Medical history			List current medication	
			Consider underlying or existing medical conditions	
			Any previous surgeries requiring intubation?	
			Allergies, asthma, respiratory issues?	
			Existing dysphonia – details of ENT history (medication/surgery/therapy)	
			Anxiety/depression/low mood?	

Key information			Questions to consider	SLT notes
Reflux			Voice change e.g. hoarseness lasting more than 2 weeks Y/N	
			Throat clearing Y/N	
			Feeling of a 'lump in the throat' Y/N	
			Feeling of phlegm build-up in throat Y/N	
			'Typical' signs of reflux – burning sensation in chest/throat, metallic taste in mouth Y/N	
			Sudden coughing/spasm particularly at night Y/N[4]	
Vocal hygiene			Explore potential laryngeal and vocal cord irritants:	
			Smoker (including passive smoke inhalation)	
			Alcohol intake	
			Hydration	
			Caffeine	
			Dentition/oral hygiene	
Emotion			Emotional response to stammer/voice?	
			Current/past emotional stressors?	
			Mental health and well-being history?	

[4] Checklist adapted from Reflux Symptom Index (Belafsky et al. 2002). Multiple 'Yes' answers warrant discussion with GP for further investigation, lifestyle changes and potential pharmacological treatment.

Observation: power, source and filter

Aim:

• To provide a summary of how the PWS's voice is produced with specific focus on power, source and filter to help guide the SLT and the PWS.

Table 3.3 Observation: power, source and filter

System	SLT observation	Notes
Power: **Respiration**	Observe the client's breathing pattern from the moment you greet them; what do you notice? • Diaphragmatic/clavicular/thoracic? • Upper chest/shoulder/neck tension? • Audible breathing? • Exertion/talking/at rest – is there a difference? • Voice onset – delayed or uncoordinated? • Impact of the stammer at this level?	
Source: **Voice box**	Observe the client's voice at various levels from single sound to connected speech: what do you notice? • Ability to maintain a steady pitch /i/ • Consistent vs. inconsistent phonation (vowel and connected speech) • Laryngeal elevation on phonation? (Note the position of the hyoid bone, as it may be habitually held high within the neck.) • Note any tension around the thyrohyoid and cricothyroid areas. • Impact of the stammer at this level?	
Filter: **Resonance**	Listen to how your client's voice sounds. Do any qualities stand out? • Hypo/hypernasal? • Pitch – too high/too low? • Limited in range? • Intensity – too loud/too soft? • Rate – too fast/too slow? • Impact of the stammer at this level?	

Drivers for voice change

Aim:

• To help understand that a voice problem is often the result of several interrelated factors.

i Emotional

Emotional stress results in generalised body and laryngeal tension.

Examples are:

• Being unhappy or under pressure at work
• Financial problems
• Difficulties in relationships with family or friends
• Feelings of loneliness, fear or anxiety
• Being a 'good worrier' i.e. getting worked up easily/quickly.

ii Medical

The state of the vocal cords and general medical health will affect a person's overall voice quality.

Examples are:

• Vocal nodules, polyps (which affect the way in which the cords come together and vibrate)
• Being tired or 'run down' (resulting in a 'tired' voice)
• Asthma, digestive problems, thyroid problems, heart problems, migraines etc.

iii Mechanical

The way in which a person uses his voice affects his voice quality.

Examples are:

• Excessive throat clearing or coughing (causes the vocal cords to 'slam' together)
• Straining to achieve a loud volume (may cause strain and fatigue)
• Poor breathing control and technique (insufficient power for the voice)
• Tense/tight jaw (causing poor resonance and projection).

iv Environmental

Conditions at home, work and in any leisure environment may affect the voice.

Examples are:

• Air conditioning or central heating
• Working in the presence of smoke, dust or fumes
• Smoking/excessive alcohol consumption
• Speaking over background noise e.g. machinery/people.

All of these have a drying and damaging effect on the vocal cords.

© Trudy Stewart (2020). *Stammering Resources for Adults and Teenagers: Integrating New Evidence into Clinical Practice.* Routledge.

Drivers for voice change – identification grid

Aim:

- For the PWS to be able to list any factors which they may think impact their voice performance.

Emotional factors	Health factors

Mechanical (the way you use your voice) factors	Environmental factors

Top tips for voice

Aim:

• To provide general information about voice monitoring and care.

i   Listen to your voice

It is important to listen to what your voice is telling you. Reduce your vocal demands as much as possible if your voice is hoarse. Pushing your voice can lead to significant problems. It is important to allow your vocal cords to recover and rest especially if you have an upper respiratory infection (e.g. a cold).

ii   Use good breath support

Take time to fill your lungs before starting to talk. Try not to wait until you are almost out of air before taking another breath to power your voice. Remember breath flow is the power for voice.

iii   Warm up your voice

Most people know singers warm up their voices before a performance. Many people don't recognise the need to warm up the speaking voice before heavy use, such as teaching a class, prolonged speaking over the telephone or giving a speech. When giving a speech or presentation, consider using a microphone to lessen the strain on your voice.

iv   Avoid throat clearing

Clearing your throat can be compared to slapping or slamming the vocal cords together. Excessive throat clearing can damage the vocal cords and may lead to the voice sounding hoarse and dry. An alternative to voice clearing is taking a small sip of water to alleviate the need for throat clearing or coughing. If you have a persistent cough and are concerned seek advice from your GP.

v   Do not abuse or misuse your voice

Your voice is not indestructible. Too much screaming and yelling puts great strain on the lining of your vocal cords. Be aware of your background noise, and try to avoid talking loudly if it becomes noisy. Stop if you feel your throat is dry or tired or your voice is becoming hoarse because you are straining.

vi   Do not smoke

Smoking can lead to lung or throat cancer. Direct or second-hand smoke breathed in passes over the vocal cords causing significant irritation and swelling. This can make the voice very husky, hoarse and weak. Talk to your GP about smoking cessation support in your area.

vii   Get acid reflux treated

Untreated gastroesophageal reflux, laryngopharyngeal reflux is a common reason for excessive throat clearing and can affect voice performance. Visit your GP if you have signs and symptoms of reflux.

© Trudy Stewart (2020). *Stammering Resources for Adults and Teenagers: Integrating New Evidence into Clinical Practice.* Routledge.

viii Avoid caffeine and fizzy drinks

Excessive amounts of tea, coffee, fizzy drinks or alcohol cause dehydration and can worsen acid reflux symptoms.

ix Drink water

Stay well hydrated by drinking plenty of water; six to eight glasses each day is essential to maintaining a healthy voice. Sipping throughout the day or steam inhalations (a cup of hot water is enough) can help.

x Get help

Voice problems arise from a variety of sources including voice overuse or misuse, infection, cancer or injury. If you have experienced changes in your voice that have persisted longer than 2 to 3 weeks or you are concerned discuss this with your GP. An assessment by an ENT (ear, nose and throat) doctor should be carried out and following this you may be referred to see a speech and language therapist who specialises in voice.

Taking care of your voice

Aim:

• To provide optimum vocal hygiene and care throughout the therapeutic process, particularly when working with direct speech change.

Table 3.4 Taking care of your voice: the dos and don'ts

DO ✓	DON'T ✗
Consider your medication: • antihistamines • diuretics • decongestants • hypertensive medication • Parkinson's disease medication • antidepressants These are examples of medications that can affect the voice.	Don't shout or scream (especially if you are upset).
Adjust your volume to the situation and use amplification when available and especially in environments where there is background noise. This can help protect and conserve the voice.	Don't raise your pitch as well as your volume.
Reduce your intake of tea and coffee (with caffeine) – they are diuretics and can also be drying to the throat.	Don't rely on your voice alone to get others' attention.
Drink plenty of water, especially when talking a lot.	Don't force a whisper.
Use a good supply of air whilst speaking.	Don't work when you are ill and really should be at home.
Avoid excessive use of the phone.	Don't depend on throat lozenges/sprays for hydration; you could damage your vocal cords.
Try to keep a good relaxed posture when talking.	Don't talk above background noise.
Look after yourself; take a break. It is important to recharge your batteries.	Don't strain your voice through singing, acting or just talking a lot.
Try breathing in steam to moisten your larynx and consider humidification in dry environments.	Don't talk a lot when you have a sore throat, cold or flu.

DO ✓	DON'T ✗
Monitor changes in your voice quality.	Don't clear your throat a lot.
Eat a healthy diet, and try to keep fit and well.	Don't smoke or drink a lot (especially spirits). Avoid second-hand smoke, which can irritate your mouth, nose, throat and airway.
See your doctor if you have any problems with heartburn or acid reflux. Unmanaged reflux could affect your voice.	Don't cough a lot to try to get up phlegm – seek treatment.

Reflecting on posture for speech
Aim:

- For good voice a person's whole body needs to be well balanced
- The spine should be relaxed and comfortable, allowing the discs between the vertebrate to expand
- The neck should feel free and not tense.

i Check

Do you tend to do any of these things?

› Lean back as you stand

› Lock your knees

› Pull in your lower back

› Fold your arms

› Cross your legs automatically as you sit

› Throw your head back as you speak.

These things restrict good voice. Try to avoid them.

ii Change

> › Learn to hold your body loosely and easily.
> › Think about moving your head slightly forward, and then lifting it, so your skull feels well balanced on your spine.
> › Think of your back as lengthening and widening, so that your spine is well aligned.

Look in a mirror to see how you are standing.

iii Care

For your back, your neck and your voice:

› Spend some part of each day lying with your head, neck and back in a comfortable relationship

› Carry out targeted relaxation as shown by your speech and language therapist.

Your voice sounds best when your whole body posture is easy.

Relaxation and re-setting the larynx

Aim:

- To aid relaxation and open up the throat (pharynx)
- To address potential muscle tension in the extrinsic and intrinsic muscle groups in the head, neck, shoulders and pharynx
- To encourage a feeling of control over tension (constriction) and reduce discomfort along the vocal tract
- To encourage and practice 're-setting' of the larynx in a wide, low position to support voice freedom.

These exercises are designed to help release the 'triangle of tension' (i.e. tension in shoulders, head and neck) so commonly associated with voice problems. Listen to your body and focus on observing any tension or tightness you may find.

If any of these exercises are painful, **stop**!

Breathe easily whilst you are doing the exercises. **Do not** hold your breath.

Do the exercises slowly about three to five times and feel the muscles stretching just a little.

i Shoulder rotations

Rotate your shoulders forwards slowly five times, then back five times.

ii Shoulder shrugs

Raise your shoulders to the ears – **hold** – let go. Press your shoulders down – **hold** – let go. Repeat five times.

NB: Adding a gentle breath in through the nose as you raise your shoulders and slowly exhaling through the mouth as you slowly lower them can add an extra level of relaxation to this exercise.

iii Neck stretches

Keeping your back and shoulders straight, slowly look over each shoulder in turn. Only go on as far as is comfortable, and hold for a couple of seconds as you look over each shoulder.

iv Throat and neck

Smooth down the sides of the voice box using the thumb and forefinger. Locate your strap muscles (prominent when you turn your head to the side). With your finger and thumb gently smooth down from behind your ear to your clavicle. Repeat this 3–5 times. Add oil/moisturiser to help keep this movement smooth and easy.

© Trudy Stewart (2020). *Stammering Resources for Adults and Teenagers: Integrating New Evidence into Clinical Practice.* Routledge.

v Widening, stretching and lowering of the larynx

- Slowly tilt your head up and back and feel the stretch in your throat. Place your bottom jaw over your upper teeth. Work towards holding for 15 to 20 seconds. This is a very important exercise for stretching the muscles around the larynx.

- Place your thumb and forefinger gently on either side of your larynx and feel the lowering and widening of the larynx between your fingers as you do the following:

  ○ Curl the tip of your tongue back along the roof of your mouth towards the soft palate.

  ○ Yawn or a try a polite yawn (behind closed lips).

Remember, you may have to do this a number of times throughout the day. Your SLT should have shown you how to carry out the exercises safely and correctly. Listen to and respond to any tension you may feel within your larynx by actively relaxing the muscles and re-setting.

Attending to the breath

Aim:

- To see the connection between breath and voice and the whole body
- To raise awareness of breath flow in different activities
- To see that breath flow i.e. without tension has a positive impact on voice sound and experience.

i   Sit quietly

In a chair or on your bed. This breath flow should feel easy, not too deep and inaudible. It is rhythmic like the ebb and flow of the sea; hence its name: *tidal breathing*.

ii   Get physical

Depending on your level of fitness perform a physical activity that will push your rate of breath flow:

› Walk up and down stairs

› Jog on the spot

› Go for a run.

What do you notice? Place your hand on your chest and feel the increase in the rate of in- and out-breath. It may also be noisy, but it is still automatic.

iii Speaking

Read aloud; talk with a friend face to face or on the telephone. Notice how you use your breath for these speaking situations. Your breathing is likely to have moved from the automatic to a more conscious coordination of inspiration and exhalation to accommodate what you need and want to say.

iv Singing

Whether this is at an amateur/singing a simple song level right up to the high vocal demand of a performance, there is a shift on how we use and coordinate our breath. A person will use his breathing differently from when he just talks. Notice, as with speaking for longer periods of time, abdominal or 'costal breathing' is used to support the length of time and effort required for the performance. Place one hand below your navel and one hand above to feel this in action.

© Trudy Stewart (2020). *Stammering Resources for Adults and Teenagers: Integrating New Evidence into Clinical Practice.* Routledge.

Vocal warm-up

Aim:

- To introduce a short vocal warm-up to improve the quality of the sound and help prevent vocal injury

- To see vocal warm-up as a way to keep in good voice and not just for performers.

i Warm-Up 1, Breath Relaxation

Releases tension often associated in the breathing mechanism that can interfere with effective voice production. Ordinarily, if there is tension when breathing, that tension radiates to the voice box muscles.

- Take a normal breath and then exhale. Make sure your shoulders and chest are low and relaxed.

- Repeat a number of times, making sure that your breaths are focused low in the abdomen and that there is no associated chest, neck or shoulder tension while breathing.

- You can place one hand on your abdomen or the side of your ribcage to remind you to keep the focus low and away from the chest and shoulders.

- Hold an 's' sound like a hiss when you exhale.

- Build up how long you can hold on to a slow and easy 's' using a low and relaxed breath.

ii Warm-Up 2, Jaw Release

Reduces tension in the mouth and jaw area during speaking and singing.

- Place the heels of each hand directly below the cheek bone.

- Pushing in and down from the cheeks to the jaw, massage the facial muscles.

- Allow your jaw to passively open as you move the hands down the face.

- Repeat several times.

iii Warm-Up 3, Lip Trills

Releases lip tension and connects breathing and speaking. Releases tension in the vocal folds.

- Place your lips loosely together.

- Release the air in a steady stream to create a trill or raspberry sound. First try making a quiet lip trill like a horse.

- Then turn on the volume and trill like you are pushing a toy car for a child.

- Hold the sound steady and keep the air moving past the lips.

- Next try to repeat the b-trill (volume on) gliding gently up and down the scales.

- Don't push beyond what is comfortable at the top or bottom of the scale.

iv Warm-Up 4, Tongue Trill

Relaxes the tongue and engages breathing and voice.

- Place your tongue behind your upper teeth.
- Exhale and trill your tongue with an 'r' sound.
- Hold the sound steady and keep the breath connected. Now try to vary the pitch up and down the scale while trilling.
- Again, don't push beyond what is comfortable at the top or bottom of your scale.

v Warm-Up 5, Buzz

Improves the resonant focus of the sound and continues work with maximal stretch on the vocal folds.

- The mouth postures are easily made by pretending you are sucking in spaghetti with an inhalation.
- On exhalation make the 'woo' sound. It will be a buzz-like sound.
- Hold the sound steady for two or three attempts.
- Now use the woo sound to go up and down the scales.

vi Warm-Up 6, Humming

Highlights anterior frontal vibrations in your lips, teeth and facial bones.

- Begin with lips gently closed with jaw released.
- Take an easy breath in and exhale while saying 'hum'.
- You should hum gentle glides on the sound 'm', feeling a tickling vibration in the lip/nose area.
- Gently glide from a high to a low pitch as if you were sighing.
- Gently humming, feeling the focus of the sound on the lips is an excellent way to also cool down the voice.

© Trudy Stewart (2020). *Stammering Resources for Adults and Teenagers: Integrating New Evidence into Clinical Practice.* **Routledge.**

Exercises to brighten up a tired voice

Aim:

- These exercises can optimise the closure of the vocal cords, open the pharynx (throat) wider
- These exercises can help to relax your throat, but you should find out which of the exercises opens up the throat and makes the voice more resonant again.

Your SLT should have modelled and checked that you are doing these safely and correctly.

Whining

Aim: Designed to be relaxing for the voice. If your voice breaks or is effortful or strained, stop and do not continue.

How to:

i Say the word 'running'

ii Isolate the 'ing' part of this word and repeat in isolation over and over

iii Think about where your tongue is i.e. back of tongue connecting with the soft palate

iv Place your tongue in the 'ing' position

v The whine sound should be quiet like a puppy would make when it is locked in the kitchen and wants to get out!

vi Practice for 30 seconds.

Mirening

Aim: To reduce the tension in the larynx. It involves singing down the nose without over articulating the sounds (i.e. try not to exaggerate the lip and tongue movements compared to when you sing normally).

How to:

i When you are mirening, pinch your nostrils. If you are doing it correctly, this will make your voice disappear completely. This is because all the sound is going down your nose, and when you pinch your nostrils, the sound cannot escape

ii Start with a song you know well or a nursery rhyme.

Sirening

Aim: To practice moving from thick vocal folds (chest voice) into thin vocal folds (head voice).

How to:

i Place your tongue in the 'ing' position as your therapist has shown you

ii Keeping the tongue in the high position quietly produce a sound then move up in pitch on a glide to a high note. You should feel you are working hard with your tongue muscles and also with the constriction release

iii When you get to the point where your larynx starts to tilt to make the vocal folds stretch to get the high pitch you may notice a 'glitch' or a break. If this happens there is too much tension in the larynx. Try again with more constriction release and if necessary a slight dip of the chin downwards as the pitch rises. Work on eliminating the glitch but do not strain the voice.

© Trudy Stewart (2020). *Stammering Resources for Adults and Teenagers: Integrating New Evidence into Clinical Practice.* Routledge.

Lip trill/tongue trill

Aim: To brighten and lighten the voice and reduce laryngeal effort.

How to:

i   Sit upright with shoulders relaxed

ii   Voiceless lip trills – like a horse

iii   Then try to turn the volume on – like a toy car

iv   Voiceless tongue trills – like a cat purring

v   Turn the volume on like a telephone ringing

vi   Glide up and down the pitch with both voiceless and voiced sounds.

Straw work

Aim: To optimise the closure of the vocal folds, open the pharynx (throat), helping the client 'feel' an open throat position, less effortful voicing and an improvement in sound/voice quality.

How to:

i   Sit upright with shoulders relaxed

ii   Place straw to lips with lips pushed forward in an 'oo' shape

iii   Ensure the sound produced is aimed down the centre of the straw

iv   Breathe in gently through the nose and produce a 'doo', and focus the sound down the straw

v   Remember the sound produced should be effortless

vi   Practice gently gliding up and down pitch on 'doo'

vii   Try everyday simple songs to build up strength/resonance and easy voicing.

Remember, ALL exercises should feel easy and relaxed. Listen for clear and crisp voice. 'Quality not quantity'. If you start to tire, take a break.

References

Awad, R., Shamil, E., Gibbins, N., Aymat, A. and Harris, S. (2019). From voice clinic to operating room: Are we out of tune? *Journal of Voice*. (In Press), On-line January.

Belafsky, P.C., Postma, G.N. and Koufman, J.A. (2002). Validity and reliability of the reflux symptom index (RSI). *Journal of Voice*, 16(2), 274–277.

Boone, D.R., McFarlane, S.C., Von Berg, S.L. and Zraick, R.I. (2014). *The Voice and Voice Therapy* (9th Edition). Boston: Pearson.

Cooper, M. (1979). The voice problems of stutterers: A practical approach from clinical experience. *Journal of Fluency Disorders*, 4(2), 141–148.

Craig, A. and Tran, Y. (2006). Chronic and social anxiety in people who stutter. *Advances in Psychiatric Treatment*, 12, 63–68.

Erickson, S. and Block, S. (2013). The social and communication impact of stuttering on adolescents and their families. *Journal of Fluency Disorders*, 38(4), 311–324.

Estill, J. and McDonald Klimek, M. (2005). *Primer of Compulsory Figures: Level Two: Figure Combinations for Six Voice Qualities*. Santa Rossa, CA: Estill Voice Training Systems International.

Guitar, B. (2013). *Stuttering: An Integrated Approach to its Nature and Treatment* (4th Edition). Philadelphia: Lippincott Williams & Wilkins.

Harris, S. (2017). Speech therapy for dysphonia. In T. Harris and D. Howard (eds.), *The Voice Clinic Handbook*. Braunton, Devon: Compton Publishing Ltd.

Jones, S.M. (2016). *Laryngeal Endoscopy & Voice Therapy: A Clinical Guide*. Braunton, Devon, UK: Compton Publishing Ltd.

Mathieson, L. (2001). *Greene & Mathieson's The Voice & its Disorders* (6th Edition). London: Whurr Publishers.

Rosen, S. and Howell, P. (2010). *Signals and Systems for Speech and Hearing* (2nd Edition). Amsterdam: Emerald Group Publishing Ltd.

Rubin, J.S and Greenberg, M.J. (2002). Psychogenic voice disorders in performers: A psychodynamic model. *Journal of Voice*, 16(4), 544–548.

Russo, M.A., Santarelli, D.M. and O'Rourke, D. (2017). The physiological effects of slow breathing in the healthy human. *Breathe* 13: 298–309.

Salihović, N., Junuzović-Žunić, L., Ibrahimagić, A. and Beganović, L. (2009). Characteristics of voice in stuttering children. *Acta Medica Saliniana*, 38(2), 67–75.

Stemple, J.C., Glaze, L.E. and Klaben, B.G. (2010). *Clinical Voice Pathology: Theory and Management*. San Diego, CA: Plural.

Stemple, J.C., Roy, N. and Klaben, B.K. (2014). *Clinical Voice Pathology: Theory and Management* (5th Edition). Plymouth: Plural Publishing.

Sundberg, J. (1987). *The Science of the Singing Voice*. Ithaca, NY: Cornell University Press.

Turnbull, J. and Stewart, T. (2010). *The Dysfluency Resource Book* (2nd Edition). London: Routledge.

Verdolini-Marston, K., Sandage, M. and Titze, I.R. (1994). Effect of hydration treatments on laryngeal nodules and polyps and related voice measures. *Journal of Voice*, 8(1), 30–47.

Ward, C.E. and van As-Brooks, C.J. (2014). *Head and Neck Cancer; Treatment, Rehabilitation, and Outcomes* (2nd Edition). Plymouth: Plural Publishing.

4 | Narrative practice
Identifying and changing problem stories about stammering
Mary O'Dwyer and Fiona Ryan

This chapter describes how a therapist works with the stories of life experiences told by a PWS. The research literature regarding stammering shows that SLTs have been interested in the stories of individuals who stammer for some time (Corcoran and Stewart 1998, Klompas and Ross 2004, Plexico, Manning and DiLollo 2005, Beilby et al. 2013).

Van Riper (1971) defined stammering as: "A stuttering behaviour consists of a word improperly patterned in time and the speaker's reactions thereto" (p. 15).

A speaker's reaction to his stammering both influences and is influenced by stories about himself and his stammering. Working with these stories can help bring about the changes which a PWS seeks when he goes to therapy. The part these stories play in the development of stammering as a problem is discussed here. Specific processes within narrative practice are explained and illustrated with clinical examples from teenagers and adults. Exercises are included to invite the reader to reflect on the processes and develop questions and an understanding of narrative practice. We will start by exploring some of the terms used in this chapter such as "narrative" and some important concepts which underlie this approach.

Narrative/story

White and Epston (1990) use the terms "narrative" and "story" interchangeably to refer to the personal accounts which a person tells about his life. "Narrative" is a term used frequently today in many different settings, for example, journalists and politicians refer to the narrative around the topic being discussed. Elliot (2005) suggests that the simplest definition of narrative can be traced back to Aristotle in his *Poetics* and that it is "A story with a beginning, a middle and an end" (p. 7). Bruner (1986) writing as a psychologist, states, "Narratives deal with the vicissitudes of human intentions" (p. 16). Bruner has written extensively on how a person makes meaning or sense of his experiences. He has linked perceptions with social and cultural background and discussed how culture influences beliefs and intentions, which in turn influence story telling or narrative. He also focused on how the mind uses narrative as a way of thinking and of constructing possibilities. In this way, an individual uses narratives to deal with problems and find solutions that fit for him in his context.

In this chapter, we use "narrative" and "story" interchangeably, and we use these terms to refer to the stories which a PWS tells. Sometimes a person tells stories which focus specifically on stammering and how he makes meaning around that experience. At other times, a story focuses on his wider life and experience. Explanations of other terms which are used in this chapter are:

Dominant narrative: the key or main story that a person tells or believes about himself

Problem or problem-saturated narrative: if the dominant story the person tells about himself does not fit with his hopes, dreams and values, it is said to be a problem story. If the person views the story of the problem as a reflection of his own identity and that the problem is internal to himself (White 2007), his narrative may be said to be problem saturated

Thick description: a detailed and rich description which is gathered by the therapist. In order to gather this level of detail, it is necessary for the therapist to be like an investigative reporter and also not to presume that the client's meaning for any word is known to the therapist, e.g. if a client says, "Well, stammering has me avoiding", then it is important to explore what does "avoiding" mean to the client including the detail of when, where, who and how

Centres: placing the client and his experiences and knowledges[1] as the focus of therapy rather than the expert knowledge of the therapist

Externalisation: the process by which a person objectifies the problem and sees the problem as separate to himself

Externalisation conversation: the conversation between the client and the therapist where the problem is externalised

Unique outcome or sparkling moment: a story, action or time when the person acted in a way that was different to the problem story

Reauthoring: the process by which the person is encouraged to tell and develop stories about his life that are "out of step" with the problem-based story (White 2007)

Meaning making: thinking and reflecting on an experience or a step taken while developing an understanding of how this action makes sense to the person and how it connects with other events in his life, relationships, values and sense of self

Mapping: a process of documenting a conversation visually so that it is summarised. A therapist can map the stories told by a PWS, and this practice helps her and her client see how stories develop and, importantly the connection between action, meaning and identity. Templates for maps are presented in **Resources 4.1** and **4.3**

Power relations: Michael White's use of this term in narrative practice is influenced by Foucault, a French philosopher (1980). Foucault wrote about modern power in contrast to traditional power. In traditional power, an authority wields power over its subjects. In modern power and in democratic societies, an individual has power, and there is a collective sense of power which is connected to an idea of what is normal. Thus, for any minority there are power relations at work, as they are outside what is considered normal. Members of a minority group may experience a sense of not having power as a result of being judged "not normal". This concept can be applied to a PWS as a member of a minority group. Power relations are also evident in the clinic room. In narrative practice, a therapist endeavours to respect the power of the client

Agency: when a client makes choices and recognises that he has choice, can take a position and express a view about a problem or an exception to the problem

---

[1] Narrative Practice uses knowledges rather than knowledge to draw attention to the idea that there are multiple aspects to knowledge.

Deconstruct: in narrative practice means to examine something and to explore it in detail while deciding one's position regarding it. For example, to deconstruct a discourse about a PWS not being confident could involve exploring this idea, checking if it makes sense or is true for an individual or other people, reflecting on why it may have developed and whether it has value for a person.

Templates and handouts

Templates are provided, along with handouts of questions useful for both externalisation and reauthoring conversations. There are exercises after Table 4.3 and Table 4.4 providing opportunities to reflect on the narratives and the questions used to elicit the responses. This chapter takes a "case story approach" (Carlson, Epston et al. 2017) to introduce NP. We will introduce the key processes through the words of individuals who stammer and invite the reader to engage with each of them and their stories. As part of this engagement, readers can explore their responses to the stories and complete the exercises following Tables 4.3 and 4.4.

Narrative therapy/practice

Narrative therapy (NT) was developed in the 1980s by Michael White and David Epston as described in the book *Narrative Means to Therapeutic Ends* (White and Epston 1990). Since then, the ideas of NT have been developed, with further work emerging from the Dulwich Centre in Adelaide, Australia, and other centres around the world. Books and a website recommended for further reading can be found at the end of this chapter.

NT focuses on:

• Personal narratives

• The meanings a person attributes to experiences and actions

• The conclusions he comes to regarding his identity.

Morgan (2000) states that "Narrative therapy seeks to be a respectful, non-blaming approach to counselling and community work, which centres people as the experts in their own lives" (p. 4). While a client comes to therapy with problem-based stories, a central premise of NT is that it is possible to reauthor these stories as less problem-based and more focused on strengths and resources.

More recently, NT practitioners have begun to use the term "narrative practice" as opposed to therapy. This acknowledges that narratives are being used therapeutically across many areas and that "practice" may reflect a more equal sharing of power than "therapy". We have chosen to use the term "narrative practice" (NP), as there are many times when a therapist, a PWS, along with his family and teachers, share stories about stammering in ways that result in reflection and change.

Relationship between action and meaning

NP takes the view that there is a relationship between action and meaning as portrayed in a person's story; actions reflect an underlying value system. Helping a PWS become aware of the specific meanings which he gives to his experience of stammering is a key step in realising how stammering impacts his identity. This centres the voice and knowledges of the person seeking help and decentres the voice of the therapist.

Bruner (2004) describes how narratives are played out on the dual landscapes of action and consciousness. He explains, "There is a landscape of action on which events unfold . . . a second landscape, a landscape of consciousness, the inner worlds of the protagonists involved in the action" (p. 698).

This second landscape has to do with emotions, thoughts, motivations, dreams and wishes. These two landscapes are connected and influence each other.

Case study 1 – David

David was aged 13 when he took part in the conversations presented here. He was initially referred to SLT regarding delayed language development when aged 2. He was discharged after two years and re-referred when aged 13 years. Language assessment indicated mild receptive and expressive language difficulties. Stammering was also diagnosed, and he was included in a therapy group of five teenagers. He presented largely with covert symptoms, and his overt stammering behaviours were mainly prolongations. He was eager to learn information about stammering, as he knew very little about it. He drew a picture of his stammer, which can be seen in Figure 4.1. A map of an externalising conversation between David and his therapist is presented in Table 4.1. (The Table should be read from the bottom up.) This map includes the therapist's questions to help the reader understand the process involved. Mapping the client's responses in this way provides a summary of the process and importantly makes visible the connections between action and meaning. The process of an externalisation conversation will be explained in detail later in the chapter.

Figure 4.1 David's drawing – Stutterman

Table 4.1 David's completed statement of position map 1 (Read from bottom up)

CATEGORY OF ENQUIRY	David's response (with some of therapist's questions included)
JUSTIFYING THE POSITION – WHY? **LINKING WITH HOPES, VALUES AND AMBITIONS**	T: What kind of things are important to you, what do you value? David: Bravery and brains, like being smart T: Does Stutterman fit with bravery and brains? David: No, he's selfish and he is trying to put misery into people's lives T: Do you think bravery helps you with Stutterman? David: Like if people weren't brave and fought against Stutterman they wouldn't talk at all T: Does your brains help you with Stutterman? David: I kind of know how to get rid of him
POSITION – WHERE DO YOU STAND ON THIS?	T: Are you okay with Stutterman in your life or do you want less of him or more of him? David: Less of him would be ideal but like it's not the end of the world if you get him
EFFECTS ACROSS DOMAINS OF LIVING	David: Oh God I'm going to stutter again It just gets a bit annoying every time you want to say something. I would like to get rid of annoyance and be happy T: Why do you think it would be important to have less of him? David: So . . . stuttering in general can be quite frustrating T: Is there any time Stutterman doesn't cause annoyance? David: No not always. Like if I'm very happy and I stutter . . . like it might ruin it just a bit but I'd still be happy T: Where does he show up? David: If I'm sleepy I sometimes stutter. In the evening. In the evening if I stay up too late T: What does Stutterman get you to do? David: Stutter T: And in what way? David: Repetitions at times T: How does Stutterman get people to think about you? David: He tries to bring back memories that you don't like for a person that's suffering from Stutterman T: Do you like your memories about Stutterman? David: Not really, he's a Supervillian

CATEGORY OF ENQUIRY	David's response (with some of therapist's questions included)
	T: How do you know Stutterman is there?
	David: Every time I can feel him when I stutter
	T: Where do you feel him? How do you feel him?
	David: I can feel him in my head, he can turn big and small
CHARACTERISATION OF PROBLEM/ NAMING	David: Stutterman is a villain who is trying to make everyone stutter
	T: When did you first meet Stutterman?
	David: When I was about 4
	David describes Stutterman while looking at the picture he has drawn – see Figure 4.1.
	David: That's me and that's him trying to break into my head and he's invisible
	He is trying to break the cords
	He is invisible
	He has like a lance and he's trying to disturb the strings – like the cord
	These are all his supports to help him break into my brain and he is invisible

Case study 2 – John

John was a man in his 30s who did not like to talk about his stammering in work situations and referred to it as:

> an unfortunate topic and you don't necessarily enjoy talking about it, but you benefit from talking about it. It's like, it's like a death in the family, do you know, nobody is happy, it has happened or you don't want to talk about it really, but you, I suppose, you have to, like, you know?

John did talk about his stammering with his partner, children and a few close friends. However, he tried to avoid using the telephone at work, as he worked in a large shared office. He had not spoken with his manager about other options, such as making calls from a different office. When asked about this by the therapist, he said "but wouldn't that be avoidance"? The therapist focused on avoidance and asked John to tell her more about this area. See Figure 4.2 for a map of this conversation. In NP a drawing or map of the conversation is usually made, and a client will copy or photograph it.

Bringing John's meaning making to consciousness is facilitated by asking questions such as:

• "By not talking about your difficulty with colleagues or supervisors at work, what are you valuing?"

• "What is of value to you that has you not talking to people about the difficulty you experience with making calls in the office?"

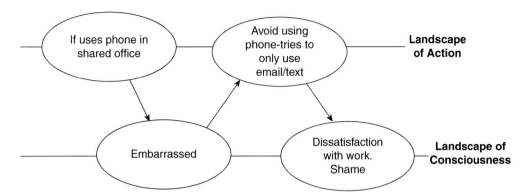

Figure 4.2 Landscapes of action and consciousness – John

This linking between actions and meaning is a core component of NP.

Acts of resistance

NP uses this understanding of two landscapes to identify an action which resists or defies the problem story. The importance of this action is then acknowledged by connecting it to thoughts, emotions, dreams and ambitions preferred by the PWS and which provide a better fit to how he wants to see himself and live life.

Case study 3 – Owen

Owen was a 16-year-old who had started to answer more questions in class. An extract from a therapy session focusing on this action of answering questions as an act of resistance and the possibilities it may lead to in the future is presented below. The links made between actions and their meanings are represented in Figure 4.3.

T: What name would you give this action?

Owen: (hesitates) I don't know

Owen and therapist decide to just call it "answering questions in class".

T: What were you standing up for by taking this step?

Asking this question sought to bring the meaning associated with the action to consciousness. Owen needed to think, and the therapist prompted him with a further question:

T: What was important for you when taking this step?

Owen: Confidence

T: Having taken this step and developed confidence what is now possible for you?

Owen: I don't know

T: Think about how you might be in different situations, like different places you go every day

Owen: I will be able to tell people what I want

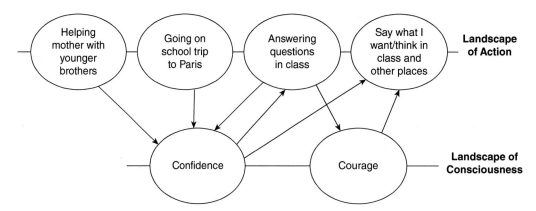

Figure 4.3 Resisting the problem story – Owen

The development of narratives

A PWS needs to recognise that power relations (such as cultural and institutional influences) are at work when he develops problem-based stories around his experience of stammering. In order to rewrite or reauthor the stories, he needs to develop a sense of agency. The process of exploring alternative stories involves meaning making. Through meaning making, a person can centre his knowledges about himself and his stammering rather than centring other, more widely held knowledges. He then develops a sense of agency and gives himself permission to hold an alternative view. In this way, he acknowledges the power relations in his life, which may include his relationship to his stammering and reaction to stories others hold about stammering. He can then address changing the nature of these power relations if he wishes.

Narratives and the development of stammering

It is not just a child who needs to make sense of the onset of stammering in his life but all the others around him, such as parents, siblings, friends, other relatives and child minders. These other narratives influence each other. Over time if a child's narrative about himself as a PWS becomes problem based, then this narrative will not support him in living as he wishes. The problem story will be established, which in turn will lead to actions and stammering behaviours which support and maintain the problem story and restrict participation in life.

Narrative/self/identity

McAdams (2013) defines narrative identity as "the internalized and changing story of your life that you begin to work on in the emerging adult years" (p. 62). NP supports a person in the development of his preferred identity. Van Riper (1971) and Sheehan (1970) both considered the impact of stammering on the PWS's "self-concept", and both discussed this in relation to communication and stammering in social situations. For a PWS, the experience of being seen to stammer in, for example, school or work impacts profoundly on his sense of social self. O'Dwyer, Walsh and Leahy (2018) studied narratives from six men who stammer and found that their ability to value imperfection rather than seek perfection was key in developing a sense of self, particularly a social self, which allowed them to be who they wanted to be.

Case study 4 – Adam

Adam is in his late 30s and, like John, is not comfortable talking about his stammering at work. He initially rails against "acceptance" of stammering. However, during an early narrative session Adam realises that "I'm going to spend my life as a stutterer. That's me". Through the narrative process he recognises that:

> There are kind of other aspects of me that I would be proud of. . . .
>   There is swings and roundabouts so okay with speaking, my presentation isn't as clear and sharp as it should be, but I've got an fantastic bubbly personality or whatever and in my professional life.

As he moves through the reauthoring process, he says, "I suppose before I would let's not be ruled by it. Let's try and overcome it". Adam's narrative of being a PWS expands to encompass that of a successful professional.

Narratives and cultural factors

Working with the narrative of a PWS brings into focus the realisation that his story is influenced by discourses in society about stammering. This work helps to deconstruct these wider discourses so that an individual does not base his story and identity on unquestioned widely held ideas about stammering. Instead he learns to rely on his preferred story and identity which fits with his values and ambitions for living.

A child who stammers will be influenced by significant others in his environment who may subscribe to dominant discourses (such as "stammering is not normal") and normalising judgements. This may influence his sense of self and the development of identity. Helping a child or adult who stammers to develop awareness of these processes is a first step in supporting them to develop preferred identities. NP advocates working with a PWS and significant others (e.g. parents and teachers) to deconstruct these dominant discourses by challenging them. For example, by reflecting on the truth of some ideas which are taken for granted, such as "people who stammer cannot be confident" or "if I stammer, it is better not to attract attention in class by answering questions".

Epston (2004) and White (2007) present a view of therapy as co-research, where a therapist and client investigate:

• The effects of problems on the client and other people

• The influences of the client on problems

• The multiple realities and multiple identities that are always available to him.

Applying these ideas in therapy leads to conversations about the meanings which a client ascribes to being a PWS and the possibilities for adopting new or different identities which fit better with the hopes and ambitions he has. In addition, this can result in changes in his stammering and avoidance behaviour. Ryan (2018) found that a client's engagement with new possibilities resulted in positive actions involving employment, education and increased social participation. Reduction in the impact of stammering on both family and work life was also identified by the participants.

Narratives and a social model of stammering

Working with the narratives of a PWS fits well with a social model of stammering. This model acknowledges the impact of a disorder which is congruent with NP's focus on the experiences, values, hopes and dreams of the person at the centre of therapy.

In a letter from Mac, a 23-year-old woman (whom the reader will meet later in this chapter), it is the impact of stammering rather than the "biological" or "medical" that is debilitating. This letter was written following her attendance at an intensive programme and extended the narrative conversation with the clinician.

> When I'm really struggling with it, when it becomes something I hate – prevents me from being happy, interacting with other people without them thinking I'm a freak, etc. [sic] It gets me really depressed and I despise it.

Narrative practice and the role of the therapist

The role of the therapist is to facilitate the development of a narrative that makes sense of and gives value to the experience of the person by recognising possibilities and areas for transformation (Charon 2006, 2012, Kleinman 1988, Mattingly and Lawlor 2001). This role involves close questioning of the person at the centre of the story. The therapist embraces the role as an investigative reporter, not directing, not advising or problem solving but engaged in picking apart how the problem works (White 2005, 2007). The therapist's own story will impact on therapy in particular:

• Her story about what is important in working with a PWS

• Her identity as a therapist

• Her working collaboratively.

Therapist's story: reflections

Working narratively has been an evolving story for our own clinical development. We have come to realise there are no "better questions", just different ones. Key to the development of narrative questions is the act of actively reflecting. Here is an example from an SLT's reflective journal following one narrative conversation:

> DVD review of RT's sessions: I am caught by the client–therapist interaction. I am thinking of questions I could have asked, things I could have should have probed further, critiquing my use of narrative therapy.

Reviewing past sessions can be a very useful process both with another therapist or the client at the centre of the story. A second therapist can ask what the thinking behind a question was; the client can reflect on the process and the impact of certain questions. This approach acknowledges the shared expertise of client and therapist.

Narrative practice processes

NP contains key processes including:

• Externalisation of the problem, i.e. the process by which the person is separated from the problem

• Identifying the unique outcome

• Reauthoring the story

• Definitional ceremonies.

The processes do not necessarily follow in a linear fashion, though the externalisation process is usually the starting point (White 2007). The beginning is the dominant problem-saturated narrative, which may be full of problem stories of stammering and its effects (Leahy, O'Dwyer and Ryan 2012). However, there will be stories that fall outside the problem-saturated one. These other stories may be preferable to the dominant one. With every "performance" or telling of a dominant story within NP, that story can be reauthored (Epston 2004).

Narrative practice: externalisation

In the process of externalisation the person is separated from the problem (White 2007). This separation of the person from the problem allows a client to observe how he relates to the problem. As a result, he develops a sense of agency and chooses how he wishes to relate to it. The starting point is separation (Morgan 2000). A "thick and rich" description (White 2000) of the problem is elicited, that is one which is full of description and detail using White's statement of position map 1 (Table 4.2).

Table 4.2 Template for statement of position map 1 (Read from bottom up)

JUSTIFYING THE POSITION – WHY? **LINKING WITH HOPES, VALUES AND AMBITIONS**	Finally, the person is asked to justify his evaluation of its influence. In this way the externalising conversation opens up possibilities for him to view his life in a different and new way.
POSITION – WHERE DO YOU STAND ON THIS?	In the third stage of enquiry, the person is asked to take a position on the problem: whether he is satisfied with its influence on his life.
EFFECTS ACROSS DOMAINS OF LIVING	This is followed by a rich description of the manifestations and effects of this problem "the pest". This rich description requires a detailed examination of all facets of the problem. The development of the problem-saturated narrative is examined by the therapist and individual, with past and present examples of the problem described in detail (White 2007). This process allows the person to be aware that the problem is the problem; the person is not the problem – a fundamental shift in understanding for the person with the problem (White and Epston 1990).
CHARACTERISATION OF PROBLEM/NAMING	In the first stage the person is encouraged by the therapist to describe the problem which has brought him to therapy. The person is encouraged to describe the problem in his own words and from his own perspective. In one example provided in what follows, the client begins by naming the problem "the pest".

Some notes about maps and tables: White (2007) developed statement of position maps to chart externalisation and reauthoring conversations. Statement of position map 1 is used to chart the externalisation conversation. A sample map is included (Table 4.2). Tables are to be read from bottom up, as that is how the narrative develops. Table 4.2 describes each stage in detail.

Some notes about questions: NP invites the therapist to ask questions in a particular way. When an individual comes to therapy, he generally talks about what brought him to therapy. The therapist asks questions from a position of curiosity without imposing her own agenda. The client usually provides an account of what has led up to his decision to seek help.

Narrative questions for externalisation

i   Open questions

Initially, there is an opportunity for the therapist to ask open questions; for example,

- Can you tell me about the problem/predicament that has brought you here?

It is important to check in with the person about the line of questioning:

- Are these questions okay with you?
- Is there something else you prefer to talk about?

ii   Ask questions to gather information about the problem in different situations:

- Can you tell me more about the problem?
- How would I know that the problem has shown up?
- When did this problem show up?
- Where else does the problem show up?
- Is there anyone else who knows about the workings of the problem?

iii   Ask questions to clarify information:

- At what point did this happen?
- How old were you then?

iv   Ask questions about the person's position on the problem:

- How do you feel about this?
- Where do you stand on this?
- What it your position on this?
- Is this a positive or negative development?

v   Ask questions that allow the person to justify his position on the problem:

- Why is/isn't this okay for you?
- Why do you feel this way about this development?
- How come you're taking this stand/position on this development? (White's workshop notes 2005)

Externalisation in practice

At this point, some individuals from our clinical practice will be introduced. In telling their stories we hope that the reader will have a greater understanding of the externalisation process. In each narrative described here, the therapist's questions and the person's responses are provided. Further sample questions for externalisation and reauthoring are included in *Resources 4.2: Questions for Externalisation* and *4.4: Questions for Reauthoring.*

Case study 5a: RT

This externalisation conversation with RT took place on an intensive residential programme. Externalising questions are included, and RT's responses are mapped.

RT's story

RT was a 38-year-old man who had stammered since early childhood. His stammering was characterised by severe blocks and many secondary behaviours. At the time the therapy took place he was unemployed, though he wished to return to education. RT had attended a number of different programmes addressing his stammering over many years. He felt frustrated that stammering still impacted his life. Therapy with an NP focus began with a discussion of the problem that brought him to the clinic. He described his stammer and his early years as a child who stammered. This detailing of his stammering history led to the naming of the problem as "the pest". In the following section, some of the questions the therapist asked are included.

Externalisation stage 1: naming the problem
The first step is for the therapist to refer to the problem as separate from the person. This is done by simply calling it "the problem" as opposed to "your problem" or "your stuttering". The therapist might ask, "Can you tell me about the problem that has brought you here today?" or "When did 'name of problem' first appear in your life?"

T: Can you tell me what you call this problem? Does it have a name?

RT: The Pest

Externalisation stage 2: mapping the effects of the problem
In stage 2, the therapist asks questions to elicit the effects of the problem. The therapist is generally curious about:

• Where the problem shows up

• What are the consequences for the problem in the person's life.

It is important to obtain as much detail as possible about the workings of the problem. This enables the individual to take a position on the problem later (stage 3). It is usual to start with a recent or "near" experience of the problem and then to ask the person: "Are there other times when this problem was present in your life?"

The "pest" has impacted RT's education and employment.

T: What has this 'Pest' led you to do?

RT: Left school . . . (the Pest) had taken control . . . couldn't concentrate

Used to think . . . (the Pest) will always be in control

Stutter stopped me from getting jobs I wanted, ended up working in jobs bad [sic] paid, working for people who treat me badly

Externalisation stage 3: taking a position on the problem

In asking the person if the effects of the problem are okay with them, the therapist is asking him to take a position on the workings of the problem. RT was angry about the effects the problem had on his life. In taking this position, RT experienced a change in how he saw the problem and a new sense of agency. He acknowledged his anger and an opportunity emerged for him to make changes.

T: How did the 'Pest' have you feeling?

RT: I got angry

Externalisation stage 4: justifying the position

In the final stage the person is asked to justify the position he has taken on the problem. RT was "angry" about the problem. This anger was justified because he felt frustrated with how his life had been impacted by "the Pest". Acknowledging this frustration, he named the values that were important to him, values that were in some way blocked by "the Pest".

T: Is this okay with you that the problem has you feeling like this?

RT: No

T: Why is it okay/not okay?

RT: Frustration that's kind of doing something

T: What is it that you value, that is important to you?

RT: My speech, my well-being, happiness, my future

Case study 6a: Mac: narrative practice and covert stuttering

Narrative practice can address the impact of covert stuttering on the life of a PWS. Mac's stammer was covert; she had few overt symptoms but at the time of therapy lived a life of limitations and avoidance.

Mac's story

Table 4.3 outlines an externalisation conversation that took place with 23-year-old Mac. Mac attended an intensive residential programme for adults who stammer and had not attended any other programme. Mac described a life of avoidance and frustration in which she could not express herself fully. She had dropped out of college and was unemployed but active in animal welfare and rights groups. Initially she described the problem as one of always being in the dark. With careful questioned she describes the effects of "being in the dark", especially in relation to her interactions both in school and at home. It had led to a lack of participation in these situations. However, through the course of the conversation she decided she was "quite angry" with how the problem had impacted her life. This anger was justified because she had a "right" to be heard. With this acknowledgment of her "rights" as a PWS it is notable how the expressions she uses are congruent with her awareness of welfare and rights for animals. When Mac uses the terms "judgement" and "rights", it demonstrates how NT is led by the understandings and real-world experiences of the person themselves and not by any terms introduced by a therapist

Table 4.3 Mac's completed statement of position map 1 (Read from bottom up)

CATEGORY OF ENQUIRY	Mac's Response	
JUSTIFYING THE POSITION – WHY?	T:	And how does that fit with these, what does that tell us about you?
LINKING WITH HOPES, VALUES AND AMBITIONS	Mac:	I have a right just like anybody else
POSITION – WHERE DO YOU STAND ON THIS?	T:	How does 'judgement' have you feeling?
	Mac:	Would make me quite angry
		I'm here to not be afraid really not be afraid of any judgements that I have perceived people may have or people do have. That would have been the principal reason why I avoided
EFFECTS ACROSS DOMAINS OF LIVING	T:	And what has this judgement lead you to do? Are there other effects in terms of your social life, your family life, your study life . . . ?
	Mac:	When I'm having bad days, there is a complete lack of communication
		I'd like to share, and most of the time I would feel so anxious and so worried that I would stammer . . . I wouldn't be brave enough to answer
		Sometimes I feel like there is not much point in being there if I can't speak about it
		I have days where I just feel so low or so fed up that things are very difficult
CHARACTERISATION OF THE PROBLEM/NAMING	T:	The story we've heard so far, the problem is . . .
	Mac:	Afraid of any judgements that I have perceived people may have or people do have. That would have been the principal reason why I avoided. . . . Always felt I was in the dark

Externalisation stage 1: naming the problem

Mac started by telling her story of stammering. As the therapist listened, she summarised using the client's own words and prompted for a name or the client's belief about the nature of the problem.

T: The story we've heard so far, the problem is . . .

Mac: Afraid of any judgements that I have perceived people may have or people do have. That would have been the principal reason why I avoided. . . . Always felt I was in the dark

Externalisation stage 2: mapping the effects of the problem

Mac gave a rich and detailed description of the impact of "judgement" across many aspects of her life. It had led to her feeling "in the dark". The therapist asked questions about home, school, education, work and relationships.

T: And what has this judgement led you to do? Are there other effects in terms of your social life, your family life, your study life . . .?

Mac: When I'm having bad days, there is a complete lack of communication

       I'd like to share, and most of the time I would feel so anxious and so worried that I would stammer . . . I wouldn't be brave enough to answer

       Sometimes I feel like there is not much point in being there if I can't speak about it

       I have days where I just feel so low or so fed up that things are very difficult

Externalisation stage 3: taking a position on the problem

Here the therapist:

• Summarised the effects of the problem

• Talked Mac through the map taken at the time of the story

• Asked her to take a position on the problem.

T: How does 'judgement' have you feeling?

Mac: Would make me quite angry

       I'm here to not be afraid really not be afraid of any judgements that I have perceived people may have or people do have. That would have been the principal reason why I avoided

Externalisation stage 4: justifying the position

Documents had a powerful role in the telling and retelling of this story. Mac kept a folder with the photos of the statement of position maps and her artwork on her lap during subsequent sessions. In later sessions she looked over the folder as she reflected on the problem of "judgement".

The therapist summarised the story using her map (drawn on the whiteboard) and asked whether the "anger" fit with the story.

T: And how does that fit with these, what does that tell us about you?

Mac: I have a right just like anybody else

Reflection exercise 1 (adapted from Carlson et al. 2017)

In the following exercise the reader is invited to explore his/her responses to Mac's externalisation conversation. Reflect on the questions in Table 4.3, in particular how the questions offer opportunities for the client to identify her values. It might be important for the reader to note alternative questions that could be asked to elicit a rich description of the problem.

Reflective questions for the reader:

• Is there any question that resonates with you in particular?

• How does this question capture your imagination?

• How does this question have you feeling/thinking?

- Are there any other questions that you feel it might be useful to ask?

- What did these questions lead Mac to consider that she may not have considered before?

- Write two further questions that you might ask Mac about the effects of the problem across her daily life and relationships.

Reauthoring

The second map described by White (2005) outlines the conversation eliciting the exceptions to the problem-based story. These exceptions or "unique outcomes" identify the occasions when the problem was not dominant and the person could act or perform in a way that was preferable. This conversation describes how a detailed description linked strongly to the experience of the PWS is arrived at. When beginning to use NP, it is difficult to identify an exception or a unique outcome. Applying the concept of "absent but implicit" may solve this difficulty. The variability of stammering means it is easy to identify times when the problem is less dominant. However, a PWS may be prompted to seek therapy at times when he considers his stammering to be "worse than ever". One way of identifying a time when the problem was not so dominant is to enquire about the times when the problem was not as bad as now. This will lead the way into a reauthoring conversation.

Unique outcome

This unique outcome is "mapped" in White's statement of position map 2. Statement of position map 2 outlines a rich and detailed description of the time when the problem is **not** present. The structure of the conversation would be:

- A rich description of the initiative or step taken

- Exploring the impact of this step on the person's relationships with himself and others

- Describe his experience of this step. "Would you like more of this initiative?"

- "Why take this position on it?"

- "What does it tell others about what you value?"

This identification of a "unique outcome" is the turning point in NP. It is the entry point to the reauthoring process, the creation of an alternative story. This exception to the problem story is then linked over time to past actions, embedding this exception into the person's new story and creating the possibilities of future actions. As the exception or "sparkling moment" (Leahy, O'Dwyer and Ryan 2012) is mapped by detailed questioning, the person is asked to take a position on it and then to justify the position. In taking a position the person identifies the values that are important to him, connects these values to the action taken and identifies possible future actions.

Therapist's story: reflections from SLT's journal

In a further extract from her reflective journal an SLT noted some of the challenges in the identification of unique outcomes.

> I fell into the trap, I viewed the story as significant and I see from watching back that I appeared to be trying to convince him that it was significant. Must remember what White (2007) wrote: it is only a unique outcome if the person consulting the therapist judges it to be so.

Narrative questions for reauthoring:

i   Naming the initiative or step taken

Here the therapist asks open questions:

- Can you tell me about this step?
- What was the step/action you took that day?
- Can you tell me more about it?

ii Ask questions to map the effects/potential effects of the unique outcome/exception:

- Can you give me another example of another time you displayed "determination, persistence and never giving up"?
- Who knows this about you?
- Who would have said you were capable of these things?

iii Ask questions about the person's position on the initiative/step:

- How do you feel about this?
- Where do you stand on this?
- What is your position on this?
- Is this a positive or negative development?

iv Ask questions that allow the person to justify his evaluation of the initiative/step:

- Why is/isn't this okay for you?
- Why do you feel this way about this development?
- How come you're taking this stand/position on this development? (White's workshop notes 2005)

Reauthoring in practice

Guidelines for reauthoring: suggested starting points

Reauthoring focuses on the neglected stories. These stories attest to what is valued, the stories that reflect hopes, values and dreams. For the therapist it is important to listen carefully, focusing on the "unsaid hints". Inexperienced practitioners can use the following guidelines for a conversation:

I want you to tell me a story.

This story is about you and something you did or a time that you acted in a particular way that stands out to you.

It might be that it appears to be different to the way you usually act.

This structure has proved useful in leading the way to alternative stories. With time and practice a therapist can listen carefully for openings within the stories the client tells without recourse to the earlier exercise.

Case study 5b: RT: reauthoring stories: "speaking out, without words of course"

RT described a time when he "spoke out" but "without words". His actions allowed him to express his feelings about dance, which he hated. This resulted in positive effects, including spending time with his dad. In describing his actions, he reported that "he does not do the obvious" and he valued his mind and this "eccentricity". In the NP sessions, RT went on to talk about other times that he did not "do the obvious", surprising himself and others. As he recognised and valued this he realised what was possible including "I can work on what I've heard, what I've been told, to be less kind of, less kind of judgmental of myself. And I've learnt that things are good. There is a path, kind of steps I can take, to improve my speech" (Ryan 2018).

Stages for reauthoring conversations

There are four stages within the reauthoring process. These stages are mapped out in what follows with reference to RT, Adam and Mac and their reauthoring sessions. Suggested questions are provided for each stage.

Stage 1: involves the definition of the unique outcome/exception. The therapist might ask:

- "What was the step/action you took that day?"
- "Can you tell me more about it?"

T: So it was a big step to speak out, do you not normally speak out?

Adam: Em . . . actually thinking about it. I do it to something that has to be spoken about, be it . . . or whatever . . .

T: Can you tell me more about this experience? What was it that you did?

RT: I turned left and exited the stage. Without using words of course. . . . I don't do the obvious

Stage 2: maps the effects/potential effects of the unique outcome/exception in various situations in which these effects might be seen. The therapist will carefully use the client's key words and phrases:

- Can I ask some questions about "not doing the obvious/being persistent/speaking out/ hope"?
- There were other times you have fought off "the tiredness" and the "bad speech" to open up new possibilities?

T: How long have you had this 'hope' inside?

Mac: If you are talking from when I actually knew that I had all this difficulty, since I was 16, 17, five years. . . .

T: How did this 'speaking out', well how did it have you, and how did it have your parent's feeling?

RT: I laughed but I remember my mother's face. She was red. My Dad decided he would take me to football matches every Saturday instead

Stage 3: The person is invited to take a position, to evaluate the effects of this unique outcome. Here the therapist might ask some of the following questions:

• Is this okay with you?

• How do you feel about this?

• How is this with you?

• Where do you stand on this?

• What it your position on this?

• Is this a positive or negative development?

• What does that tell us about you?

T: What does that tell me about you?

RT: I just [clicked fingers] happened, I just got the idea I was just like [demonstrates motorbike]

T: About what you value?

RT: Eccentric kind of

Stage 4 calls for the justification of the evaluations that from the previous stage. The therapist will ask the person to take a position on their evaluation:

• Why is/isn't this okay for you?

• Why do you feel this way about this development?

• How come you're taking this stand/position on this development?

• Would you tell me a story about your life that would help me to understand why you would take this position on this development?

• What does the change that happened the other night, what does that say?

• What does that change say about what is important to you?

T: Okay, eccentric. Do you value that in yourself, it's sort of unpredictable?

RT: I do

T: You value that?

RT: My mind the way I think, inside like, I'm laughing

As a final point within the reauthoring conversation the therapist asked RT: "If your story had a title, what would it be?" His title links with the time he spoke out without words (by walking off stage in the middle of a dance competition) and the values he holds dear.

RT: Acts of defiance, you get busy living or you get busy dying.

Case study 6b: Mac: persistence, determination and never giving up

Table 4.4 outlines what happened when Mac decided she could be quite persistent. Getting off the bus at the wrong stop in an isolated area because she was afraid to ask the driver for information led to a frightening experience. She described how she found her way out of the darkness with "persistence" and "determination". This, she discovered, was not a

Table 4.4 Mac's statement of position map 2 (Read from bottom up)

Category of Enquiry	Response	
Stage 4: Intentional understandings of this experience and understandings of what is accorded value	T:	It is important . . .
	Mac:	To be happy, just to get there
		I have a right
Stage 3: Experience of this development	T:	and how does that fit with these, what does that tell us about you?
	Mac:	I can build up the courage to do it and that I have learned that I have a right to, I have a right
		Just I am a strong person, if I wasn't strong person; I wouldn't even be here today kind of a thing, I have to say so
		I did have these hopes and aspirations inside when I was a lot younger, but I wouldn't really have developed as a person yet . . .
		I didn't make a wrong turn. Everyone had been looking frantically for me around the town and my boyfriend had been so worried. I was really proud of myself
Stage 2: Initiative in relationship	T:	Can you give me another example, is this the only time you displayed determination, persistence and never giving up?
	Mac:	Talking in terms of being determined, sometimes the weather is bad, I'd still go sometimes a lot of people don't turn up and like a lack of human power or people power means just get washed out, nobody really wants to listen to you
	T:	So it's really important to try and attend. . . . It is very important for you to be there. Is there another event in the past we have always said this about you, when you were younger, are there other times when you have shown pride, determination, never giving up?
	Mac:	This happened earlier as well. I just same word same primary, secondary, sometimes when a teacher would say, does anyone have a response to that or whatever. I had a burning urge to say because I feel like it's a really good response. I'd like to share. . . .
		On occasion, I have spoken out, even though it's difficult and I got through it
		In terms of seeing me as determined and courageous, would definitely be my partner, Eoin. He knows the best
Stage 1: Characterisation of initiative (what was the step you took that day?)	T:	Can you tell me more about this experience? What was it that you did?
	Mac:	I was determined to get to my destination. I never gave up. I can be quite persistent

new phenomenon for her. She identified other examples of persistence and determination (turning up in bad weather for demonstrations) that fit with her values of having "rights" and "being heard".

Acknowledgment of rights, for her, led to awareness of actions she was able to take.

Reflection exercise 2 (adapted from Carlson et al. 2017)

In this second reflection exercise readers are invited to explore their responses to a reauthoring conversation. Consider, in particular, how the questions offer opportunities for the client to identify his values and how this might lead to further action. Consider the questions and responses given by Mac.

• Is there any aspect of Mac's story that resonated with you?

Highlight words, phrases or expressions that exemplify Mac's determination, persistence and never giving up.

• What did identifying these values lead Mac to consider that she may not have considered before?
• Are there other questions that come to your mind when you read Mac's answers?
• Write two further questions that might encourage Mac to expand on her experience of this development.

Documents and narrative practice

In NP, documents are used in different contexts to further develop the story, increasing the impact of therapy "fourfold" according to Epston (1998). They can be used to supplement the face-to-face sessions by providing a permanent record of key moments. Documents remind a person of how his story has changed over time, giving a sense of history. They serve as conversations carried out on paper (Pentecost 2008). Documents can thicken stories and lend more authority to the stories being told (Speedy 2008).

How to create documents

The therapist during a narrative session may map out, on a whiteboard/sheet of paper, key words or phrases used by a client. This is useful, as it allows the therapist time to reflect on what she is hearing and gives the person a visual overview of his story. This document may take the form of an enlarged statement of position map (Table 4.2) highlighting key words and phrases used by the person themselves. Alternatively, two lines representing landscape of action and consciousness can be drawn on which the key words may be plotted and connected by arrows, as demonstrated in Figure 4.2. In the creation of the map, the therapist will repeat key words, clarify meanings and request further elaboration. In this way the document is co-created with the person. At the end of the conversation, a photograph of the map or a copy may be given to both parties, serving as a shared record.

Summary and concluding remarks

NP engages with the stories a person tells to make sense of his life. The processes of externalisation and reauthoring are illustrated in this chapter with stories from our clinical practice. Through the process of externalisation, a person takes a position as separate from the problem and evaluates the effects of the problem. From this, a sense of agency develops, which allows him to recognise steps he has to take in line with his desired outcomes. This leads into the reauthoring process. Narrative practice, while recognising the value of narratives, has developed these processes to enable a therapist to help move a client from problem-based narratives to narratives that fit better with his hopes, values and dreams.

Template for statement of position map 1 – externalisation conversation

Table 4.5 Template for statement position map 1 – externalisation conversation

HOPES/VALUES WHY?	
POSITION – WHERE DO YOU STAND ON THIS?	
EFFECTS ACROSS DOMAINS OF LIVING	
CHARACTERISATION OF PROBLEM/ NAMING	

Questions for externalisation

4.2.1 Questions for naming the problem

Do you have a name for this problem?

If this problem had a name what would it be?

Tell me about the problem/why you are here today.

Talk about "the stammer" not "your stammer".

Can you draw it?

Can you tell me a bit about P (the problem)?

When did P first appear in your life?

Is there a picture or image that describes the problem?

Do you think we have the right name for the problem, or is there a better word to describe it?

4.2.2 Questions to elicit effects

Can you tell me more about this problem?

When did it first emerge/arrive/show up?

Where does it show up now? At home/workplace/school/with peers?

Tell me what it is like for you to be living with the *problem name*.

Have you noticed any situations in particular that the *problem name* shows up?

How does the problem make you feel?

Do other people notice the problem?

Does the problem affect your behaviour in situations?

How does the problem affect your behaviour in situations?

Tell me about when the problem shows up.

How would I know it is around?

What does the problem get you to do?

Are there places where it shows up often?

Does the problem get in the way of ordinary everyday tasks?

How does the problem get you to think about yourself?

Does the problem affect the way others see you?

© Trudy Stewart (2020). *Stammering Resources for Adults and Teenagers: Integrating New Evidence into Clinical Practice.* **Routledge.**

4.2.3 Questions to elicit person's position on the problem

Where do you stand on this?

What is this like for you?

How is this for you?

Say a bit more about your experience of this.

Is this okay with you that the problem has you feeling like this?

Are you happy with its place in your life now, or would you like it to expand or shrink or change in some way?

Is this okay with you?

How do you feel about this?

What relationship would you like with the problem now?

How might that play out in your life?

4.2.4 Questions to elicit the person's justification of this position

Why is it okay/not okay?

Why do you think this is what you want?

How come you are taking this position?

How does it fit with your hopes for your life?

Is it linked to values that are important to you?

How does this fit with the person you want to be?

Template for statement of position map 2 – reauthoring conversation

Table 4.6 Template for statement of position map 2 – reauthoring conversation

CATEGORY OF ENQUIRY	RESPONSE
JUSTIFYING THE EVALUATION **INTENTIONAL UNDERSTANDINGS OF THIS EXPERIENCE AND UNDERSTANDINGS OF WHAT IS ACCORDED VALUE** (Why was this important for you, what does it tell me about what you value?)	
EVALUATING EFFECTS OF ACTION/ UNIQUE OUTCOME **EXPERIENCE OF THIS DEVELOPMENT** (Tell me how this was for you.)	
EFFECTS OF ACTION/UNIQUE OUTCOME **INITIATIVE IN RELATIONSHIP**	
CHARACTERISATION OF INITIATIVE/ NAMING & DESCRIBING THE ACTION/ UNIQUE OUTCOME (What was the step you took that day?)	

Questions for reauthoring

4.4.1 Characterisation of initiative/naming and describing the action/unique outcome

Choose an action you took that seemed to go well. (Therapist may notice an exception.)

Describe what you did.

What words or images come to mind as you describe it? (Therapist may need to ask follow-on questions to ensure a rich description of the action.)

4.4.2 Effects/connections of this action/unique outcome/initiative in relationship

What do you think was the turning point that led to this action being possible?

What does this action/this initiative/this event have you thinking about yourself?

What effect does it have on your sense of who you are?

What has it got other people thinking about you? Saying about you?

What areas of your life does this action impact? Home? Work? Friends?

Can you think of any step earlier in your life that was in any way linked with these hopes or intentions? And go further back into your history? Are there links with events and actions from when you were an adolescent . . . or from your childhood?

What has this step got you to understand better?

What other events/ideas/actions/beliefs from other areas in your life might be connected to this action?

Who might really understand the importance of this?

What does this exception/initiative/action make possible in the future?

4.4.3 Evaluating the effects of this action/unique outcome/experience of this development

What was your experience of this action and its effects?

Is it okay with you?

What position do you take on it?

How do you feel about this?

How is this by you?

Where do you stand on this?

Is this a positive or negative development?

How well does it fit with the things you believe in?

4.4.4 Justifying the evaluation/intentional understandings of this experience and understandings of what is accorded value

Why do you think this is what you want?

How does it fit with your hopes for your life?

Is it linked to values that are important to you?

How does this fit with the person you want to be?

How does it fit with the things you believe in?

What does this say about what is important to you?

Why is/isn't this okay for you?

Why do you feel this way about this development?

How come you're taking this stand/position on this development?

Would you tell me a story about your life that would help me to understand why you would take this position on this development?

References

Beilby, J.M., Byrnes, M.L., Meagher, E.L. and Yaruss, J.S. (2013). The impact of stuttering on adults who stutter and their partners. *Journal of Fluency Disorders*, 38(1), 14–29. https://doi.org/10.1016/j.jfludis.2012.12.001

Bruner, J.S. (1986). *Actual Minds, Possible Worlds*. Cambridge, MA: Harvard University Press.

Bruner, J.S. (2004). Life as Narrative. *Social Research*, 71(1), 691–711. https://doi.org/10.1007/s10780-008-9039-2

Carlson, T.S., Epston, D., Haire, A., Cortillo, E., Lopez, A.H., Vedvei, S. and Pilkington, S. (2017). Learning Narrative Therapy Backwards: Exemplary tales as an alternative pedagogy for learning practice. *Journal of Systemic Therapies*, 36(1), 94–107.

Charon, R. (2006). *Narrative Medicine: Honouring the Stories of Illnesses*. Oxford: Oxford University Press.

Charon, R. (2012). *Narrative Medicine*. Oxford: Oxford University Press.

Corcoran, J.A. and Stewart, M. (1998). Stories of stuttering: A qualitative analysis of interview narratives. *Journal of Fluency Disorders*, 23(4), 247–264. https://doi.org/10.1016/S0094-730X(98)00020-5

Elliott, J. (2005). *Using Narrative in Social Research: Qualitative and Quantitative Approaches*. London: Sage Publications.

Epston, D. (1998). *Catching up with David Epston*. Adelaide: Dulwich Centre Publications.

Epston, D. (2004). From empathy to ethnography: The origin of therapeutic co-research. *International Journal of Narrative Therapy and Community Work*, 2, 31.

Foucault, M. (1980). *Power and Knowledge: Selected Interviews and Writing*. New York: Pantheon Books.

Kleinman, A. (1988). *The Illness Narratives: Suffering, Healing, and the Human Condition*. New York: Basic Books.

Klompas, M. and Ross, E. (2004). Life experiences of people who stutter, and the perceived impact of stuttering on quality of life: Personal accounts of South African individuals. *Journal of Fluency Disorders*, 29(4), 275–305. https://doi.org/10.1016/j.jfludis.2004.10.001

Leahy, M.M., O'Dwyer, M. and Ryan, F. (2012). Witnessing stories: Definitional ceremonies in narrative therapy with adults who stutter. *Journal of Fluency Disorders*, 37(4), 234–241.

Mattingly, C. and Lawlor, M. (2001). The fragility of healing. *Ethos*, 29(1), 30–57. https://doi.org/10.1525/eth.2001.29.1.30

McAdams, D.P. (2013). *The Redemptive Self: Stories Americans live by* (Revised Ed.). New York: Oxford University Press.

Morgan, A. (2000). *What is Narrative Therapy? An Easy-to-Read Introduction*. Adelaide: Dulwich Centre Publications.

O'Dwyer, M., Walsh, I.P. and Leahy, M.M. (2018). The role of narratives in the development of stuttering. *American Journal of Speech and Language Pathology*, 27(3S), 1164–1179. https://doi.org/10.1044/2018_AJSLP-ODC11-17-0207

Pentecost, M. (2008). A Letter to Robyn: Explorations of the written word in therapeutic practice. *International Journal of Narrative Therapy and Community Work*, 1, 17–27.

Plexico, L., Manning, W.H. and Dilollo, A. (2005). A phenomenological understanding of successful stuttering management. *Journal of Fluency Disorders,* 30(1), 1–22.

Ryan, F. (2018). *Stories from the Other Side: Outcomes from Narrative Therapy for People Who Stutter* (Unpublished Thesis).

Sheehan, J.G. (1970). *Stuttering: Research & Therapy*. New York: Harper & Row Publishers Inc.

Speedy, J. (2008). *Narrative Inquiry & Psychotherapy*. New York: Palgrave Macmillan.

Van Riper, C. (1971). *The Nature of Stuttering*. New Jersey: Prentice Hall.

White, M. (2000). *Reflections on Narrative Practice*. Adelaide: Dulwich Centre Publications.

White, M. (2005). *Workshop Notes*. Adelaide: Dulwich Centre Publications.

White, M. (2007). *Maps of Narrative Practice*. New York: W.W. Norton Co.

White, M. and Epston, D. (1990). *Narrative Means to Therapeutic Ends*. New York: W.W. Norton Co.

Further reading

Logan, J. (2013). New stories of stammering: A narrative approach. In *Stammering Therapy from the Inside: New Perspectives on Working with Young People and Adults*. Guildford: J & R Press Ltd.

Morgan, A. (2002). Beginning to use a narrative approach in therapy. *International Journal of Narrative Therapy and Community work*, (1), 85–90.

https://dulwichcentre.com.au/is a link to an important website for narrative practice; many resources can be accessed including free on-line training.

5 | Principles of avoidance-reduction therapy

Jonathon Linklater

This chapter will give an overview of avoidance-reduction therapy for stammering. This therapy was developed by Dr Joseph Sheehan, a psychologist who also stammered. Vivian Sheehan, Joe Sheehan's wife, was a highly skilled speech-language pathologist and continued their work after his death in 1983 until her own death in 2008. This chapter updates some of the Sheehans' work with practical ways to adapt its use in everyday settings with clients. Reflections are made on my own research and clinical work using avoidance-reduction therapy with clients of all ages in group and individual sessions.

This approach aims to uncover stammering; it enables stammering to be seen and heard, for a client to show it to his clinician, his friends and family, colleagues, the man in the shop and the woman on the bus. Avoidance-reduction therapy leads the client to realise that the people he meets in his life generally don't care about stammering as much as he thinks they do. This therapy gives permission to the PWS to stammer. "Learning how to stutter more easily is core to avoidance-reduction therapy" (Sheehan 1975).

To speak or not to speak

Sheehan (1975) proposed that stammering had a theoretical basis in role conflict. In their final piece of writing together, published after Joseph Sheehan's death, Joseph and Vivian Sheehan's summary was "stuttering is perpetuated by successful avoidance, by the successful suppression of outward stuttering behaviour and the substitution of false fluency or by inner patterns of stuttering" (Sheehan and Sheehan 1984, p. 147). Put simply, the PWS wants to speak, but has fear of stammering, he holds back, and as a result, this approach–avoidance conflict results in observable features of stammering. Sheehan argued that stammering was exacerbated by trying not to stammer and attempting to be a fluent speaker; thus, the PWS had not accepted the role of stammerer.

When stammering occurs, Sheehan suggested that this act satisfies the fear of stammering and is ultimately resolved; the block is released, or the struggle reduced, when the fear of stammering has been sated. This idea led to avoidance-reduction therapy as a way to work with a PWS. The important goals of avoidance-reduction therapy are to confront and reduce fear and to become more comfortable with stammering and being a PWS. This should lead to less stammering in the long term.

For an adult undergoing and completing this type of therapy Sheehan states:

> The result is a person who accepts himself and adjusts freely to either the stutterer role or the alternating normal-speaker role, who struggles minimally against himself when he stutters and who feels freedom and comfort in the speaker role whether he stutters or not. Combination of self-acceptance with role acceptance leads to freedom and ease in the speaker role, with prevalent fluency as the ultimate product.
> (Sheehan 1970, p. 22)

While this chapter updates avoidance-reduction therapy for a clinician working today, the ideas presented are based on many years of clinical use. To help a clinician and her client working in this way, the chapter will give practical ways to reduce avoidance and challenge thinking on stammering.

Therapy: theory and practical application

The therapy outlined in the literature appears sequenced and linear. Vivian Sheehan, Shanks and Mereu (2005) suggest that assignments and exercises should be completed in order. However, a key point noted from my discussions with and observations of Vivian Sheehan during a visit in the early 2000s is that exercises were not always completed in chronological sequence. Although therapy is linear and logical, working through the five stages of therapy (outlined in what follows), it is not delivered in a dogmatic fashion. A client would be directed to specific assignments and exercises when appropriate for the individual. Vivian Sheehan wrote, "what is important is not the time it takes to complete an assignment, but how well you do it" (Sheehan, Shanks and Mereu 2005, p. 3).

Beginning therapy: "you can stutter your way out of this problem"

I encourage both clients and clinicians to read Sheehan's "Message to a stutterer" (2005). (Message to a stutterer can be found online hosted by the Stuttering Foundation of America www.stutteringhelp.org/message-stutterer.)

This short piece outlines the principles of therapy and can be both reassuring and uncomfortable. Key lines in the message echo the experience of the PWS while signposting the challenges ahead. Sheehan states, "You can stutter your way out of this problem" (Sheehan, Shanks and Mereu 2005, p. 6). Outlining his thesis, he writes, "you don't have a choice as to whether you stutter but you do have a choice as to how you stutter" (Sheehan, Shanks and Mereu 2005, p. 6). These are defining sentences and may provoke a discussion between a therapist and PWS. It is important that the clinician offers her client the option to counter Sheehan's claim and discuss the point that attitudes and feelings associated with stammering may have an impact.

In my experience, having presented "Message to a stutterer" to clients to take away and read, most will return for a second session. Many clients talk to me about the lines that jump out at them and give a well-meaning challenge to their current belief system. A popular line that can introduce an alternative way of looking at stammering is, "your stuttering doesn't hurt you; your fluency doesn't do you any good" (Sheehan, Shanks and Mereu 2005, p. 5). Once client and clinician can move to a more objective attitude towards stammering, change may begin to happen. The clinician will encourage her client to go ahead and talk – no matter whether he stammers or not.

> The next time you go into a store or answer the telephone, see how much you can go ahead and speak in the face of fear. See if you can accept stuttering so that your listener can do the same. In all other situations, see if you can begin to accept openly the role of being someone who will for a time stutter and have fears and blocks in speaking. But show everyone that you don't intend to let stuttering keep you from taking a part in life. Express yourself in every way possible and practical.
> (Sheehan, Shanks and Mereu 2005, p. 7)

The iceberg of stammering

Joseph Sheehan is perhaps best known for the analogy of the iceberg of stammering. Applied to therapy, openness about stammering leads to a reduction of the part of the iceberg below the surface exposing the iceberg to the air. Sheehan wrote, "For an adult or an adolescent mature enough to tolerate it, public presentation of the self as a stutterer has major therapeutic effects. The portion of the iceberg exposed to the sunlight of public view melts away more quickly" (Sheehan, Shanks and Mereu 2005, p. 73). Introducing (or reminding) a client about the iceberg analogy can give a sense that changing stammering is possible. It also suggests that this change will be gradual, with a strong foundation and lasting benefits. There is no aim for fluency; and if strategies are applied, there should be no significant relapse. No relapse? Can such a claim be made? Allow me to elaborate. A PWS will continue to demonstrate stammered behaviours while this therapy continues and after he leaves therapy. Consequently, if he is using more open stammering strategies there will not be a great fall from this notion of 'fluency'.

Levels of avoidance

Sheehan's theory and therapy suggested that avoidance operated on several levels:

> Approach-avoidance conflict in stuttering may occur at five fairly distinct levels:
>
> • word level – conflicting urges to approach or to avoid the speaking of a feared word [e.g. A client may say that she cannot say words beginning with 's']
>
> • situation level – to enter or not enter a feared situation [e.g. a client he may not want to order in a coffee shop or apply for a new job because of his stuttering]
>
> • feeling – to express or inhibit the expression of heavy emotional content [e.g. being assertive with someone and expressing negative feedback]
>
> • relationship – to enter into or to avoid certain kinds of interpersonal relationship [e.g. being less likely to engage in friendships]
>
> • self-role, or egoprotective – accepting or rejecting role-expectations, especially those for intellectual achievement [e.g. not fulfilling ones potential or challenging expectations].
> (Sheehan 1975, p. 119)

Stewart (2012) suggested an extension to the five levels and proposes an additional level she called an avoidance of "intention to behave".

Turnbull and Stewart (2010) note that the levels of avoidance are often intertwined, especially important to consider when working on these in therapy. They are unlikely to be sequential i.e. when a client works on one level, for example ordering something in a shop while a colleague just happens to be present, he may find that he has to say a feared word which requires him to be more open about his speech in front of with someone he knows.

Furthermore, Turnbull and Stewart (2010) suggest that the clinician asks the client to determine his own hierarchy of avoidance, ranging from what is easiest to stop avoiding through to the most difficult to stop avoiding. The SLT cannot assume that all clients find work at, for example, situational levels more difficult than self-role.

Action therapy

How can avoidance be tackled? Sheehan's therapy was predominantly delivered in a group format in which discussion would take place and ideas could be explored, challenged and better understood. In addition, avoidance-reduction therapy is action therapy, so a client needs to be 'in action'.

Sheehan suggested the following phases of avoidance-reduction therapy:

• Self-Acceptance Phase – involves acknowledging the stammer, reducing elements of denial and becoming more open about it

• Monitoring and Exploring Phase – the individual begins to analyse his stammering in a more systematic and less emotional way and take responsibility for it

• Initiative Phase – here a PWS begins taking action; he will approach more by increasing his talking and going into feared situations

• Modification of Pattern Phase – the client begins to change the way in which he stammers and the way he talks (e.g. using voluntary stammering and hurrying less)

• Safety Margin Phase – a natural progression of the work carried out. This is done by resisting ideas of relapse and continuing to stammer in a more comfortable way.

In the initial stages of avoidance-reduction therapy a client may find that he starts to stammer more than he had previously. This brings with it a challenge to the PWS; he can avoid situations/not stammer openly and in so doing will not fulfil his potential, or alternatively, he can stammer in a different way, care less and get on with living his life. It can be valuable to have these conversations with a client. Some PWS will embrace the change quickly, while some PWS will reflect that this is difficult and need support to move on.

Sheehan's idea that 'you know how to be fluent, you don't know how to stammer' is central to therapy. I have used the line 'learning how to stammer' many times in therapy sessions with varying expressions of understanding, insight and incredulity on the face of my clients. Some PWS have accepted this as a logical route, while other PWS have questioned my sanity! (As a teenager, I was very sceptical when my speech and language therapist suggested it to me as a viable option, and it took a few years for the idea to start to make sense and for me to be ready to work on it.)

Who can use avoidance-reduction?

While this book is designed for adults, I do use a modified version of avoidance-reduction therapy with teenagers and children who are aware of stammering and, crucially, are bothered by it.

In terms of adults, a PWS with a more overt stammer may increase his sense of 'control', though control is not the intention or the vehicle of therapy. Avoidance reduction can be used even if there are very few overt stammering behaviours – i.e. where a person can appear to be very fluent on the surface. A PWS with a more covert stammer may be able to reveal part of his iceberg in a gradual manner.

Doctoral study data (Linklater 2017) examined who this form of therapy would work best for. Data suggested that level of education had no effect on the reduction in severity that a PWS reported; those who had left school at sixteen years of age fared just as well as those who had studied to third-level education. Age, gender and family history also had no bearing on therapy. Therapy carried out in residential or non-residential settings had similar outcomes. Severity was not a predictor of how impact was reduced or if people were more likely to relapse.

The following sections outline principles of Sheehan's basic therapy procedures, and suggested assignments can be found in the Resources section at the end of this chapter.

Outline of Sheehan's exercises

Establishing eye contact

Making eye contact with people is one of the keys to interpersonal communication. It may have been a natural response over the years for a PWS to look away at the point of stammering. There are several possible reasons for this including the need to distract himself to increase fluency or not wanting to experience shame of stammering and the reaction of others. Poor eye contact also conveys feelings of being ill at ease during stammering. However, if a PWS is looking away he does not know how his communication partner is reacting. He needs to challenge his presumptions about other people's reactions to his stammer. He may find that people do not care about his stammering as much as he thinks they do.

In this first assignment the speaker will attempt to maintain eye contact during conversation.

See **Resource 5.1: Eye Contact**.

Open discussion of stammering

The object of this assignment is for the PWS to discuss stammering with a number of people. Sheehan's intention here was to "begin accepting your role as a stutterer by discussing stuttering with friends and acquaintances with whom you will be more tempted to show your stuttering" (Sheehan, Shanks and Mereu 2005, p. 13). The client can design a short questionnaire about stammering and make notes of the responses. See **Resource 5.2: Open Discussion of Stammering**.

This exercise gives the client real-life experience of discussing stammering, something he may be most uncomfortable talking about. Typically, many people find that once the speaker and listener know stammering may take place, then stammering is likely to decrease.

This subtext of this exercise is to challenge the PWS's own views on stammering (e.g. do others think and/or care about stammering in the same way as he does?) and for him to be more open about stammering.

Exploring one's own stammering behaviours

Sheehan outlines the purpose of this assignment thus:

> We want you to explore your stuttering, and invite you to do the same. Oddly enough, you probably don't know what you do when you 'stutter'. Because it's unpleasant, you've probably covered it up from yourself as well as others.
> (Sheehan, Shanks and Mereu 2005, p. 14)

Sheehan suggests looking at the crutches or behaviours that a PWS uses in order to reduce the fear of the unknown. In the first instance, the PWS lists the many types he uses regularly e.g. eye blinks, head movements, filler sounds or phrases such as "em" or "you know".

Keeping notes like this is useful to monitor progress. It can be difficult for a client to see his progress at various points in therapy. Therefore, notes allow a client and clinician to reflect on progress that has been made.

See **Resource 5.3: Exploring One's Own Stammering Behaviours**.

• Formal self-assessments such as OASES (Yaruss and Quesal 2006) and WASSP ((Wright and Ayre 2000) can be used for identification purposes, this is directed at the client's stammering behaviours in a more specific way. I would use one of these more formal outcome measures at initial assessment prior to using the Sheehan checklist with adult clients. Alternatively a self-assessment checklist could be used like the one described in the DRB (Turnbull and Stewart 2010).

Setting goals and making assignments

Sheehan writes about setting goals and designing and carrying out assignments. These goals and assignments should be specific to the client in question. Examples are:

• Talk to one new person about stammering this week

• Maintain eye contact when stammering with three people each morning

• Monitor speech when talking in shops five times this week.

A recurring theme in Sheehan's approach is "Success is not fluency; facing fear and doing what is agreed upon is achieving success" (Sheehan, Shanks and Mereu 2005, p. 17). Sheehan also notes that the PWS can positively mention his stammering during these assignments. There is no need to apologise for stammering. If he has a block, he can let a friend or colleague know that he is actively working on his stammering and has been attending speech and language therapy. This can open up a supportive dialogue.

Sheehan also invites the client to reflect on his own stammering and why he is undertaking therapy. See **Resource 5.4: Reflections and Making Changes**.

Learning the language of responsibility

The underlying aim behind this assignment is that a client will increasingly take ownership and responsibility for his stammering behaviours. If a person is going to make attitudinal and behavioural changes in his speech he must take responsibility and move towards action. He cannot hope that someone else will work on his stammering on his behalf.

This ownership of stammering will be reflected by a shift in the language that a PWS uses; rather than *my hand moved* or *my eyes blinked*, which suggests something else was controlling the behaviour or as if a mysterious force is causing stammering, he will say *I* moved my hand, *I* blinked my eyes. See **Resource 5.5: Learning the Language of Responsibility**.

Again this activity encourages a person to be more objective about stammering and less emotional. Stammering is something he does, not something that happens to him. Sheehan directs this comment to the PWS: "You are doing the doing" (Sheehan, Shanks and Mereu 2005, p. 19).

Monitoring behaviours

Sheehan wants the PWS to become curious about his crutches and be able to describe them. These exercises are designed to get a client to monitor his behaviour; to observe consciously what he does. Questions such as "What are you doing that is getting in the way of speaking more naturally?" can help this process. In my experience, once this monitoring has begun, many behaviours reduce immediately. Sheehan suggests that "you can make faster progress by alert monitoring than by continuously trying to present your crutches" (Sheehan, Shanks and Mereu 2005, p. 20). Practically, the client is asked to pick one crutch and monitor it in two situations for two days. Monitoring should include noting which words the crutch is used on and what happens before, during and after its use. This process should be repeated with another crutch for the next two days. Monitoring can then be expanded to a larger sense of speech. In time the PWS should be able to accurately describe what he does in much the same way as a clinician might.

Initiative and fear seeking

Sheehan writes, "in stuttering therapy you never stand still" (Sheehan, Shanks and Mereu 2005, p. 21). The client is asked to approach situations more rather than avoiding.

He must taking the initiative and seek out feared situations.

> You progress much farther and speak much better if you keep seeking out feared words and situations instead of just letting them happen to you. Unless you continue pushing into the frontiers of fear and difficulty, you tend to lapse into retreat and the fear mounts. When you initiate an avoided situation, you succeed in challenging your fear.
> (Sheehan, Shanks and Mereu 2005, p. 21)

The PWS is invited to pick specific situations each day to work on his speech and to note how he stammered, his reactions and/or the reactions of others.

See **Resource 5.6: Initiative and Fear Seeking**.

Counting successes and failures

This section is designed to challenge a PWS's existing beliefs about success and failure in relation to stammering. Perhaps prior to starting avoidance-reduction therapy or a stammering-modification approach, a PWS would regard success as any form of fluency. By implication, hiding his stammering away from public view would have been perceived as a good thing. In contrast, he will feel that any form of stammering was a failure or something negative.

Sheehan et al. write:

> In the new approach, covering up or using a crutch is a failure even if the most immediate effect is that you sound more fluent. And stuttering openly and more easily counts as a success that can increase your security and eventually your ease of speaking.
> (Sheehan, Shanks and Mereu 2005, p. 20)

This is one of the more significant parts of Sheehan's work. It designed to challenge existing beliefs about success (hiding stammering) and failure (stammering badly or uncomfortably in front of someone); a block is not failure, nor is fear a failure.

See **Resources 5.7: Successes and Failures** and **5.8: Successes and Failures Grid** for suggested activities.

Exposing the iceberg

The intention of activities so far has been for the PWS to allow his stammering to be seen by other people and gradually expose his iceberg.

In this exercise the client is requested to draw his own 'iceberg of shame and guilt' in different situations over a number of days. The top part of the iceberg/the exposed section is *open stammering behaviour* (blocks, tension), while the lower part/the submerged section is *concealment behaviour*. Gradually, his stammering iceberg should move from a greater number of hidden items (false roles, crutches, fear, avoidance, guilt) to more open stammering behaviours (blocks, eye contact, monitoring). The visual representation can be beneficial for a client to reflect on progress by comparing and contrasting) and to target areas to work on between therapy sessions.

Stammering openly and easily

Sheehan's original piece of writing invites the client to allow his stammering behaviours to be seen.

The PWS is asked to cover up less and let his stammering come out. He is encouraged not to hide, but to continue blocking and begin to tolerate the lack of fluency.

Once this toleration of stammering begins, then his fear will decrease.

Resisting time pressure

The exercises of resisting time pressure are straightforward. Both a PWS and his clinician know that a PWS experiences both internal and external time pressure. The aim of these assignments is therefore for the PWS to develop an increasing ease when under time pressure and essentially cultivate an unhurried manner of speech. This idea of not hurrying is subtly different to the unhelpful advice of others who often suggest that if the PWS 'slows down' his rate of speech then his stammering will be reduced.

The first stage in this section is for the PWS to become more aware of time pressure and begin to act accordingly. The PWS must develop a sense that he can talk when he wants to and not in response to someone else's urgency. Again, this moves him towards exercising choice. Ultimately if he can learn not to hurry he is likely to reduce his stammering and increase fluency.

Being less hurried and being more deliberate are also linked to the PWS planning what he wants to say before he says it. This necessitates the individual engaging in positively planning what he wants to say, rather than scanning ahead for words he feels he cannot say. He may be so hurried that he begins to speak before he is ready to. Sheehan suggested that the rate of response, not the rate of speech, is what needs to be changed.

See **Resources 5.9: Resisting Time Pressure** for the exercise associated with resisting time pressure.

Pausing and phrasing: use of silence

The exercise of pausing and phrasing follows neatly on from resisting time pressure. The PWS is often so hurried to get as far as he can along a train of thought without stammering that his phrases and sentences can become longer than they need to be – much like this one! In this assignment the PWS starts to become more comfortable with silence and not fear it as much.

Any moment of silence or pause for a client is frequently associated with stammering and a feeling that he might not be able to start or restart speech. Thus, playing with pauses takes away some of this uncertainty and unpredictability.

A PWS can practise this activity by reading aloud and putting elongated exaggerated pauses into his reading. Longer pauses can be used in practice settings but are not intended for use in real situations, where he should be more natural in his delivery and less hurried.

Similarly, the clinician should make it clear that there is no intention for the PWS to talk like a robot in everyday speech. Rather he should become able to handle natural pauses and choose when to pause rather than have the stammer dictate unexpected and unwanted pauses.

Sheehan et al. write:

> Breathing, one of the most conditionable of responses, is notoriously associated with fear states. Lapsing into silence is a natural defensive biological reaction. Part of your built-in time-pressure system as a stutterer is that you never pause for breath except in the 'dead stops' before feared words. You need to learn to phrase normally so that you do not begin speech on residual air.
> (Sheehan, Shanks and Mereu 2005, p. 34)

See **Resource 5.10: Pausing and Phrasing** for exercises on pausing and phrasing.

Reducing struggle and stammering forward

Throughout avoidance-reduction therapy Sheehan is leading towards an easier way of stammering. Sheehan wants the PWS to notice where he struggles and to question "Why did I force so much?" To stammer in a relaxed way is counter-intuitive when many PWS have thought that trying harder would result in increased fluency.

The clinician can encourage her client to stammer forward. Sheehan et al. describe this:

> In learning to stutter forward, it is important to eliminate 'dead stops', to begin feared words with movement and sound just as you begin non-feared words. You should stutter so that your listener can see and hear your blocks clearly enough to be able to describe them.
> (Sheehan Shanks, and Mereu 2005, p. 39)

This is tied into Sheehan's ideas of encouraging approach rather than avoidance. "Keep moving forward" is a mantra that can applied to this aspect of therapy. Once more, this is not about being fluent, it is about the PWS going into situations and speaking even though he thinks that he will stammer. This is reframing the ideas of success.

Voluntary stammering

Voluntary stammering (i.e. stammering on purpose) is not singularly Joseph and Vivian Sheehan's creation, but they advocate that it is a way to learn to stammer more easily. They note, "it will not reduce the frequency of stuttering. Quite to the contrary it should increase frequency, but with a change in form" (Sheehan, Shanks and Mereu 2005, p. 40). They do, however, add their own flavour and characteristics and suggest the slide as their preferred technique: the prolongation of the first consonant in a word.

Clinical trials by Sheehan and Voas (1957) reported that the slide is more effective than the bounce (e.g. buh, buh, buh bounce). While the latter variant may be useful in desensitising some clients, in my view the slide keeps the client moving forward and challenges the approach-avoidance conflict. It counteracts 'holding back', which can be one aspect which perpetuates stammering for the client.

Vivian herself cautioned that voluntary stammering should not be the only strategy a client takes away from therapy. It should be tied in with eye contact, pausing and phrasing and resisting time pressure and part of a repertoire of skills that the clinician will show her client. In particular it links closely with openness in stammering: for the client to show that he is a PWS and he is working on being more comfortable with stammering. He is choosing when to stammer.

The clinician can advise her client that he does not need to use voluntary stammering on every word in every sentence for the rest of his life. Instead he should vary it and use it as much as possible in, first, comfortable situations to become more natural with it and then later in more difficult situations. The client should start using it on non-feared words and progress to using it on feared words. A hierarchy can be drawn up by the client and SLT in order to be more strategic about where and when to use voluntary stammering.

Many clients find it useful to understand the basic phonetic nature of sounds when learning about voluntary stammering. Discussing which sounds are easier and more difficult can be illuminating for PWS. A clinician knows that fricatives are easier to slide on due to their manner of production. However, plosives are more difficult, and therefore an easier onset or softer release may be recommended for use on these sounds. Initial vowels can be problematic for a PWS. In this instance it is suggested that a client slide on the first emphasised consonant in a word e.g. avvvvvoidance. However, some words may not allow for this strategy, so some flexibility is suggested, with sliding on vowels remaining as an option for the client.

Voluntary stammering aims to reduce the impact that stammering has on a PWS's life. By practising voluntary stammering and using it in daily situations the PWS can gradually learn to stammer more comfortably.

See **Resource 5.11: Voluntary Stammering**.

Exercising choice

With the introduction of voluntary stammering, the PWS will have a greater choice as to how and when he stammers.

A clinician can help a client to exercise his choice in when to stammer. She could facilitate a discussion around this area and enable the PWS to select some situations. Alternatively the following options could be talked through:

• Voluntarily stammer with the first person you talk to each morning

• Stammer voluntarily in ten different situations through the day

• Stammer voluntarily with someone who you know well each day.

Safety margin and tolerance for disfluency

The ideas presented in the safety margin exercise are important in moving into the maintenance stage of therapy. This exercise encourages the client to let his stammering sound 'worse' than it needs to.

Sheehan suggests that the fear of stammering also leads PWS to *not* work on his speech: the fear of failure and making a mess of speaking opportunities is powerful.

The ultimate aim of the safety margin exercise is for the client to get used to the bumps and bobbles of everyday speech. Sheehan et al. write:

> The more fear you can satisfy ahead of time the less chance fear has of building up and catching up with you. . . . To help you keep from straining for perfect speech you can make use of the 'safety margin'. If you use it properly you can gain much security about hanging onto the successes that you have achieved.
> (Sheehan, Shanks and Mereu 2005, p. 55)

Voluntary stammering and development of safety margin for the client allows his stammering to be seen and his speech to be less than perfect. By doing this he can 'over-satisfy' the fear and build for fluency. Sounding less than perfect allows a gradual acceptance and tolerance of the natural bobbles and disfluencies that all speakers encounter and means the PWS becomes less sensitive to these over time.

See **Resource 5.12: Safety Margin** for activities associated with safety margin.

Direct natural speech attempts

As therapy progresses, the client is encouraged to make more direct attempts on feared words without use of his old crutches. This is part of a wider change for him to become a more natural and effective speaker who chooses pauses, inflections and the words he uses rather than feel that some aspect of stammering can limit his communication.

Adjusting to fluency

For all the talk of stammering in avoidance-reduction therapy, the client must now start to accept the new role of a more fluent speaker. Sheehan writes about the 'giant in chains' complex, whereby the PWS essentially believes that "if only I could sort out my stammering then all my other problems will be solved". Realising that a reduction in stammering will not solve all his problems can be one of the more difficult points for the client in therapy. "Just as in the early phases of therapy you had to accept your role as a stutterer, so in the later phases, you have to accept your role as a more normal speaker" (Sheehan, Shanks and Mereu 2005, p. 58). This can be a challenge for a PWS; many of his other difficulties in life may still remain, he can just deal with them with more fluent speech.

The clinician should also raise the idea that other people in the client's life may react differently to a new style of speaking and perhaps to the change in assertiveness that this shift brings. Occasionally roles may change. His spouse, family members and friends may find that they are no longer required to order food in a restaurant for him or telephone on his behalf. While most vested parties will respond positively to the client's change, a minority may feel superfluous or even resentful where once they were more important.

Non-reinforcement and cancellation

Sheehan points towards the neurology of stammering in these exercises; he notes the "motor or instrumental side" to stammering in addition to the emotional and attitudinal sides that take main focus. Sheehan argues that whenever a trick is used it strengthens the habit of crutches, and this must be challenged. He suggests monitoring where the moment of release takes place in stammering and where the fear subsides. Then the PWS will stammer smoothly and openly beyond this point of release i.e. making this block longer than it needs to be. This work centres on reducing fear and bringing about "reinforcement of a newer and smoother style of stuttering" (Sheehan, Shanks and Mereu 2005, p. 59).

Avoidance-reduction therapy offers the PWS two ways to weaken his struggle in stammering and to reinforce the easier stammering: the pull-out or the cancellation. Both of these techniques are described fully in DRB (Turnbull and Stewart 2010), and readers are directed to this text for more detail.

How to carry out avoidance-reduction therapy with limited sessions

The clinician is often time bound in how long she can work with clients. She may only have a limited number of sessions. In these instances, it would be useful if she focuses on some of the fundamental points of avoidance-reduction therapy and its principles. While doing this, a healthy explanation of why she is choosing particular exercises can have a far-reaching impact. "He [the client] must accept responsibility for making changes, though it is the therapist's responsibility to provide him with a better modus operandi" (Sheehan 1975, p. 146). She can provide her client with the most basic of tools outlined here:

• Increasing openness and acceptance

• Eye contact and self-monitoring

• Voluntary stammering

• Hurrying less

• Developing a safety margin

• Redefining ideas of success and failure associated with stammering.

She should state and restate the reasons behind learning to stammer more easily and becoming more comfortable with stammering. Essentially, these overarching themes are in 'Message to a stutterer'. However, for a PWS a lifetime of conditioning takes time to change. Using some of this time to cultivate independence for the client is invaluable, i.e. suggesting ways that her client can work without her and how he needs to become his own clinician.

Conclusion: approach-cultivation and avoidance-reduction

The idea behind avoidance-reduction therapy is simple; but it can be difficult to implement. Part of the challenge with this therapy is to make avoidance reduction part of everyday life. An attitude to approach, instead of avoiding, is essential. Put simply; avoid less, approach more.

After working as a speech-language pathologist specialising in stammering for more than sixty years, Vivian Sheehan cautioned:

> If a therapy or device results in immediate fluency, it is probably a trick, so forget about it. In fact, you should expect more stuttering for a time. You should just change *how* you stutter – with ease, acceptance, eye contact with the listener, and continued communication. Get a feeling of success from *not avoiding*. Finally, never try to be fluent. Easy speech comes with acceptance of the role of a stutterer and on becoming a *good* one. With easier speech, fluency will be a natural result – with time! Do not expect instant miracles. Remember, you are changing habits that developed over a lifetime.
> (Sheehan, Shanks and Mereu 2005, p. 3)

Reflecting on my own stammering and the stammering of some of the clients I've worked with, it appears that avoidance-reduction therapy can work for different people in different ways. What I might have initially thought of as a potential success or end point for a client was redefined by the client themselves, and I had to adjust my sights accordingly. Thus, there is no completion point with this type of therapy; there will always be different levels of client satisfaction. However, I suggest that there is likely to be a level of maintenance that is required, be it daily, weekly, monthly or less frequently. There is a sense that topping up is helpful, or, as Sheehan suggested, mowing the lawn of avoidance.

Many PWS might argue that their stammering has hurt them; I cannot argue this point. However, it maybe that the attitudes around stammering, from himself and/or from others, have been the bigger problem. Can a PWS adopt an attitude that stammering is okay, and can his attitude to stammering be neutral? Stammering is neither good nor bad, but thinking makes it so. To achieve that belief, the transformation may take many small steps, but there is hope and it is possible to change.

Acknowledgement

Some of Sheehan's avoidance-reduction therapy worksheets were adapted as part of the Dublin Adult Stuttering course, which was designed with my esteemed colleagues Noreen Keane and Dr Duana Quigley.

Eye contact

Points for a clinician to raise with a client

- Good eye contact is a good foundation for communication; it puts you and your listener at ease. However, maintaining eye contact while stammering can be a challenge for clients. But with a little practice, it can be empowering to stammer more comfortably and maintain eye contact.

- A hierarchy system may be used to support the change to increased eye contact.

Instructions for a client

- As a first step, try keeping eye contact with yourself in the mirror. (This may be a challenge, and it may feel uncomfortable.) Read aloud a paragraph and notice what you do.

- Build this up and try maintaining eye contact while talking on the phone while looking into the mirror – make eye contact with yourself as a starting point.

- Maintain eye contact in a conversation with a friend, colleague or boss. Write down what you feel afterwards.

You may find that you over-stare at times or you may lose eye contact – this is to be expected. You may have been looking away while you stammer for most of your life. The good news is that it will get easier – so keep trying.

Practical activities

A It can be helpful to make observations that keep you focussed. As you grow confidence and have less difficulty making eye contact you can make the activity more interesting by answering the following questions:

- How many different eye colours did you see today? List them.

- Was anyone wearing glasses?

- Did anyone look away more than you did?

B It is likely that you will stammer in these situations, but that's okay – that's why we're doing this.

- Write down ten words you stammered on while maintaining good eye contact.

- Introduce yourself with good eye contact – don't worry if you stammer. How did you react? How did your listener react?

Open discussion of stammering

Information and instructions to a client

Sheehan suggests asking people you know questions about stammering. This increases openness around stammering and allows you to show listeners what your stammering is really like. Once you have tried this exercise, he suggests asking a stranger the same questions. It can be quite daunting to go up to someone you don't know and start talking about stammering – especially when you stammer! However, the rewards can be significant.

Select a public place, look for an approachable face and introduce yourself. Let the person know that you are doing a 'speech and language therapy assignment' and carrying out a survey, would they mind answering a few questions, it won't take long etc.

If they say yes, that's great – go ahead and ask your questions! If they say no, be polite and thank them for their time. This 'rejection' is unlikely to be anything relating to you and your stammering – we move on! This exercise is all about disclosure and being more open about stammering. Even asking a stranger is evidence of success.

Remember not to take any negative answers personally. Imagine how you would respond if you were asked questions on an unfamiliar topic; you might reply with a less well-informed response than you would prefer.

Make notes and report back to your speech and language therapist about how you felt about this exercise.

Sheehan's questions and additional ideas are suggested below. Make sure you can answer the fact-based questions yourself before you start talking to people!

- Have you ever known any other stammerers?
- How does my stammering affect you?
- What do you think causes stammering?
- What do you think people can do about their stammering?

Additional questions could be asked:

- Do you know what percentage of the population stammers?
- Do you think more males or females stammer?

Make up at least one question that you are interested in e.g. Do you think that stammering runs in families? Do you think that people who stammer should have jobs that require a lot of talking?

© Trudy Stewart (2020). *Stammering Resources for Adults and Teenagers: Integrating New Evidence into Clinical Practice.* **Routledge.**

Exploring one's own stammering behaviours

Notes for the clinician

Sheehan's Speech Pattern Checklist allows for a more clinical look at stammering. It may be the first time that your client has looked at his stammering so closely. It can be useful to make a copy of the Speech Pattern Checklist and refer to it later in therapy to compare against potential changes that he has made. Some clients may be skilled at self-analysis of their stammering behaviours, while others may require more guidance and support.

Notes for the client

Sheehan devised a Speech Pattern Checklist which allowed for more clinical analysis of stammering by a person who stammers. This assignment is designed to tune you into your stammering. Ultimately, it would be helpful if you could become more objective about your stammering; you will then care less about it. Examples from Sheehan's original worksheet are suggested as well as space for other suggestions.

To be completed by the client

Monitoring and Exploring

1 How do I avoid stammering?

- I give up when I have difficulty

- I substitute words

- I pretend to think of what I want to say

- I change the order of words

- I begin to speak when someone else is talking

- _____

- _____

2 How do I postpone stammering?

- I pause

- I beat around the bush

- I repeat previous words and phrases (running start)

- I use fluent asides

- I pretend not to hear

- _____

- _____

© Trudy Stewart (2020). *Stammering Resources for Adults and Teenagers: Integrating New Evidence into Clinical Practice.* **Routledge.**

3 What "starters" do I use?

- I introduce unnecessary words, sounds or phrases

  e.g. well, uh, em, you know, actually

  _____

- I use a stereotyped movement
- Shift my body
- Clear my throat
- Blink my eyes
- Move an arm or hand
- Move a leg or foot
- Click my fingers
- Yawn

- _____
- _____

4 What distractions do I use?

- I speak in a monotone
- I assume an air of self-confidence
- I try to think of something else

- _____
- _____

5 How do I get out of my stammering block?

- I try to force the word out
- I pause and then finish the word
- I keep repeating the sound until I can say the word
- I become tense: my lips, head or some part of my body tremors
- I go back to the preceding word or phrase

- _____
- _____

6 Additional reflections

- Do any of these behaviours change in different situations?

- _____

- Do any of these behaviours change from week to week?

- _____

- Are there any times when you do not need to use tricks or avoidances?

- _____

- What do these reflections tell you about the variability of your stammering? Do you think you can change these behaviours?

- _____

© Trudy Stewart (2020), _Stammering Resources for Adults and Teenagers: Integrating New Evidence into Clinical Practice._ **Routledge.**

Reflections and making changes

Notes for the clinician

As part of Sheehan's section on exploring stammering behaviours, he suggests that a client also reflect on the impact of stammering and why he is making changes now. The later part of the activity is more action based, where he can monitor and reflect on his stammering in everyday situations.

To be completed by the client

• List the ways in which stammering has had an impact on your life

_____

_____

• Why do you want to do something about your stammering now?

_____

_____

• If you suddenly gained control over your speech, how would your life be different?

_____

_____

• List

  a) Five speaking situations in which you have difficulty

_____

_____

_____

_____

_____

  b) Five speaking situations that you usually avoid

_____

_____

_____

_____

_____

Go into some of these situations and record the outcome even if you may stammer 'badly'. Note what you did before, during and after stammering.

© Trudy Stewart (2020), *Stammering Resources for Adults and Teenagers: Integrating New Evidence into Clinical Practice*. **Routledge.**

Learning the language of responsibility
Information and instructions for the client

> Your stuttering is not something that happens to you, but something that you do.
> (Sheehan, Shanks and Mereu 2005, p. 19)

Before you can make changes in your speech, you need to take responsibility for your stammering. This exercise is designed to get you to see that "you are doing the doing". It shows that many of your stammering behaviours are things that you do rather than things that happen to you. With improved identification of what you do when you stammer you will be able to reduce your tricks and avoidances.

Practical activity

Notice how you talk and describe your stammering. If you notice that you are describing it as something happening to you rather than something you do – rephrase and say it again differently. For example, "My eyes closed when I stammer" can be changed to" I closed my eyes when I tried to say your name".

• Notice five times in a day that you do not use the language of responsibility.

_____

_____

_____

_____

• Notice five times in a day that you do use the language of responsibility.

_____

_____

_____

_____

Initiative and fear seeking

Information and instructions to a clinician and client

Sheehan wants the client to seek out feared words and situations rather than waiting for them to happen. By going into situations that the person who stammers would usually avoid, Sheehan, Shanks and Mereu (2005) outline four points of importance:

- If you find yourself avoiding a situation, then you need to put yourself in that feared situation

- To succeed, it is sufficient that you enter the situation. Rate yourself not on fluency but on meeting the challenge

- Anticipate difficulty but[1] stutter forward and openly

- Your readiness to stutter in itself will make things easier in the long run.

(p. 21)

Over the next week, pick one situation each day where you will specifically work on your speech. Start with familiar situations but also look at the situations that you typically avoid.

Make notes on the following after each situation:

- What you did before, during and after stammering.
- Who did you talk to?
- How did you feel afterwards?
- What were your three most successful situations?

---

[1] stutter and stammer are the same. The term stuttering tends to be used in other countries such as USA and Australia, while in the UK stammering is used.

© Trudy Stewart (2020). *Stammering Resources for Adults and Teenagers: Integrating New Evidence into Clinical Practice.* **Routledge.**

Successes and failures

Information and instructions to a clinician

At various stages in therapy it is important to challenge what the person who stammers thinks of as successes and failures. The following sheet can be introduced to change the perception of what the PWS sees as success and to challenge this idea.

Information and instructions to a client

This activity challenges what you think of as successes and failures. There are spaces for you to record your own ideas. Pin this on the noticeboard at home or keep it with you as you go about your day. You will need to remind yourself of these ideas, especially the notion that being fluent is not a success. Saying what you want to say should be regarded as more of a success.

Count it as a success if you:

- Establish eye contact before beginning to speak
- Stammer forward without using tricks
- Stammer but bring the sound in immediately
- Complete any feared word you started
- Stammer with good eye contact
- Observe exactly what you did when you stammered (e.g. closed your eyes, repeated the first letter, tensed your lips)
- Choose feared words instead of 'easy words'
- Mention your stammering casually without shame
- Go out of the way to talk in a difficult situation (e.g. make a phone call you didn't have to make)
- Cancel any failure.

Others

- _____
- _____
- _____
- _____
- _____

Count as a failure if you:

- Lose eye contact while stammering
- Use an easy word instead of a difficult word
- Substitute or avoid using a word that you need to
- Avoid talking in situations
- Cover up your stammering with tricks
- Try to talk fluently at any cost
- Respond quickly and automatically to every little pressure in the situation
- Show embarrassment which puts your audience ill at ease
- Use a starter, filler or back up and start again
- Stop halfway through a block.

Others

- _____
- _____

© Trudy Stewart (2020). *Stammering Resources for Adults and Teenagers: integrating New Evidence into Clinical Practice.* **Routledge.**

Successes and failures grid

Information and instructions to a client

The following grid can be used to turn **Resource 5.7: Success and Failures** into a more visual record of the changes that you are making. You can use Sheehan's ideas of successes and failures and add in your own suggestions too.

Suggestions for areas to work on

- Establishing eye contact before speaking
- Entering situations to work on speech
- Completing any feared word
- Mentioning your stammering.

Table 5.1 Successes and failures grid

	Establish eye contact	Enter situations to work on speech	Complete any feared word	Mention your stammering without shame . . .		
Mon						
Tues						
Wed						
Thurs						
Fri						
Sat						
Sun						

R5.8

Resisting time pressure

Information and instructions to client

Time pressure is something that many people who stammer react to, which can in turn lead to more stammering. By becoming more aware of time pressure you can become less reactive and move towards choosing when to speak. Time pressure can be either external or internal. Two activities are set out to work on resisting time pressure. The first is observational; the second is a practical activity for you to use with your speech and language therapist in clinic.

External time pressure

• Observe how much you are put under time pressure by other people (not by those who wait patiently).

• Collect examples of situations where you are put under time pressure (e.g. by a bus driver, shop assistant, a person on the telephone etc.).

• _____

• _____

• _____

Internal time pressure

• Observe how you put yourself under time pressure.

• Collect examples of situations where you put yourself under time pressure (e.g. when you go to order in a shop, when you introduce yourself, when you speak on the phone).

• _____

• _____

• _____

Sheehan outlines some ways that you can notice time pressure. Do you do any of the things listed here?

• Trying to cover up silence with filler words and noises

• Answering questions before the other person has finished speaking

• Getting other people to take your place in a queue

• What else do you do?

• _____

• _____

© Trudy Stewart (2020). *Stammering Resources for Adults and Teenagers: Integrating New Evidence into Clinical Practice.* Routledge.

Practical activity: the yes/no game

Information and instructions to clinician for the yes/no game

The clinician should ask the client questions at first. The client should try to resist time pressure when being asked questions. The roles may be reversed after a few rounds of questioning and when time pressure has been adequately resisted.

Information and instructions to a client

The yes/no game is a way to play with a sense of time. It challenges how quickly or slowly a person might reply. It aims for you to be less hurried in responses. It allows you to become more comfortable with silence. This can be useful as it may desensitise you to the moments when you feel that you are blocking or stammering.

You must resist time pressure with the questions that are asked of you. However, the catch is that the person must not reply using "yes" or "no". Instead, he/she must respond appropriately without either term i.e. "that is correct" or "I don't think so".

Tip: Quick tag questions ("Are you sure?" or "Really?") are a good way to catch out the person responding in this game.

Pausing and phrasing

Information and instructions to a client

Read the following sentences in a less hurried manner. Each "/" in a sentence is intended to be a pause. Try to make these pauses as long as possible, they should be exaggerated in the practice session with your speech and language therapist. Pauses in everyday conversations do not need to be as long. However, it can be quite empowering to use *really* long pauses. This undoes some of the discomfort that has been associated with silent blocks. Vary the length of your pauses. Play around with your pauses. Try to enjoy the silence rather than feeling a need to hurry on to the next word or phrase. The intention is not for you to 'slow down' for this exercise; the rate of your words and phrases can remain at a typical rate, but the pauses are crucial. Essentially, don't hurry.

- The boys ran / down the cliff.

- In the morning / we saw / the airplane.

- The club / will meet / at seven thirty.

- Paint the car / a dark blue.

- Those green leaves / are turning brown.

- If you need more paper / come to me / and I will give you some.

- The waiter tripped / and dropped / the tray of cold drinks.

- If it is too cold / or / if it rains / we will meet inside.

- When the paper comes / we will read the story / on the front page.

- We saw them play / on Wednesday evening / in the auditorium.

Exercise

Take a page from a newspaper or magazine and mark the places where you will pause. Try this with a page online; you can't mark the page online, so you'll have to figure out your pauses as you go.

Note: Though fluency may increase, this exercise is not about reading fluently. The space in between the words is what you should be interested in. Don't hurry!

© Trudy Stewart (2020). *Stammering Resources for Adults and Teenagers: Integrating New Evidence into Clinical Practice.* Routledge.

Voluntary stammering

Information and instructions to a client

Voluntary stammering is one of the most powerful tools that can change your stammering *and* change how you feel about it. Sheehan writes: "You don't have a choice as to whether you stutter but you do have a choice as to how you stutter" (Sheehan, Shanks, and Mereu 2005, p. 5). By using voluntary stammering you are learning to reduce your struggle and tension, and you are choosing to stammer in an easier way. You are becoming more open about stammering. Instead of avoiding, you are approaching sounds and words, and you are moving forward.

Sheehan listed eight criteria for good voluntary stammering. They are:

- Voluntary stammering should be done with good eye contact
- Voluntary stammering should be used on words that you do not fear
- To stammer voluntarily, you prolong the fffffirst sound of the wwwwword (not the voooooowels in the miiiiiddle)
- Voluntary stammering uses a shift or movement, not a position
- Good voluntary stammering is unhurried
- Voluntary stammering is varied in length from word to word
- When you are using voluntary stammering in a situation, do not speak fluently immediately afterwards
- Voluntary stammering is done with a smooth release.

Exercise

Try these phrases using voluntary stammering. Remember to sssssslide!

- FFFFFFrozen ffffffood
- Shshshshrimp is a shshshshell fish
- A fffffffoggy frosty Friday
- LLLLLLLight the candle
- Spring has sssssprung
- Robin rrrrredbreast
- Elllllllllllastic is strong and stretchy
- Ninety-nine nnnnnname
- ShShShShow me again.

© Trudy Stewart (2020). *Stammering Resources for Adults and Teenagers: Integrating New Evidence into Clinical Practice.* **Routledge.**

Practical activities

Information and instructions to a client

Reading

Read a paragraph from a newspaper or magazine using voluntary stammering – underline the words that you will slide on before you start to read the piece. First do this in front of a mirror, and then with a partner. Get used to making the slides long enough for listeners to hear. Let them know you are stammering.

Conversation

Choose three sounds that you like to slide on – e.g. sounds such as m, s, f and w. Have a three-minute conversation with someone, and try to slide on each sound at least three times.

Reflection: Was it easy to use voluntary stammering in the conversation? Was it difficult? What happened over the course of three minutes?

Practical activity: using voluntary stammering in everyday situations

Information and instructions to a client

The idea is to make voluntary stammering part of your regular speech. Use it when you get on the bus, use it when you ask for something in a shop, use it when you pick up the phone or use it when you read a story to children. You could even record your voicemail message with a slide; it lets lots of people know that you stammer in a very efficient manner!

Look at words or phrases that you use regularly in everyday life – pick some of these to slide on e.g. "good mmmmmorning", "ssssssee you later", "wwwwwhat time?", "thank yyyyyou".

• Write your phrases here:

• _____

• _____

• _____

© Trudy Stewart (2020). *Stammering Resources for Adults and Teenagers: Integrating New Evidence into Clinical Practice.* Routledge.

Safety margin

Information and instructions to a client

Safety margin is a way to build in tolerance for disfluency. All speakers experience some level of disfluency in their speech; this is a way for you to become more comfortable with the bobbles and glitches that occur. The more fluent you try to be, the more likelihood there is that you will stammer. By using more voluntary stammering than you need to, you won't be as surprised when you have a block, and you will have a more solid foundation for fluent speech in more challenging situations.

Exercise

Pick five situations in which you can make your stammering sound *worse* than you need to. Use voluntary stammering in these situations on non-feared words. Monitor the number of slides that you use in each situation.

1

2

3

4

5

How did you feel after you had used more voluntary stammering than you needed do?

_____

_____

What happened to your fluency?

_____

_____

What happened to your stammering?

_____

_____

Maintaining a safety margin

Information and instructions to a client

Sheehan asks in what kind of situation it would be important to maintain a 'margin of safety'. Furthermore he asks the all-important question of *how* you would carry this out.

What situations would it be important to maintain a safety margin?

_____

_____

_____

Ahead of these important events – like a work meeting, a presentation, a job interview – how can you develop a safety margin?

_____

_____

_____

© Trudy Stewart (2020). *Stammering Resources for Adults and Teenagers: Integrating New Evidence into Clinical Practice*. **Routledge.**

As a way of keeping track, Sheehan suggests an exercise to monitor speaking situations with two columns of speaking situations: +margin and -margin. In the +margin, note where you use more voluntary stammering and over-satisfy the fear; in the – margin, make a note of where you don't use much voluntary stammering and the fear is under-satisfied.

+ margin	- margin
1	1
2	2
3	3
4	4
5	5

Repeat this exercise every day for one week. Report back on what you find.

References

Linklater, J.P. (2017). *Effectiveness of Avoidance-reduction Therapy for Adults Who Stutter* (Doctoral Thesis). University of Limerick.

Sheehan, J.G. (1970). *Stuttering: Research and Therapy*. New York: Harper & Row.

Sheehan, J.G. (1975). Conflict theory and avoidance-reduction therapy. In J. Eisenson (ed.), *Stuttering: A Second Symposium* (pp. 97–198). New York: Harper & Row.

Sheehan, J.G. and Sheehan, V.M. (1984). Avoidance-reduction therapy: A response suppression hypothesis. In W.H. Perkins (ed.), *Stuttering Disorders* (pp. 147–151). New York: Thieme-Stratton.

Sheehan, J.G. and Voas, R.B. (1957). Stuttering as conflict. I. Comparison of therapy techniques involving approach and avoidance. *Journal of Speech and Hearing Disorders*, 22(5), 714–723.

Sheehan, V.M., Shanks, P. and Mereu, S. (2005). *Easy Stuttering: Avoidance-Reduction Therapy*. Santa Monica, CA: Sheehan Stuttering Center.

Stewart, T. (2012). Avoidance in adults who stutter: A review and clinical discussion. *Polish Forum Logopedyczne*, 20, 20–29.

Turnbull, J. and Stewart, T. (2010). *The Dysfluency Resource Book*. London: Routledge.

Wright, L. and Ayre, A. (2000). *WASSP: The Wright & Ayre Stuttering Self-rating Profile*. Bicester: Speechmark.

Yaruss, S. and Quesal, R.W. (2006). Overall assessment of the speaker's experience of stuttering (OASES). *Journal of Fluency Disorders*, 31(2), 90–115.

6 | Integrating mindfulness into therapy with people who stammer

Carolyn Cheasman

What is mindfulness?

Definitions

In the past decade mindfulness has become a term familiar to most people with articles appearing regularly in the press. However, there are many misconceptions, and so I will begin this chapter by defining the term. Since working with mindfulness myself I have found the following definition useful: "Mindfulness is paying attention in a particular way: on purpose, in the present moment and non-judgmentally" (Kabat-Zinn 1994, p. 4).

Shapiro, who has written widely on mindfulness, elaborates on this definition, stating: "Mindfulness is more than just moment-to-moment awareness. It is a kind, curious awareness that helps us relate to our ourselves and others with compassion" (Shapiro 2013).

Thus, the aim is to cultivate a particular quality of awareness – one that is imbued with a friendly, kindly curiosity. For me this signals a moving towards, a 'gentle approach' to our experience, and this may be different to the way a PWS brings awareness to his experience of stammering.

Misconceptions

One common misconception is that mindfulness is a relaxation technique. We can see from this definition that it is not; if a person is tense and brings a friendly interest to sensations of tension he is being mindful. He can pay attention to the totality of his experience, both external events (sights, sounds, tastes, smells) and internal events (thoughts, feelings and body sensations).

This brings up another common misunderstanding that mindfulness is about emptying the mind or not having any thoughts. With mindfulness training, this same friendly interest can be applied to thinking, and an individual can develop a different experience of space between himself and his thoughts.

Being present

The challenge is that generally a person is not in the present moment, as thinking whisks him into the past or future. He is not paying attention deliberately and is often being very judgemental about his experience. A lack of awareness in the present moment means living life on automatic pilot (Crane 2009). When on autopilot, a person will not be present to what is actually happening in the moment, as he is somewhere else in his head. Often carried away on a stream of thinking, his mind gives him thoughts for much of the time; this is normal and is just what the human mind does.

The 'doing' mode

Language-based ways of processing experience are helpful for activities such as planning, analysing and goal setting and are often described as the 'doing' mode of mind (Crane 2009). However, this doing mode can be unhelpful for dealing with internal experience e.g. trying to manage grief. It tends not to work and often leads to unhelpful attempts to fix, control or suppress, which may increase the underlying difficulty. When caught up in streams of thinking and reactivity, a person's mind is in 'doing mode'. Thoughts lead to other thoughts, and before he is aware, an individual has tumbled into an internal experience which bears little relationship to what is happening. These are some of the challenges to mindful awareness; minds wander, judge experience and compulsively try to fix things.

Learning to be mindful

The good news is that mindfulness is a trainable skill. In contrast to doing mode, mindful awareness is described as 'being' mode, and this can be cultivated through formal and informal approaches. A person starts to pay attention to internal experience in an interested way and lets go of trying to control. Mindfulness does not aim to get rid of unhelpful thoughts and feelings. Instead, it develops an awareness of direct and natural human reactions and distinguishes these from the layers added by the mind. This is a key point: learning to notice not just internal experience but reactions to this. Mindfulness helps cultivate sensory-perceptual processing as opposed to language-based processing (Boyle 2012). Through non-judgemental noticing in the absence of attempts to change or fix anything, mindfulness practice helps cultivate greater acceptance of aversive experience.

Relationship to stammering

Whilst stammering presents on the outside as particular types of disruptions to speech fluency, it is far more than just a set of speech behaviours. As Yaruss (2007) states, "stammering is more than just stammering" (p. 314).

The behaviours are often accompanied by streams of thinking, strong feelings before, during and after moments of stammering and frequently go along with attempts to hide or avoid. Many believe that the person's attempts to avoid feed the whole stammering dynamic (Sheehan 1970, Starkweather 1999, Van Riper 1973). In looking at the relevance of mindfulness to stammering Boyle (2012) identifies two key areas: the psychosocial domain and the sensory-motor domain. In my own writing I have come to similar conclusions and describe much of stammering as automatic pilot activity (Cheasman 2013). Both of us conclude that awareness and acceptance are key aspects of mindfulness training that are helpful to a PWS.

Stammering modification therapies aim to help reduce negative emotional reactivity to the threat and experience of dysfluency (Van Riper 1973). These approaches invariably incorporate traditional behavioural methods to help this process, commonly called desensitisation. Mindfulness training supports this through increasing the ability to simply notice, open up to and make space for emotional reactions. This in turn leads to a reduction in emotional reactivity and develops emotional regulation skills (Hölzel et al. 2011). In addition, mindfulness practice addresses the unhelpful avoidance behaviour head on, encouraging acceptance, which can lead to a reduction in anxiety. This acceptance is not resignation but rather an active 'allowing' and creation of helpful conditions for a PWS to apply stammering modification techniques. Broadly speaking, if a person can:

a   allow himself to stammer and

b   be less reactive in that moment

he may have less physical tension and be more able to use strategies such as in-block modification (Van Riper 1973).

The use of techniques is challenging in part because speech patterns are habitual. It is hard for a PWS to consistently apply techniques learnt in therapy in the outside world. Mindfulness is clearly relevant here, as it increases the ability to maintain attentional focus; an ability which is relevant regardless of the therapeutic approach.

The literature

There is now an extensive literature base on mindfulness and its application to many areas. Kabat-Zinn has written widely on the relevance of mindfulness in a generic way i.e. to human beings in general. He developed an eight-week mindfulness-based stress management (MBSR) programme (Kabat-Zinn 1996), and this has been comprehensively researched (Gu et al. 2015). MBSR was developed by Segal, Williams and Teasdale, (2002) into mindfulness-based cognitive therapy (MBCT), an eight-week programme designed specifically for people recovering from depression. They include a strong rationale for how mindful awareness can help a person step back from negative thinking cycles and rumination. There is a rigorous evidence base for MBCT for depression (Gu et al. 2015), and NICE, the UK institute for clinical excellence, recognises MBCT as an intervention to prevent relapse in people recovering from depression. There is now a range of MBCT courses for a variety of difficulties (Baer 2003). A growing body of neuroscience literature gives a 'hard science' evidence base for how mindfulness has its effects in relation to brain structure and function (Davidson et al. 2003, Gu et al. 2015, Hölzel et al. 2011).

A small but growing group of writers has given a rationale as to why mindfulness training could be helpful to a PWS (Boyle 2011, Plexico and Sandage 2011). Fairburn et al. (2009) indicated that mindfulness training could help to reduce fear and anxiety as well as increase positive speech attitudes, locus of control and problem-focused coping behaviours. Cheasman (2013) describes the development of an eight-week MBCT programme for a PWS and Beilby, Byrnes and Yaruss (2012) a programme for a PWS integrating stammering therapy and acceptance and commitment therapy (ACT). ACT is a mindfulness-based approach. (See chapter 7 on ACT in this book.)

Relevance of mindfulness when working with a PWS

I have identified three key ways in which mindfulness can be relevant to an SLT:

• Becoming a more mindful therapist

• Incorporating mindfulness interventions into therapy

• Personal well-being benefits.

This chapter will elaborate on points 1 and 2.

Being a mindful therapist

Studies since the 1990s have revealed that the strongest predictors of therapy outcome in the psychotherapy field are rooted in the qualities of the therapist and the resulting therapeutic relationship. "It might almost be said that the relationship is the treatment" (Duncan and Miller 2000) (See also chapter 1 Stewart and Leahy). The qualities patients attribute to a positive therapeutic relationship include empathy, warmth, understanding and acceptance (Lambert and Barley 2001). Thus, the challenge to be a more effective therapist is, to a large degree, the challenge of finding ways to help cultivate the qualities shared by excellent therapists. Whilst an SLT working with a PWS is not practising psychotherapy her client who stammers is, nevertheless, being offered a relationship where challenging thoughts, feelings and experiences can be explored and worked with. Bien (2006) comments that the mindful therapist considers diagnosis broadly and sees the person as a whole, looking beyond any label he may come with. A therapist working with a PWS should know the need to look beyond the label, stammering, and the need to understand each unique PWS.

Karunavira (2019) summarises the main helpful therapeutic skills and qualities specifically trained by mindfulness as being:

• Attentiveness

• Affect tolerance

• Radical acceptance

• Empathy and compassion

• Congruence.

It is interesting to note that these qualities mirror much of what Carl Rogers describes as being the essential components of person-centred counselling (Rogers 1951).

Paying attention: Every clinician knows the experience of a wandering mind during therapy and accompanying draining feelings. Mindfulness practice is an antidote to a wandering mind. All events, including boredom or anxiety, are invitations to notice and include in attention. When a therapist is alert and attentive to all of her experience, fascination is a natural response. Genuine attention leads to both parties becoming more fully awake to the purpose in hand. Over time, the capacity for moment-by-moment attentiveness is strengthened. When a client meets a therapist who is undistracted he can tangibly feel her interest and *know* he has been fully heard. To give grounded, wholehearted attention is a gift that can be offered to all clients. Bien (2006), comments, "in the context of mindful therapy it is essential to listen deeply. Yet we cannot become capable of deep listening in the therapy room if we do not practice mindfulness elsewhere" (p. 24).

Affect tolerance: This is an enormously important quality in the therapeutic alliance. If a therapist cannot tolerate her own difficult emotions, how can she be fully open to her clients' difficult feelings? Far from providing a safe environment for exploration, a therapist's own intolerance of feeling may prematurely eclipse the client's freedom, and there is the danger of becoming reactive in the face of strong emotion. Mindfulness practice invites ongoing interest and so tolerance of difficult emotions or body sensations. The SLT's receptivity in the face of difficult emotional content allows an ethos of open, uncensored exchange. In this climate very strong emotions can be 'reappraised' and so lived with (Hölzel et al. 2011).

Practicing acceptance: Mindfulness practice strengthens the essential quality of acceptance each time attention is returned to the object of awareness, regardless of it being pleasant or unpleasant. Everything is repeatedly and equally welcomed. In this way self-acceptance becomes stronger as awareness is *turned towards* all that arises, including the so-familiar draining patterns of self-criticism that can reduce the therapist's creative responses. The importance of a radical acceptance towards the client's story and being is obviously crucial.

Empathy and compassion: Mindfulness practice is a potent method for cultivating empathy. It offers a way to change the therapist's relationship to suffering by surrendering her need to reject it. Her own suffering offers an opportunity to become openhearted rather than merely oppressed. Compassion for others arises from the recognition that no one is exempt from suffering and that everyone wishes to be safe from it. Compassion and empathy toward others become natural expressions of this growing perception of interdependence.

Congruence: To be a real and authentic person in the therapy relationship is what is meant by congruence, and this quality is, according to Rogers (1951), perhaps the most powerful element of the alliance. To be fully aware, open and non-reactive moment by moment forms the basis of congruence. So it is clear that unless a therapist can have that present-moment awareness of her own internal experience, she will not be able to offer her genuine presence to her client.

Bien (2006) gives some suggestions around incorporating mindfulness practice into everyday work contexts. These include ideas such as allowing time to be present before the first appointment, walking mindfully from the waiting room to the therapy room, and, rather than filling every gap with admin tasks, having a few minutes of mindful breathing in between sessions. Bien also talks about the mindful therapist starting and ending sessions on time.

Since what a therapist is mainly offering in the therapeutic alliance is 'herself', it is fundamentally important to be the best she can be, including being fully present without striving. For the therapist working with a PWS, mindfulness practice, as an ongoing exploration of *who* and *what* she is and of her world, is a potent means to this end. As is repeatedly advised before flying, 'Make sure you secure your own oxygen mask before attempting to help others'!

Incorporating mindfulness interventions into therapy

There are two broad ways in which mindfulness interventions can be used in therapy with a PWS:

• As a primary intervention i.e. to deliver a mindfulness-based cognitive therapy (MBCT) or mindfulness-based stress reduction (MBSR) course

Delivering programmes such as MBCT requires training to become a mindfulness teacher and is therefore not appropriate to most SLTs.

• To support other therapy approaches

The focus of this chapter will be on how a therapist can include mindfulness activities to support the primary approach in a management programme for a PWS.

If mindfulness is to be incorporated into therapy it is helpful to:

• Do this as early as possible, as it can be supportive of other therapy aspects. For example, if a stammering-modification approach, such as block modification (Van Riper 1973), is the primary approach, then being more mindfully aware is likely to assist the identification, desensitisation and modification stages

• Provide the client with sufficient understanding of the nature of stammering to help him make sense of the relevance of mindfulness. This will prepare him and mean he is also less surprised by the experiences arising from mindfulness practices

• Enable a client to understand that stammering is more than just the behaviour. Having the opportunity to 'tell the story' which is likely to happen at the start of therapy will help here

• Use a model such as the stammering iceberg (Sheehan 1970). This will help a client understand that thoughts, feelings and attempts to hide are all intrinsic parts of the difficulty.

Using mindfulness in sessions: Initially it is likely that a mindfulness practice would be introduced in a session to help develop the core skill of cultivating mindful awareness. Mindfulness practices can be included at the start of sessions to help the client 'arrive' and be present in the now.

They can also be incorporated at the end of a session, again marking a boundary as the client transitions into the next part of his day.

Within sessions practices may be used at times when there is strong emotion to help bring stability if feelings are overwhelming and/or to help a client 'sit with' a strong feeling. Mindfulness practices can help to develop an attitude of friendly interest in emotional sensations as he tackles avoidance-reduction in his everyday life.

A PWS often has a strong 'control agenda'. He may wish to control the thoughts, feelings and behaviours. This is understandable, but attempts to control are frequently unhelpful and, as has been said, feed the difficulties. Mindfulness training is not a 'treatment' and is not a 'fix it' intervention. Nevertheless, a client may consciously or unconsciously recruit mindfulness to become part of the control agenda. For example, a PWS may want to use it to make feelings go away as opposed to making space for them. It is important for his therapist to be alert to this possibility.

There are clients for whom mindfulness training is contraindicated. These include an individual:

• With a history of trauma

• Who is grieving/close in time to a major bereavement

• Who has a substance abuse issue

• Who has a diagnosed psychosis or other significant mental illness.

Mindfulness practices

A selected range of practices can be used by a therapist who is not a trained mindfulness teacher. Such practices can be used to:

• Introduce mindfulness

• Teach the basic skill of focusing on an object and working with the wandering mind

• Help with emotional regulation and grounding

• Help approach and be present with difficult thoughts and feelings.

Unscripted guided practices are preferable as the therapist is more likely to be guiding from her own experience and therefore more present. However, a clinician may begin by using some form of written guidance (please see suggestions on the following pages and the Resources section at the end of the chapter). The tone and manner of guidance is just as important as the words used. It is important to offer clarity combined with a gentle and invitational tone. Adopting a hypnotic tone is unhelpful; the intention is to help a person wake up to his experience rather than drift off to sleep. The invitational tone is usually demonstrated through the use of the present participle; for example, saying "noticing any sensations of the breath moving in the abdomen" as opposed to "notice any sensations", which has more of a commanding air. Phrases such as "gently and firmly bringing the attention back to the breath", "as best you can, bringing a friendly curiosity to your experience" and "congratulating yourself when you notice your mind has wandered" are also commonly heard. The language and tone are all designed to help a client cultivate this particular quality of non-judgemental, kind and friendly awareness that are central to Kabat-Zinn's definition. The best way to learn how to guide practices is to listen to some of the many guided practices available. Readers of this chapter are advised to follow the link to the mindful health website to access a range of short practices: www.mindfulhealth.co.uk.

Introducing mindfulness – the raisin exercise

Mindfulness can only be learnt experientially; a person needs to be an active participant. The raisin exercise, as described by Segal, Williams and Teasdale (2002), is the most well-known practical introduction to mindfulness. (A script is included in **Resource 6.1: The Raisin Exercise**.)

The practice is then followed by a particular form of inquiry to help the client reflect on his experience and to draw out key learning points. Each participant is encouraged to share his direct sensory experience, and the therapist models openness, non-judgement and a friendly curiosity. The following is an example of the type of exchange that might happen. In an eight-week course an inquiry process generally follows a practice. Here is an example of the type of inquiry that might take place after the raisin exercise.

T: So, that was an eating meditation – I am really interested to hear something about your experience – would you be willing to share anything you noticed in that practice?

C: I was amazed at the taste

T: That's interesting – can you say what you noticed about the taste

C: It was just so sweet – I realise I don't usually ever really taste raisins properly – I just stuff them in

T: That's really useful – thank you for sharing it and it illustrates really well that eating is something that we as humans often do on what we call automatic pilot. We are apparently eating but because we are often somewhere else in our heads, we are not fully present to the experience of eating

We can see from this that open questions lead to the client describing some of his sensory experience. This is then normalised, and a teaching point about automatic pilot is drawn out.

C: When I smelt it my mind took me back to a memory – I remember my mother making the Christmas cake

T: Mmm can you say how you experienced the memory – was it maybe words or pictures

C: I could see the kitchen really clearly

T: Was there a feeling going along with it?

C: Just kind of nice and warm

T: Were you aware of that feeling at all in your body?

C: Yes, I was I think – like a warm feeling in my chest

T: Thank you – isn't it interesting how our minds time travel like this – and even when someone is guiding us to the present the mind isn't having anything to do with this and just goes off on its journeys

In this inquiry the client is asked if he is aware of any feelings and particularly any sensory experience in the body connected to the feeling. This time a learning point to do with the mind time travelling is drawn out.

It is beyond the scope of this chapter to go into more detail about inquiry but readers are invited to see Segal, Williams and Teasdale (2002) and Crane (2009) for more description of how to lead an inquiry process.

The raisin exercise is a powerful way to introduce mindfulness because it is so ordinary. What could be more ordinary than eating a raisin? And yet so much about the nature of the human mind can be learnt from it. After guiding the practice a comment such as: "So that was an eating meditation" can be made. This gives the sense that mindfulness and meditation are not esoteric or other worldly experiences. The practice naturally leads to other forms of informal practice e.g. showering, teeth cleaning, making tea etc., and this in turn can lead to bringing more mindful awareness to speaking i.e. just noticing in the absence of trying to change anything.

Flaxman (2017), drawing on the work of Crane (2009) and Williams and Penman (2011), identifies key learning points that can arise from the raisin exercise:

• The ability to recognise the difference between mindful awareness and autopilot
• Reflecting on how much is missed out on in a busy life through inattention
• Seeing how bringing attention to something very simple can often transform the experience
• Starting to normalise mind wandering – this is just what our minds do.

When working with a PWS this inquiry can be followed with open questions about:

• Whether participants can see any relevance to stammering
• Learning points related to the benefits of awareness
• Automatic pilot
• The mind getting 'hooked' by memories or thoughts.

Teaching the basic mindfulness skill

Breath and body meditation
(see link to audio file on p. 158)

This practice is a good entry point into more formal mindfulness practice. The recommended audio file is 16 minutes long, which someone new to practice often finds a manageable amount of time to find to practice. An individual can be encouraged to cultivate the basic attentional training skill of intending to focus on an object, in this case the breath and body. When he notices his mind has wandered, he can gently but firmly bring it back. Once again, the focus is on physical sensations, e.g. the sensation of the breath entering and leaving the nostrils and the gentle rise and fall of the abdomen on the in-breath and out-breath. A key aspect of meditation and other practices is not just the development of attentional focus but an understanding of how the mind works, enabling a refocusing so that thoughts and feelings are not overwhelming. It is for this reason that mindfulness is positioned in the insight group of meditation practices as opposed to being a purely concentration practice. When first introducing this to a client the practice can be followed by a brief inquiry. This will often bring up mind wandering and, significantly, how the person related to his mind wandering i.e. how judgemental he was about this.

The body scan
(see link to audio file on p. 158)

The body scan practice is introduced at the start of 8-week MBSR and MBCT courses and is seen as a key way:

• To start to cultivate open and friendly interest to experience

• To work with mind wandering

• To develop more awareness of sensations in the body.

Body scans vary greatly in terms of length from 10 minutes to 45 minutes. The mindful health website includes a 23-minute version on CD 4. Whilst the practice is generally done lying down it can also be done in a sitting position. As a therapist, it would be important to have one's own experience of the body scan prior to leading it. In relation to stammering therapy this is generally not used as a regular feature of sessions but could be introduced in a session. The client could then be guided to resources to practise it at home if he would like to. It can be used with groups, and short, adapted body scans are used with children. Body scan practice can help to nourish the soothing system. It is also relevant to cultivating acceptance, as a participant is guided to notice and open up to uncomfortable sensations in the body. These sensations could be physical pain or discomfort, or they might be emotionally based. Overall, the practice can facilitate the process of becoming more aware of body-based sensory experience i.e. getting out of the head and into the body and moving away from language-based processing. It can offer a first glimpse of experiencing thoughts and emotions as sensations in the body and can be a revelation to a person. Boyle (2012) describes adapting it for a PWS by putting more emphasis in the guidance on the articulatory tract, noticing any sites of tension and begin to notice how certain thoughts and feelings can lead to an increase of tension in these areas.

Shorter grounding practices

FOFBOC (feet on floor, body on chair) (see *Resource 6.2: FOFBOC – Feet on Floor, Body on Chair*)

The mind is often scattered and lost in thought because it is working away in the background, trying to fix and sort things out. At one level, a scattered mind can get in the way of simple appreciation of the present moment, and at another, more risky level, it can lead into potentially unhelpful emotional territory. For example, the mind of a PWS might get carried into unhelpful time travel with anxious thoughts about what might happen in an upcoming speaking situation or painful memories of previous experiences. In this very brief practice, the aim is to learn to recognise and step out of more scattered autopilot states and come back to the here and now using the skill of paying attention to a chosen physical anchor in order to gather and settle the mind.

A FOFBOC practice could be used at the start of a session to help the person 'arrive' or during the session if things are becoming unhelpfully overwhelming. It might also be helpful after a debriefing conversation about the week just gone or a particular speaking situation before transitioning into the next part of the session, where new content might be about to be introduced. It is a very functional practice which a client can easily incorporate into his everyday life.

The three-step breathing space
(Segal, Williams and Teasdale 2002) (see link to audio file on p. 158)

This is another short grounding practice to help a person step out of autopilot and reconnect with the present moment. It takes about 3 to 4 minutes.

The first step of the practice is about taking stock or 'reading a person's internal weather' and so has a broad field of awareness. An individual is invited to simply notice his thoughts, feelings and body sensations and, as far as possible, to make space for them all to be present i.e. it is not about trying to get rid of anything. In step 2 the attentional field is narrowed down to the breath with guidance around feeling the breath sensations and working with mind wandering. The attentional field is expanded again in step 3 to include a wider sense of the whole body, posture and facial expression.

Basic instructions for this are given in **Resource 6.3: Three-step Breathing Space**. It is important for a therapist to practise the breathing space herself before guiding it for a client.

The three-step breathing space is another very functional practice that can be incorporated into everyday life. When it is introduced it is helpful to encourage a client to anchor it to specific activities in his day e.g. morning coffee, just before or after switching the computer on or just before or after making a phone call.

Stop and drop – take a pause

A less formal and shorter way to help grounding and coming back to the present moment is 'stop and drop', which is literally just 'stop or pause' and 'drop' i.e. bring one's attention to your feet on the ground.

Being with difficult thoughts and feelings

The responding breathing space

(Segal, Williams and Teasdale 2002) (see link to audio file on p. 158)

This elaboration of the basic three-step breathing space is specifically designed for when a person is troubled in thoughts or feelings. The first two steps are very similar to the standard breathing space. The first step might include some additional guidance around putting experiences into words, for example, saying silently 'there is a feeling of anxiety' or 'self-critical thoughts are here'. In the third step when the awareness is widened out to the body there is specific guidance around bringing attention to any sensations of discomfort, tension or resistance. A participant is encouraged to take his attention to those feelings through 'breathing into the sensations' on the in-breath and then 'softening and opening' on the out-breath. On the out-breath a client can practise saying phrases such as "I can be with this" or "I don't like this and I'm practising being with it – let me feel it".

This practice can be very helpful in sessions when strong feelings are around. For example, a client might be talking about a speaking situation, either from the past or one yet to happen, which is bringing up strong feelings of anxiety, and the therapist might introduce the responding breathing space to give the client the experience of responding to difficult thoughts and feelings in a very different way to usual. This use of mindfulness can be highly supportive to the desensitisation process. Whilst the aim of desensitisation over a period of time is to help a client have less strong emotional reactions to speaking and stammering, this can be misunderstood by both a client and therapist as meaning the process is about not having a feeling or having less of a feeling. However, it actually involves allowing and making space for the difficult feelings that will almost inevitably come up when an individual steps out of his comfort zone and faces some of his fears. The process of desensitisation is about experiencing difficult feelings which, over time and through exposure, start to lessen. Mindfulness practices such as the responding breathing space which are designed to enable turning towards uncomfortable sensations can be very supportive here.

Informal practice ways of being with difficult thoughts and feelings

The responding space is a formal practice to help cultivate a different way of being with difficult experience. Mindfulness may also be used less formally in sessions to help a client 'sit with' and open up to emotion. For example, if someone is feeling very anxious he can be asked if he would be willing to stay with the feeling for a moment, to notice how and where he is experiencing the feeling, to notice what the sensations are like. He could also be asked to notice how he is reacting to the sensations – is there any tensing or bracing? – and then invited to see what it is like to breathe into and around particular sensations. It can be helpful to start off with a few mindful breaths for grounding before moving to the particular emotion.

Introducing the idea of turning towards difficulty with a less strong experience can also be powerful for the client. For example, it might be that there is background noise or a small ache or pain, and a clinician could suggest to her client that he begin to notice his reactions to these experiences and make space for things to be here in what might be less emotional contexts.

Acceptance practices like this, whether formal or informal, are a cornerstone of mindfulness interventions and are highly relevant to a PWS where avoidance-based emotional reactivity may be present.

Home practice

If a PWS wants to develop greater mindfulness, then he needs to engage with practices outside a clinical setting. There are many resources available now to assist with home practice including a range of audio downloads and apps. These are referenced on page 158. It is also helpful to encourage a client to do some informal practice as described earlier. This is where an individual brings mindful noticing to the experience of a routine daily activity e.g. cleaning his teeth, noticing when his mind wanders off and gently bringing it back to the experience of teeth cleaning. In this way, bringing friendly curiosity to an aspect of experience, noticing the wandering mind wanders off and drawing it back to the present, are practised. When this is repeated, the 'muscle of the mind' is strengthened.

Concluding remark – the importance of personal practice

When asked to write this chapter I was initially cautious. I did not want to write a quick 'how to do mindfulness' piece, as I know this is not how it works. It will be unhelpful if a therapist recruits mindfulness into a toolkit of 'how to fix' strategies. Evidence supports the view that having one's own mindfulness practice is important if a therapist sets out to teach mindfulness to others (Segal, Williams and Teasdale 2002). This is because teaching mindfulness flows from the therapist being able to embody mindfulness. Crane (2009) explores this and writes, "we need deep familiarity with exploring it (being mode) ourselves and with seeing how 'doing mode' tenaciously reasserts itself over and over" (p. 157).

Having one's own practice can help a clinician become aware of when she moves into problem-solving mode and tries to fix issues, recognising when this is unhelpful. If she can learn to sit with and 'be with' her own difficult experience she is much more likely to be able to help another sit with his own in therapy sessions. The list of resources included here will be helpful to a therapist on a personal level. I strongly recommend that each therapist attend an eight-week mindfulness-based stress reduction for herself. In this way a clinician is more likely to be able to embody mindfulness and thus be more helpful to her clients.

MBSR courses can be found in most areas of the UK now, and the website https://bamba.org.uk/ guides people to what is locally available as does https://mindfuldirectory.org

The raisin exercise

Instructions to a client:

Therapist: We are going to start learning about mindfulness in a particular way. I am going to give you a small object in your hand, and I would like you to imagine you have come down from Mars and you have never seen one of these before – the reality is that you have never seen this one. [It is helpful to say here that at some point there will be an invitation to place the object in the mouth and eat it and that this is completely optional. It is important to leave about 10 seconds between each small chunk of guidance. A raisin is given to the client.] So, firstly picking up the object and noticing what it looks like – noticing any patterns or shapes . . . variations in colouration . . . perhaps holding it up to the light to see if it is translucent or opaque. Bringing as best you can a real and friendly curiosity to this little object. You might notice thoughts, or memories or pictures popping up and that is absolutely fine. It's just what our minds do and is completely normal. When you notice you have become distracted by thoughts just acknowledging them and gently but firmly returning your attention to the object. [This type of guidance for working with mind wandering/thinking is interspersed throughout the practice.] Now paying attention to the feel and texture of the object . . . perhaps giving it a little squeeze – noticing the two ends . . . are they the same or different? And now bringing the object to your nose and exploring through the sense of smell . . . again noticing any thoughts, memories, pictures etc. Now if you are willing placing the object in your mouth, not chewing just holding it in your mouth and again feeling its texture . . . noticing what it's like not to follow an urge to bite into it. Now starting to chew and exploring through the sense of taste – not swallowing just chewing and tasting . . . just experiencing the taste sensations . . . and then starting to swallow and paying attention to how we do this. Noticing any aftertastes in the mouth and now very importantly noticing – what does it feel like to be one raisin heavier? (This last phrase is said with a smile to indicate the practice has ended on a light note.)

FOFBOC – feet on floor, body on chair

(Bum on chair can be used when working with young people.)

A mindfulness-based grounding practice

Therapist instructions to a client:

> First establish an intention to focus your attention on anchors of felt sensations in the body to gain some space from unhelpful thinking and come to the present moment. Find a posture that can help you to rest into the support that the chair offers so you can directly sense your feet on the ground, the uprightness of your body, and get a sense of waking up so you can be alive to your present moment experience. The posture should ideally be giving a sense of wakefulness and comfort as you settle with a sense of purpose.

We then aim to connect with a physical anchor, and the guidance moves through a range of options.

i   Feet: inviting attention to the feet . . . sensing the contact of the feet with the floor . . . the contact with shoes or socks . . . noticing if the feet are warm or cool . . . noticing if there are any sensations of tingling . . .

ii Chair: noticing the sensation of our sitting-bones with the chair . . . sensations of contact and pressure as the chair takes our weight . . . maybe a sensation of weight dropping down . . . again any sensations of temperature . . . also noticing any sensations of contact with the back of the chair . . .

iii Hands: now . . . inviting interest to our hands . . . any sensations of contact . . . maybe sensations as the hands touch each other or the lap or knees . . . noticing right now, any sensations of temperature . . . warm or hot? or cool? . . . perhaps sensing the weight of our hands . . . noticing the lie of the hands . . . the fingers and the thumbs?

iv Then moving to make a choice: and now choosing between these anchors allowing our attention and interest to lightly move into whichever feels most vivid . . . most comfortable . . . or most clear and allowing this place to be the anchor for the rest of the practice.

v   Then moving to maintaining a connection with this anchor of choice as you stay with this chosen anchor as best you can for four or five breath cycles. Noticing and perhaps appreciating this part of the body . . . bringing an attitude of friendliness and care to our experience as best you can . . . noticing the mind might wander away and gently returning again and again . . . without rushing . . . without judging into the direct sensations arising moment by moment here.

All of the above can be adapted for 'standing'.

© Trudy Stewart (2020). *Stammering Resources for Adults and Teenagers: Integrating New Evidence into Clinical Practice*. Routledge.

Three-step breathing space
(adapted from Segal, Williams and Teasdale 2002)

This practice generally takes around 3 to 4 minutes – it is usually done sitting, but it can be done standing as well.

Before moving into the first step it is important to give some guidance around posture. So, for example, "Firstly making a deliberate shift in your posture to bring yourself into the present moment . . . if sitting adopting an upright, awake posture . . . if possible closing your eyes".

An hourglass or egg timer is a visual image that is sometimes used to illustrate the three steps as described in what follows.

Step 1 Awareness – the broad top of the hourglass
In this first phase guidance is given to help a participant bring awareness to three key aspects of his internal experience: thoughts, feelings and body sensations. So, noticing your thinking . . . not particularly the content of your thinking but rather the quality of your thinking right now . . . are there lots of thoughts or maybe not many . . . does the mind feel busy or quiet or dull . . . then noticing any feelings/emotions that are around right now . . . then noticing any sensations in your body . . . these might relate to emotions, there might be sensations of contact with the chair, air, clothing . . . there might be sensations of discomfort or pain. As best you can making space for all of this experience to be here, not trying to change anything . . . just reading your own internal weather right now.

Step 2 Gathering – the narrow neck of the hourglass
In this step guidance is given to help a participant narrow down the focus of his awareness to the breath. This guidance will be similar to guidance in any awareness of breath practice. So, along the lines of 'now gently gathering up your awareness and coming to the breath, feeling the whole of an inbreath and the whole of an outbreath . . . using the breath as an anchor to bring you into the present moment'. The guidance will also include instructions for working with the wandering mind as in any practice.

Step 3 Expanding – the wider lower part of the hourglass
In this step guidance is given to help a participant expand his awareness into the whole body, posture, facial expression. The practice ends with clear instruction to open the eyes if closed and move into the next part of the day.

When moving through the breathing space it is helpful to signpost each step i.e. saying Step 1 of the breathing space . . . Step 2 etc.

Responding breathing space
(adapted from Segal, Williams and Teasdale 2002)

As with the three-step breathing space the practice starts off with guidance around adjusting the posture to come to a position of dignity and wakefulness.

Step 1 Awareness
The guidance for the step 1 of the responding breathing space is very similar to the standard three-step breathing space. Again, the focus is on observing internal experience and noticing what is happening with thoughts, feelings and bodily sensations. This time there might be additional guidance around silently acknowledging and identifying experience e.g. "Saying in your mind . . . a feeling of anxiety is arising" . . . or "judging thoughts are here".

Step 2 Gathering
Guidance around redirecting attention to the breath, feeling and following the breath, gently coming back to the breath when the mind wanders as with the standard three-step breathing space.

Step 3 Expanding attention and making space for difficult sensations
Here there is guidance around expanding attention to the whole body and now there is particular guidance around 'opening and softening' into any sensations of tension, discomfort or resistance . . . "breathing into and around any sensations of discomfort" . . . "as best you can making space for the sensations" . . . "allowing them to be here as best you can" . . . "maybe saying silently to yourself 'I don't like this and I'm practising being with it' or 'let me feel it' or 'I am making space for anxiety'".

Again, there is clear guidance around ending the practice, opening eyes and 'as you move into the next part of your day, as best you can, bringing this expanded awareness with you'.

References

Baer, R.A. (2003). Mindfulness training as a clinical intervention: A conceptual and empirical review. *Clinical Psychology: Science & Practice*, 10, 125–145.

Beilby, J.M., Byrnes, M.L. and Yaruss, J.S. (2012). Acceptance and commitment therapy for people who stutter: Psychosocial adjustment and speech fluency. *Journal of Fluency Disorders*, online publication.

Bien, T. (2006). *Mindful Therapy*. Boston: Wisdom.

Boyle, M.P. (2011). Mindfulness training in stuttering therapy. *Journal of Fluency Disorders*, 36(2), 122–129.

Boyle, M.P. (2012). Mindfulness and stuttering. In P. Reitzes and D. Reitzes (eds.), *Stuttering: Inspiring Stories and Professional Wisdom* (pp. 261–271). Chapel Hill, NC: Stuttertalk Inc.

Cheasman, C. (2013). A mindful approach to stammering. In C. Cheasman, R. Everard and S. Simpson (eds.), *Stammering Therapy from the Inside*. Guildford: J & R Press.

Crane, R. (2009). *Mindfulness-based Cognitive Therapy*. Hove: Routledge.

Davidson, R.J., Kabat-Zinn, J., Schumacher, J., Roserkranz, M.S., Muller, D., Santorelli, S.F., Urbanowski, F., Harrington, A., Bonus, K. and Sheridan, J.F. (2003). Alterations in brain and immune function produced by mindfulness meditation. *Psychosomatic Medicine*, 65, 564–570.

Duncan, B.L. and Miller, S.D. (2000). The client's theory of change: Consulting the client in the integrative process. *Journal of Psychotherapy Integration*, 10(2), 169–187.

Fairburn, C.G., Cooper, Z., De Veer, S., Brouwers, A., Evers, W. and Tomik, W. (2009). A pilot study of the psychological impact of the mindfulness-based stress reduction program on persons who stutter. *European Psychotherapy*, 9, 39–56.

Flaxman, P. and Mcintosh, R. (2017). *Acceptance and Commitment Therapy for Workplace Settings*. Trainer Manual.

Gu., J., Strauss, C., Bond, R. and Cavanaugh, K. (2015). How do MBCT and MBSR improve mental health and wellbeing? A systematic review and metanalysis of meditation studies. *Clinical Psychology Review*, 37, 1–12.

Hölzel, B.K., Lazar, S.W., Gard, T., Schuman-Olivier, Z., Vago, D.R. and Ott, O. (2011). How does mindfulness meditation work? Proposing mechanisms of action from a conceptual and neural perspective. *Perspectives on Psychological Science*, 6, 537 http://pps.sagepub.com/content/6/6/537"6

Kabat-Zinn, J. (1994). *Wherever You Go There You Are*. New York: Hyperion.

Kabat-Zinn, J. (1996). *Full Catastrophe Living*. London: Piatkus.

Karunavira. (2019). Personal Communication.

Lambert, M.J. and Barley, D.E. (2001). Research summary on the therapeutic relationship and psychotherapy outcome. *Psychotherapy: Theory, Research, Practice, & Training*, 38(4), 357–361.

Plexico, L. and Sandage, M.J. (2011). A mindful approach to stuttering intervention. *Perspectives on Fluency and Fluency Disorders*, 21, 43–49.

Rogers, C. (1951). *Client Centred Therapy*. London: Constable & Robinson.

Segal, Z.V., Williams, J.M.G. and Teasdale, J.D. (2002). *Mindfulness-based Cognitive Therapy for Depression*. New York: Guildford Press.

Shapiro, S. (2013). Does mindfulness make you more compassionate. *Greater Good Magazine* Online February edition.

Sheehan, J. (1970). *Stuttering: Research and Therapy*. New York: Harper & Row.

Starkweather, C.W. (1999). The effectiveness of stuttering therapy. In N. Bernstein-Ratner and E.C. Healey (eds.), *Stuttering Research and Practice: Bridging the Gap*. Mahwah, NJ: Lawrence Erlbaum Associates.

Van Riper, C. (1973). *The Treatment of Stuttering*. Englewood Cliffs, NJ: Prentice Hall.

Williams, J.M.G. and Penman, D. (2011). *Finding Peace in a Frantic World*. London: Piatkus.

Yaruss, J.S. (2007). Application of the ICF in fluency disorders. *Seminars in Speech and Language*, 28(4), 312–322. https://doi.org/10.1055/s-2007-986528"10.1055

Audio resources

For free access to a range of short guided practices, go to www.mindfulhealth.co.uk for mindfulness meditation audio with Karunavira.

There are four CDs on the website containing a range of practices that take people through an eight-week MBCT course. Readers of this chapter are particularly guided to the shorter practices as follows:

CD 1 Awareness of breath (10 minutes)

CD 1 Short body scan (23 minutes)

CD 4 Three-step breathing space

CD 4 Responding/coping breathing space

CD 4 Breath and body meditation (16 minutes)

CD 4 Turning towards a difficulty practice

There are a range of other websites offering access to audio downloads of practices including:

Bangor University Centre for Mindfulness Research and Practice www.bangor.ac.uk/mindfulness

Center for Mindfulness UMass Medical School www.umassmed.edu/cfm

Apps

Headspace

Calm

7 | Integrating acceptance and commitment therapy into stammering therapy

Rachel Everard and Carolyn Cheasman

What is ACT?

Acceptance and commitment therapy (ACT) is an empirically-based psychological approach combining cognitive and behavioural therapies (Hayes, Strosahl and Wilson 1999). Its very name, ACT (pronounced as the word 'act'), underlines the importance placed on taking action. The phrase coined by Harris (2008), 'Embrace your demons and follow your heart', neatly summarises the two main objectives of ACT:

- To help create a full, rich and meaningful life, whilst accepting the pain that inevitably comes with living

- To teach mindfulness skills that allow a person to manage painful thoughts and feelings more effectively so that they have less impact on him.

At its heart, ACT is a mindfulness-based approach designed to develop psychological flexibility, the ability to take mindful, values-guided action. Psychological flexibility can also be described as resilience. Kashdan and Rotterberg (2010) define psychological flexibility as the measure of how a person:

- Adapts to fluctuating situational demands

- Reconfigures mental resources

- Shifts perspective

- Balances competing desires, needs and life domains.

A more accessible definition, helpful to share with a client, is 'be present, open up and do what matters' (Harris 2008).

Two different models of therapy will be briefly described here to illustrate the processes involved in developing psychological flexibility.

The hexaflex

Developed by Harris (2008, 2019), the hexaflex describes six core processes, which work together to enable greater flexibility. Listed here is each process, the first four of which are mindfulness skills and the final two are about identifying values and taking action:

- Contact with the present moment: this is the ability to pay attention to the here and now, to fully engage and connect, whether to internal experience or to the world around. The opposite is being distracted, disengaged or disconnected from the present moment

- Cognitive defusion: often referred to simply as defusion, this relates to putting distance between the self and one's thoughts, to recognise the transitory nature of thinking and to allow thoughts to come and go. The opposite of this is fusion, when a person can be caught up in, hooked or hijacked by thoughts so that they dominate awareness and influence behaviour

- Acceptance: this process involves opening up to, giving space to and allowing difficult and painful internal experiences including thoughts, feelings, memories, images and sensations. The opposite is experiential avoidance, the on-going struggle to fight against, avoid or escape from painful internal experience

- The observing or noticing self: sometimes referred to as self-as-context, this describes the part of an individual that does the noticing but doesn't judge experience. For example, when a person practises defusion, he will notice his thoughts. When practising acceptance, he will notice thoughts, feelings and sensations in his body. The observing self is therefore separate from the thinking self and represents meta-awareness, a transcendent sense of self. The opposite of the observing self is over-identification with concepts or beliefs about oneself, which can impact behaviour. For example, someone who stammers may identify with the concept 'I'm an ineffective communicator because I stammer' and as a result may choose not to pursue a career which he perceives as requiring excellent communication skills

- Values: these are personally chosen, individual qualities of on-going action that are important and make life worth living. Identification of values is an integral part of ACT. The opposite is remoteness from values, when an individual forgets or loses sight of what is important

- Committed action: this relates to taking mindful action in line with personal values. The opposite is unworkable action that takes a person away from his values and is often impulsive, reactive or automatic.

The Three Pillars

Closely related to the hexaflex is the concept of the Three Pillars (Flaxman, McIntosh and Oliver 2019), where the six core processes described before are subsumed into three pillars:

- The Noticing Pillar: this includes contact with the present moment and the noticing self

- The Open Pillar: this includes defusion and acceptance

- The Active Pillar: this includes values and committed action.

We will discuss the Three Pillars organising framework in detail later in the chapter and provide some clinical examples that a therapist should find helpful. Figure 7.1 is a pictorial illustration of the Three Pillars.

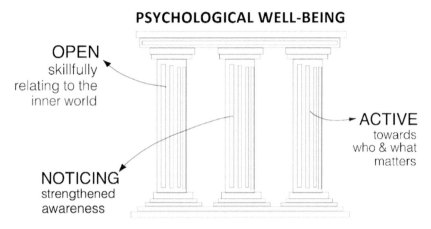

Figure 7.1 The Three Pillars

Current evidence base for ACT

ACT's appeal is universal in that anyone can benefit from developing psychological flexibility in order to improve well-being and lead a more meaningful life. ACT is also used increasingly to manage a wide range of conditions including chronic pain, anxiety, depression, obsessive-compulsive disorders, smoking cessation and weight loss. There are a number of randomised controlled trials that demonstrate its effectiveness. Steven Hayes, the original founder of ACT, usefully provides on the Association for Contextual Behavioral Sciences website a list of randomised controlled trials dating back to 1986 (https://contextualscience.org/ACT_Randomized_Controlled_Trials).

Systematic reviews also feature in the research related to ACT; as for example, the study by A-Tjak et al. (2015) which included 39 randomised controlled trials on the efficacy of ACT. The authors concluded that ACT may be as effective in treating anxiety disorders, depression, addiction and somatic health problems as other established psychological interventions, for example cognitive behaviour therapy.

There is also growing evidence in relation to the use of ACT with a PWS. The study by Beilby, Byrnes and Yaruss (2012) explored the effectiveness of integrating ACT into a group therapy programme for adults who stammer, taking place over eight weeks, with each session lasting two hours (16 hours of therapy in total). The results were impressive: the group of 20 participants demonstrated statistically significant improvements in psychosocial functioning, preparation for change and therapy, utilisation of mindfulness skills and overall speech fluency. These changes were maintained over a three-month period.

A study carried out by ourselves (Cheasman and Everard 2013), exploring the effectiveness of a three-day ACT group therapy programme, demonstrated development of mindfulness skills, greater acceptance of stammering, reduction in stammering behaviours, reduction in negative thoughts and feelings associated with stammering, reduction in avoidance behaviours and stammering being perceived as less of a disadvantage. Additional clinical data collected since 2013 shows similar positive results.

Applying ACT to adult stammering therapy

ACT appears a natural fit to stammering, given the complex and multifaceted nature of stammering and the importance of addressing the affective, behavioural and cognitive aspects in therapy (Beilby and Yaruss 2018, Harley 2015).

According to the ACT model, the main sources of psychological suffering are:

• Experiential avoidance (the on-going struggle to avoid or escape painful thoughts and feelings)

• Cognitive fusion.

The experience for a PWS reflects this through the common use of avoidance strategies (for example, avoiding words, saying less, avoiding particular situations) and fusion with painful thoughts and feelings associated with stammering (thoughts such as 'I can't go for that job because I stammer' and feelings such as shame, fear and anxiety).

The integration of ACT into adult stammering therapy supports work on increased awareness of both overt and covert elements of stammering, avoidance-reduction, becoming more open to the experience of stammering, speech change and motivation to keep going in challenging situations.

Aspects of ACT in practice

As a wide-ranging approach to therapy, ACT includes many different processes and strategies. It is not possible to include a comprehensive account in one short chapter, but our intention, as authors, is to highlight aspects that a therapist might find helpful, using the Three Pillars model as a framework. The writings of Russ Harris, particularly his workbook *ACT Made Simple* (2009, 2019) is an inspiring text for a clinician working with ACT. Readers are also recommended to access the many downloadable resources from his websites www.thehappinesstrap.com and www.actmindfully.com.au. Similarly, the work by Flaxman, McIntosh and Oliver (2019) gives a very detailed description of ACT and best practice in teaching ACT principles to others.

When used in one-to-one work, ACT tends to move from process to process organically i.e. the therapist doesn't complete work on the Noticing Pillar before moving onto work on the 'open' or 'active' pillars but rather flows from one to another depending on the client's needs. So although each pillar is presented as a discrete section, this does not necessarily indicate sequence in therapy or process in action.

Struggle is the problem – the control agenda

ACT therapy can include a stage where a client is encouraged to consider whether managing his difficulties up to the present has helped or hindered. Control strategies are often effective when an individual wants to change something in the external world – for example if the boiler breaks down, a heating engineer is called to fix it. These strategies are less effective when trying to control the internal world of thoughts and feelings. In fact, the more a person attempts to control them, the more power is given to them.

This is often highly relevant to a PWS, whose sophisticated array of avoidance strategies might be preventing him from leading the life he wants. For example, a client in our experience reported not attending meetings for fear of having to say his name. Another did not pursue his ideal career in the belief that his stammer disqualified him. At a speech level, a client may be doing everything he can to avoid or escape moments of stammering, or he might be adding extra physical tension to get through a word.

In therapy it is useful to ask these four simple questions:

• What have you tried?

• How has it worked?

- What has it cost?

- Are you open to something new?

Sometimes a client's avoidance strategies could be working for him i.e. changing the odd word here or there may not be having an impact on his ability to communicate his ideas. For another person avoidance strategies are exhausting and burdensome, and it is often at this point that he will seek therapy.

Metaphors are commonly used in ACT to help bring a concept to life. A range of metaphors can be used here with a client to illustrate that how someone responds often exacerbates the problem. Here are two such examples of metaphors to illustrate the problems associated with struggle:

- Quicksand: Ask a client to imagine he finds himself suddenly stuck in quicksand; what might he do? The most common and intuitive type of response is to panic and try to get out as quickly as possible by increasing the struggle (and sinking deeper). If someone has received some survival skills training, he might know that lying back and thereby spreading weight equally will make it easier to reach safety. The different types of responses can be compared to how a client might respond to a moment of stammering i.e. panicking and trying to escape the moment or reducing the struggle and allowing oneself to be with the moment and move forward in the word

- Tug of war with the monster: Ask a client to imagine he is at one end of the rope and at the other end of the rope is a monster which represents painful feelings such as fear, anxiety, shame, self-doubt. The more the person tugs at the end of his rope, the more the monster tugs at his end, and all the PWS's energy is taken up with the struggle. What could be done differently? The simple response is 'drop the rope'. This illustrates the point that an individual can waste a lot of time and energy caught up in his emotions, time and energy that could be better used by focusing on the things that are important.

Raising awareness of how a client can easily get caught up in struggle paves the way for introducing mindfulness skills, as illustrated by the Noticing and Open Pillars.

The Noticing Pillar

What is meant by the Noticing Pillar?

It is appropriate to start with the Noticing Pillar, positioned centrally, as noticing skills underlie the whole of the ACT approach. As will be discussed, noticing is fundamental to the Active and Open Pillars which follow.

Noticing skills can be developed through mindfulness training (Gu et al. 2015). Kabat-Zinn (1996) defines mindfulness as 'paying attention in the present moment in a particular way – on purpose, in the present moment and non judgementally' (p. 4). Harris (2009), writing from within the ACT literature describes mindfulness as 'paying attention with flexibility, openness and curiosity' (p. 8).

Whilst mindfulness is fundamental to the whole ACT approach it will not be described in detail here. Rather the reader is referred to the wider literature (Kabat-Zinn 1996, Williams and Penman 2011) and chapter 6 on mindfulness (Cheasman) in this book. It is important to note that ACT is a mindfulness-based approach (MBA), and without an individual having sufficient opportunity to develop this skill, the rest of the therapy may be just a series of 'clever' strategies. Consequently ACT becomes a 'mindfulness-lite' approach.

In general, mindfulness practices incorporated into ACT are shorter than those used in a pure mindfulness programme. Harris has recorded a range of mindfulness practices for use within ACT (www.actmindfully.com.au/product-category/mp3s/).

Harris describes how ACT mindfulness practices generally arise from a combination of three instructions:

• Notice X

• Let go of your thoughts

• Let your feelings be.

Practices in summary:

• Always contain guidance around point 1, (noticing)

• Many include instruction around point 2, (defusion)

• Less commonly include point 3, acceptance (however, it is always implied through guidance around the theme of allowing things to be as they are)

• Nearly always include guidance around bringing awareness gently back to the object of attention when the mind has wandered.

Flaxman, McIntosh and Oliver (2019) describe mindfulness as a form of mental training which helps to wake up the mind from autopilot and to gather the scattered mind. The non-judgemental quality of the attention bringing is key, and this is assisted by practices including phrases such as 'bringing a friendly curiosity', 'gently bringing attention back when the mind has wandered' and 'opening up as best you can to whatever experiences arise'.

Integrating noticing into therapy

In their ACT training, Flaxman, McIntosh and Oliver (2019) give a rationale for explicitly including a description of the distinction between 'thinking/doing' and 'sensing/being ' modes of mind. They tell participants that one of the great benefits of mindfulness training is that it helps to develop a more healthy balance between these two modes of mind. A PWS often connects with the idea that the thinking mode can be very unhelpful at times in relation to his speech and grasps that developing this other mode of mind has the potential to be valuable.

Ideas for integrating noticing into therapy for PWS include:

• The raisin exercise is commonly used to introduce mindfulness within ACT (see the mindfulness chapter 6 in this book for a full description with an example of an inquiry process)

• 'Mindfulness of your hand' (Harris 2009). The book *ACT Made Simple* includes a script for this as well as a link to an MP3 download (www.actmindfully.com.au/free-stuff/free-audio/)

• Awareness of breath and breath and body practices (see mindfulness chapter 6 in this book) are used to help cultivate the skill. Flaxman, McIntosh and Oliver (2019) incorporate the three-step breathing space (see the mindfulness chapter 6 in this book) into their ACT training programmes.

As with other mindfulness approaches a person can develop noticing skills in three main ways through:

• Formal practice

• Informal practice i.e. bringing noticing to a range of everyday activities, e.g. taking a shower

• Regular 'mindful check-ins' e.g. stop and drop (see the mindfulness chapter 6 in this book).

The concept of the observing self is implicit in the development of mindfulness skills, based on the capacity that a human being has to step back and notice his experience. The sky-and-clouds metaphor (Harris 2009) can be used to illustrate this concept. Within this metaphor the observing self is like the sky and thoughts and feelings are the weather. The weather is constantly changing – clouds can be light and fluffy or dark and threatening. There might be no clouds, or an individual might not be able to see the blue sky for the clouds. No matter what, the sky is always there, and it can contain all of the weather that is ever-changing. Through mindfulness practice the ability to access this part of the self can be developed, from which a client can safely observe and make room for difficult thoughts and feelings.

See **Resource 7.1: Take Your Mind for a Walk**, designed to develop understanding of the concept of the observing self.

By encouraging a client to carry out regularly brief formal and informal practices of noticing skills, he is more likely to be able to stay in the present moment and open up to his experience.

The Open Pillar

What is meant by the Open Pillar?

The Open Pillar relates to a client developing a different relationship to his thoughts and feelings, and this process will have already begun with the work on noticing. The key principle here is that painful thoughts and feelings are not the issue; it is how an individual relates to those thoughts and feelings which can be problematic. If a PWS fuses with thoughts such as 'I'll never get the job I want because I stammer', he may limit his career choices, which could ultimately impact his quality of life. If he is able to learn to create space between himself and his thoughts in such a way that thoughts do not influence behaviour, it will be easier for him to move towards his values, as described in the Active Pillar.

Flaxman, McIntosh and Oliver (2019) suggest there are three ways to relate skilfully to unhelpful thoughts:

• Become more aware of unhelpful thoughts

• Take thoughts less seriously

• Create space between the self and thoughts.

Parts of the Open Pillar include:

• Defusion – normally associated with creating space between the self and thinking

• Acceptance is clearly fundamental to the whole ACT way of working. Harris (2019) describes acceptance in the following way:

> Acceptance means opening up to our inner experiences and allowing them to be as they are, regardless of whether they are pleasant or painful. We open up and make

room for them, drop the struggle with them, and allow them to freely come and go, in
their own good time.
(p. 251)

Harris (2008) illustrates these points through the use of a metaphor called the struggle switch,
which PWS respond well to. This is the format a therapist might use:

Imagine that at the back of your head there's a switch, a bit like an electricity switch,
which can be on or off. When a feeling shows up, like anxiety, and my struggle switch
is on, I will fight against the uncomfortable feeling of being anxious by telling myself:
'Oh no, I hate this feeling. Why do I always feel like this? What's wrong with me?
When will I ever stop feeling this way? It can't be good for my health.' In this way I
am totally caught up with the feeling. When the struggle switch is off, I still feel my
anxiety and I don't like it or want it but I let it be and focus my energy on the things
that are meaningful to me.

Under the list of useful resources at the end of this chapter, there is a reference to a YouTube
video about the struggle switch, which can be used with a PWS.

Integrating defusion and acceptance into therapy
Defusion
Before introducing skills in this area, it is useful to provide some psychoeducation around the
nature of the human mind. The concept that the mind is like an over-protective friend, who
tells scary stories about the future or goes over past events, is often highly relevant to a PWS.
These ideas can be introduced in the following way:

Step back in time and imagine you're living as a caveman (or cavewoman), when
sabre-toothed tigers stalked the earth and there were potential dangers around
every corner. Our minds evolved at that time to protect us from real physical dangers to ensure our survival, so they would always be on the alert and warn of any
impending danger. Our minds also made sure we remained part of the social group,
as going it alone would reduce our chances of survival and producing offspring.
These two functions of the human mind, protecting us from physical danger and
making sure we fit into the social group, go some way to explaining why our minds
constantly warn us of problems ahead and compare ourselves to others, fearing
negative evaluation from others.

(These ideas are explained in a visually appealing YouTube video; see the *List of useful
resources* at the end of this chapter.)

Defusion is introduced via a variety of ways, a small selection of which is listed in what follows.
For a full description of each activity, please refer to **Resource 7.2: Defusion**.

1 A taste of defusion
2 Playing around with painful thoughts
3 Naming the story
4 Giving your mind a playful label or nickname

Cognitive fusion and defusion
Once the client gains an understanding of the nature of the human mind, cognitive fusion
and defusion are introduced through the hands-as-thoughts metaphor (Harris 2008). See the
Resources section for a description of this.

Differentiating fusion and defusion
A client may be helped by understanding the difference between fusion and defusion i.e. when a person is fused with a thought, the thought represents reality, the truth and something important which needs to be obeyed. When he is able to put some distance between himself and his thoughts, he can recognise thoughts for what they are: that is merely sounds, words, bits of language which may or may not be true or important and which may not be wise.

The transitory nature of thought
Thoughts and feelings are constantly changing, and this can be illustrated by different metaphors:

- Thoughts are like passing cars in the street – one can let them come and go or can jump up from the sofa and look out to see what kind of car it is, how fast it's going and who's driving it

- Thoughts are like suitcases going round on a conveyor belt, as at an airport. Some thoughts will come and go easily; other thoughts will stick around for longer

- Thoughts can be compared to waves on a beach, one thought coming one after another, sometimes in quick succession and some more attention-grabbing than others.

Acceptance
The actual term 'acceptance' is rarely used, as it can carry connotations of resignation, with no possibility of change. In ACT terms, acceptance is an active process which leads the way to change. An open discussion with a PWS about the nature of acceptance helps to clarify this point, and alternative terms are introduced such as:

- Making space for
- Allowing the feeling to be there
- Letting go of fighting with it
- Letting it be
- Not wasting energy in pushing it away.

The client can be introduced to a mindfulness practice called "the four steps to emotional acceptance" (Harris 2008). This requires him to bring to mind some kind of emotional difficulty, not the most significant issue going on in his life, but something which elicits uncomfortable feelings. The four steps are:

- Observe: the client is invited to bring curiosity to the feeling in his body and explores where the discomfort is, whether it has a shape, whether it has texture, whether it is on the surface or lies deeper, if it has colour and/or temperature

- Breathe: the client is encouraged to breathe into and around the feeling using long, slow breaths

- Expand: as the client breathes into the feeling, he is encouraged to create space and make room for it

- Allow: the client is invited to make space for the feeling, drop the struggle and allow it to be there.

The purpose of this exercise is to be with what is, not to make the uncomfortable feelings disappear or reduce. A reduction in feelings can be considered an added bonus but it is made clear that if the client strives for this to happen when practising expansion, then he is returning to the control agenda.

Once the client has practised these four stages, he is free to repeat this exercise whenever needed. He may also use an accompanying phrase, such as 'I don't like this feeling but I have room for it' or 'This is unpleasant but I can accept it'.

Developing a different relationship with thoughts and feelings can be illustrated through the commonly used metaphor 'Passengers on the bus'. (A cartoon version is listed in the Resources section at the end of this chapter.) As the driver, a person can steer his bus of life in any direction he chooses, but the passengers, who represent thoughts and feelings, do their best to distract, confuse and influence the driver. An individual can choose to fight or argue with the passengers, which often means the bus is going nowhere, or he can learn to accept their presence and move in the direction of what is important to him. A client is encouraged to identify his own passengers and his response to them.

Practising defusion and developing a willingness to be with what is will support the work on values and committed action as described in the next section.

The Active Pillar

What is meant by the Active Pillar?

The Active Pillar involves:

- Clarifying what really matters to a person

- Enabling him to begin to move towards those key values (committed action).

This section will give practical suggestions on how to work on these two areas.

Values clarification

Flaxman, McIntosh and Oliver (2019) define values as 'the personal qualities a person most wants to express in his or her daily life' (p. 43). Harris (2009) says that when working with a person he describes values as '. . . our heart's deepest desires for the way we want to interact with the world, other people and ourselves' (p. 191). In our experience the concept of values can be an elusive one to communicate to a client. Flaxman, McIntosh and Oliver (2019) attribute this difficulty to the fact that an individual is often more tuned in to goal-directed outcomes than qualities he wants to express. Deconstruction and elaboration of their definition is helpful:

- Personal – this is important because it differentiates a person's values from those society or others think/say should be important

- Express – this gives the link to action: 'values only come to life when they are expressed in our actions' (p. 16)

- In daily behaviour – this indicates that a person will be working on the small things he does each day and that this work will help to move him in his valued directions. This is a direct link to the 'C' part of ACT – committed action. We will return to this in the next section.

Values link to behaviour. As Harris (2009) states, if something doesn't translate into a behaviour, then from an ACT perspective it would not be seen as a value. Consequently, feeling statements such as wanting to be happy, confident, or not wanting to be anxious would not be seen as workable values because they are not underpinned by action.

Values are also not about the behaviours/reactions an individual wants from another person. They are fundamentally about what one stands for.

In personal relationships examples of personal values are being caring, loving and patient. It is immediately apparent that these terms point to qualities of action which can be applied to the personal relationships domain of a person's life. In the workplace examples include being hardworking, determined and supportive to colleagues. It is helpful to give examples like this when introducing the concept to a client.

Values are different to goals; values endure, whereas goals can be worked towards, achieved and then 'ticked off' when they have been completed. For example, if someone has a value of wanting to be a supportive colleague he might set a goal of helping a fellow worker with a new computer system. The value will continue after the colleague is competent.

Integrating values and committed action into therapy

There are a range of ways to identify values including worksheets such as the Life Compass and the Bullseye (Harris 2008). These and others can be found on www.actmadesimple.com, and a copy of the Bullseye is included in the Resources section. Our experience has shown that a client can struggle to identify his values when going straight to using one of the worksheets. We have found it helpful to start by giving lists of values from which to choose:

• Harris has developed a useful values checklist that can be found on www.actmindfully.com. au. This is a list of 38 values. A person is invited to rate how important these values are to him personally by placing a V = very important, Q = quite important, and N = not important next to each item on the list

• A Quick Look at Your Values (Harris 2019) gives a longer list of 60 values. This is also available on www.actmindfully.com.au

• Flaxman, McIntosh and Oliver (2019) provide boxes of 50 values cards created from Harris's questionnaire for a client to sort into piles. Instructions can be given as follows: 'Pile 1 are the ones that carry most personal meaning for you, they resonate with you, they ignite you in some way. Pile 2 also carries some personal meaning but don't ignite you quite as much. Pile 3 carries less personal meaning though they might still be important'. This activity is supported with visual images of a small and a large flame to communicate the idea of 'igniting'. When doing activities like this it is important to say to a client that he won't have to share his rating, as it is easy to feel social pressure to choose certain values. It is also helpful to say things like 'just go with your gut feeling' to try to prevent an individual agonising over each choice. At the end of a task like this a client will not only have identified personal values but will be starting to have a sense of which ones are really important and therefore motivating for him.

The Bullseye (Harris 2008) is a useful resource we use with groups of PWS. Having identified some personal values using one of the methods above and having identified some as being more important to him, a person is invited to use the Bullseye to plot the extent to which he is currently living by that value. The worksheet enables an individual to look at a range of values in four key life domains: work/education, relationships, personal growth/health and leisure. If he feels he is living very much in line with a value in a particular domain he places a cross close to the centre (the bullseye). If he is not so connected with the value at that point in time he places a cross somewhere further out. In our experience this is a useful tool, as it sets the scene for goal setting. Clearly, the values that lie some distance away from the centre are more likely to be priorities for work.

Integrating values identification into desensitisation work

We have run ACT-specific programmes (Everard and Cheasman 2013) and also use values identification to support avoidance-reduction work in stammering therapy programmes. Experience shows that connecting with values gives a client a bigger reason to work on a particular aim aside from issues associated with stammering. For example, a client had a goal relating to avoiding social situations less. In ACT-based values work he also identified that being friendly and sociable were qualities important to him. Recognising this enabled him to attend a new social group that he had wanted to join but had previously avoided.

Taking committed action

Having identified values a client can move on to committed action in the service of some of those values. At this point the therapy can appear more behavioural in nature with goal setting at the fore. It is important to note however that all of the work is supported by the mindfulness training. This is important, as a client stepping out of his comfort zone and doing new things is likely to encounter some difficult thoughts and feelings. Being able to connect with the present moment, defuse from unhelpful thoughts and make space for challenging emotions will be helpful in this process.

The following is an example of a client working through this process. He recounted how he needed to make an important phone call and noticed feeling nervous beforehand. He had been unwell and observed the following thoughts: 'I'm not very fluent', 'I won't get my message across'. He started the call and said to himself: 'just go for it'. He stammered on his name and thought he heard someone laughing. He had lots of feelings and thoughts afterwards including some anger. He was able to experience these as physical sensations, which he visualised and allowed to be there. He found this helpful because he could quite quickly move on whereas previously he would have spent hours 'beating myself up'.

The concept of 'towards' and 'away' moves is being increasingly used in ACT. This helps a client:

• Understand what can get in the way of moving towards his values and

• Identify what he can do to move towards expressing those personal qualities.

Towards moves: Committed action is all about towards moves, and a worksheet can be a useful resource to start the process. Having identified values the client can use a values-based action worksheet from Flaxman, McIntosh and Oliver (2019) that helps identify some recent small actions that have brought a selected value to life. Included in the Resources section (Figure 7.4) is the small values–based action worksheet. Figure 7.2 is an example of a completed small values–based action worksheet. The individual would then go on to note other small actions which would bring the value to life in the short term i.e. in the next week.

Away moves: Before starting the action phase it is helpful for a person to consider some of the inner experiences that might appear and interfere with the process of values-based action. These can include:

• Procrastination

• Anxiety

• Thoughts about others' expectations.

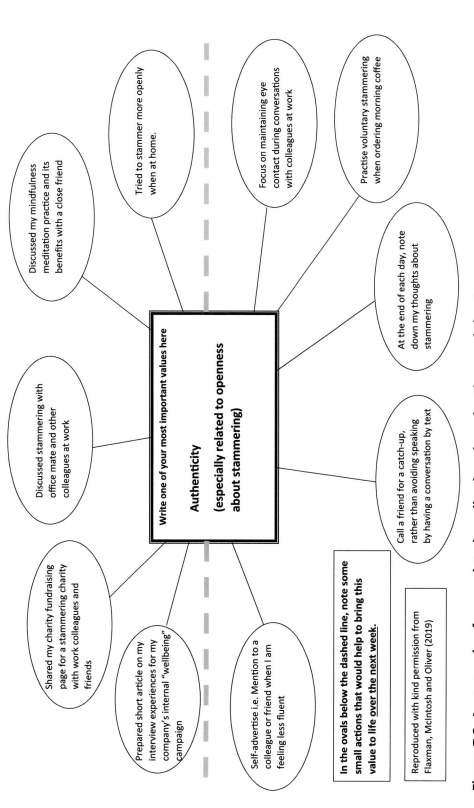

Write one of your most important values here

Authenticity

(especially related to openness about stammering)

Discussed my mindfulness meditation practice and its benefits with a close friend

Tried to stammer more openly when at home.

Focus on maintaining eye contact during conversations with colleagues at work

Practise voluntary stammering when ordering morning coffee

Discussed stammering with office mate and other colleagues at work

At the end of each day, note down my thoughts about stammering

Shared my charity fundraising page for a stammering charity with work colleagues and friends

Call a friend for a catch-up, rather than avoiding speaking by having a conversation by text

Prepared short article on my interview experiences for my company's internal "wellbeing" campaign

Self-advertise i.e. Mention to a colleague or friend when I am feeling less fluent

In the ovals below the dashed line, note some small actions that would help to bring this value to life over the next week.

Reproduced with kind permission from Flaxman, McIntosh and Oliver (2019)

Figure 7.2 An example of a completed small values-based action worksheet

173

It is these types of thoughts and feelings that lead to away moves. Writing some of these down, including putting some thoughts into quotation marks, can be a part of defusion. Responding with comments like 'Yes, isn't it amazing the stuff our minds give us' can also be helpful and normalising.

The matrix model (Flaxman, McIntosh and Oliver 2019) is often used to introduce a client to the concept of 'towards' and 'away' moves. There are two axes: the vertical axis is about the 'towards' and 'away' dimension; the horizontal axis is about internal versus behavioural experience. See Figure 7.3 for a completed example from a client that clarifies the importance of noticing.

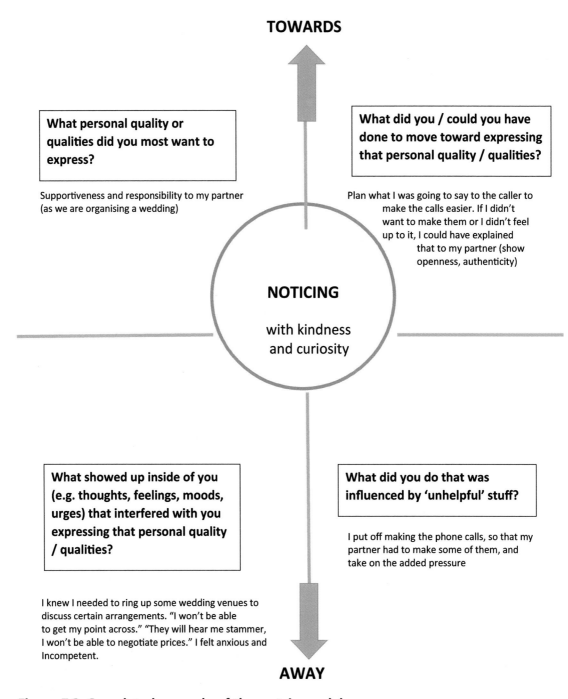

TOWARDS

What personal quality or qualities did you most want to express?

Supportiveness and responsibility to my partner (as we are organising a wedding)

What did you / could you have done to move toward expressing that personal quality / qualities?

Plan what I was going to say to the caller to make the calls easier. If I didn't want to make them or I didn't feel up to it, I could have explained that to my partner (show openness, authenticity)

NOTICING

with kindness and curiosity

What showed up inside of you (e.g. thoughts, feelings, moods, urges) that interfered with you expressing that personal quality / qualities?

I knew I needed to ring up some wedding venues to discuss certain arrangements. "I won't be able to get my point across." "They will hear me stammer, I won't be able to negotiate prices." I felt anxious and Incompetent.

What did you do that was influenced by 'unhelpful' stuff?

I put off making the phone calls, so that my partner had to make some of them, and take on the added pressure

AWAY

Figure 7.3 Completed example of the matrix model

Harris has developed a wide range of resources to help with the committed action phase of therapy. The goal-setting worksheet (see www.thehappinesstrap.com) asks a client to identify the value he wishes to work towards and then to set SMART goals. (This acronym is different in some respects to the one commonly used in speech and language therapy.) ACT SMART goals are:

• Specific

• Meaningful – the goal will be meaningful if it is values guided

• Adaptive – does this goal help you to take your life forwards in a direction that is likely to improve the quality of your life?

• Realistic

• Time-bound.

A client will use these to identify:

• An immediate goal (something simple I can do in the next 24 hours)

• Short-term goals (things I will do over the next few weeks and months)

• Medium-term goals (things I will do over the next few weeks and months)

• Long-term goals (things I can do over the next few months/years).

The beauty of this approach is that action is immediate.

Once goals have been set, the individual can then be invited to use The Willingness and Action Plan; see www.thehappinesstrap.com. This resource introduces the important concept of willingness. The client is:

• Invited to anticipate what might emerge if he takes action (compare away moves in the Matrix model)

• Asked directly what thoughts, memories, feelings, sensations, urges he is willing to make room for in order to achieve the goal.

This is where having practised making space for uncomfortable thoughts and feelings in mindfulness practice will be supportive, because this 'stuff' will frequently show up.

A client's story by Lisa Boardman

It is nearly two years since I completed "Acceptance and commitment therapy (ACT) for people who stammer", a group therapy course at the City Lit, London.

Back then, I was having a tough time in a new job and challenging workplace and after many years of living comfortably with my stammer (since previously attending City Lit in the late 1990s) my speech had started to unravel.

I had never heard of ACT, but its focus on thoughts and feelings was appealing because I knew I wanted to talk about and reflect on what was making my speech so difficult for me and I wanted to find a way through it. So I signed up for a 10-week evening class.

On the face of it the six principles of ACT did not appear particularly revolutionary, concepts like 'accepting feelings' or 'being present with others' or reflecting on core self-values or making personal commitments to action were all things I had done before – and had generally found helpful. I knew a bit about mindfulness and meditation and knew the benefits.

However, taken together, this combination appeared to produce a powerful cocktail of effects, and not just during or just after the course was finished. The effects have had a lasting positive impact on me, on my interactions at work and elsewhere, on stammering related behaviours and on life choices I have made over the last two years.

So what did I get from it? Well ultimately the eureka moment for me was realising the power of good, authentic connections with other people, and how things that interrupt that connection will generally also disrupt my fluency. That was what had been happening at work.

Good connections with others emerged as a common thread within many of the "values" I identified as most important to me whilst on the course. And I realised that my thoughts and feelings about stammering were getting in the way of my connections with other people. I had stopped really listening to others and was listening mainly to myself, to myself stammering again. I was obsessing over in-block modifications and how to get better at them, overly preparing presentations again to remove words I might get really stuck on. My head was full of thoughts and feelings of shame and embarrassment and anger about stammering so much and I was trying desperately to hold onto a sense of authority in my management role as I chaired meetings and struggled with even simple interjections.

All this left me feeling isolated and disconnected in a way I hadn't experienced for years. What I learnt on the ACT course was that it wasn't my dysfluency that was causing me that feeling of disconnect – it was because my thoughts and feelings were distracting me away from having those better connections with other people.

This realisation seemed to emerge almost simultaneously from each side of the ACT hexagon.

- Mindfulness, listening to and observing my own thoughts and feelings about others (acceptance, self as context).

- Getting to know myself, my responses to stammering, the thoughts and feelings that popped up at particular times, acknowledging them, untangling them and ultimately letting them go (cognitive defusion).

- Identifying what mattered to me most (values), what was meaningful for me. This was an integral part of the course. It's not always easy to get to the bottom of these things – so tackling them from a number of different angles was very effective at rooting out truths to enable the "commitment to action" to flow directly from something that would both inspire and drive me.

- The concept of "being present", continues to be the most helpful trigger for me when I feel anxious about communicating or start to feel disconnected. I bring myself back to the present, to the genuine desire to connect with others, and then with that anchored self, I can – and the magic happens. I have got better at watching and listening and being fully there and working with others is so much more pleasurable and satisfying because of that.

The ACT hexagon appears to have the flexibility to bend and adapt the weighting of its six principles depending on what I or others need from it and that feels like a good thing in the long term.

Importance of doing it for yourself

ACT is a powerful approach to change, and we believe it is important that a therapist tries aspects of the practice out for herself before moving to integrate some of these ideas into therapy. *The Happiness Trap* (Harris 2008) could be useful in this work, as it takes the reader through the range of processes, setting tasks. Harris says after one invitation to do a task:

> Did you do it? Remember, you can't learn to ride a bike just by reading about it; you actually have to get on the bike and pedal. . . . So, if you haven't done the exercise, please go back and do it now.
> (p. 43)

Whilst some ACT therapists say it is not necessary for the therapist to practise mindfulness, we believe it is hard to lead practices and understand the impact of mindfulness for a therapist if she has not experienced at least some formal practice herself. Likewise, values work will come alive if the therapist has identified some of her own values and done some work on goal setting and action. Flaxman (personal communication) talks about the power and value of using judicious self-disclosure when using ACT. This is humanising and normalising and again is hard to do if the therapist has not applied some of the concepts to her own life.

How to take the work forward

We hope this chapter has been a useful introduction to ACT and has given you ideas on how it would complement your therapy with an adult and young person who stammers or with another type of client. We are passionate about ACT and the difference it can make to a client's life. We hope that this introduction to the approach has whetted your appetite and given you ideas on how you can take the work forward, both personally and professionally.

Take your mind for a walk

Instructions: this exercise, associated with the Noticing Pillar, is designed to develop understanding of the observing self, the part of us that observes everything we do without judgement.

The exercise requires two people (client and therapist or two clients). Person 1 is themself and Person 2 pretends to be Person 1's mind.

The person goes for a walk, and the mind must follow.

• Person 1's job is to be in sensing mode; to feel his body, to see what he sees, to hear what he hears, maybe to notice things he might not normally notice and gently and compassionately listen to his mind.

• The mind (Person 2) does what our minds do so well and chatters away, giving some commentary on what is going on, making judgements, straying into thoughts about the past and speculating about the future e.g. wondering what might be on the menu for dinner that evening.

• After about 5 minutes, Person 1 and Person 2 then swap over, so they experience the same exercise but from the other perspective.

After the exercise, there is a debrief to find out what it was like to be Person 1 and what it was like to be Person 2. Typical comments include how difficult it can be to focus on the present when the mind is talking about the past and future.

Defusion

The exercises that follow are designed to help the client develop the skill of defusion (where he learns to gain some distance from his thoughts).

7.2.1 A taste of defusion

The therapist talks the client through these instructions and at the same time goes through the exercise herself. Participating in the exercise at the same time as the client normalises the concept that we all get caught up in our thoughts.

 i Bring to mind a painful or difficult self-judgement in the form of 'I am xxx'. Say that over and over to yourself for the next 20 seconds.

 ii Insert in front of the self-judgement 'I'm having the thought that I'm xxx'. Again say that over and over to yourself for the next 20 seconds.

 iii Finally insert an extra bit of language 'I notice I'm having the thought that I'm xxx' and say that over and over to yourself for the next 20 seconds.

The client is then asked for feedback from that exercise and more often than not will express a change in his relationship with the self-judgement.

7.2.2 Playing around with painful thoughts

 i The therapist and client together think of a commonly occurring painful thought around stammering (e.g. 'people will think I'm stupid if I stammer'). The client could then type this into a screen and then play around with the colour, the font size and the type of font.

 ii The client could then use one of his thoughts associated with stammering and play around with the thought in the same way.

This exercise illustrates that thoughts are composed of just sounds and words and are not necessarily the truth.

7.2.3 Naming the story

The therapist encourages the client to see whether his thoughts can be grouped under particular headings. For example there might be a range of thoughts that fall under the 'I can't do that because of my stammer' story. Types of thoughts that might come under this category could include 'I can't give a talk in front of my colleagues', 'I'll make a fool of myself if I ask that person out for a drink', 'I can't ask for what I really want at the sandwich shop'. The client can then learn to recognise those particular types of thoughts and can notice them by saying something to himself like 'There I go again, there's my 'I can't do that because I stammer' story'.

7.2.4 Giving your mind a playful label or nickname

The therapist introduces the idea that our minds can be prone to respond in a certain type of way, particularly when faced with something new or challenging. For example some minds go into worry mode, thinking of all the things that could go wrong. In this instance a playful label could be 'The Worry Machine' and the client can then be encouraged to notice when their worry machine is working overtime.

7.2.5 Hands-as-thoughts metaphor

This exercise is designed for the client to understand the difference between fusion and defusion and what it feels like to be totally fused, hooked by, totally caught up with a thought and what it feels like to have some space between him and his thought. The therapist talks through the following script whilst also carrying out the exercise herself.

i   Place your hands palm up on your lap and imagine that your hands are like some painful or difficult thoughts.

ii Now slowly raise your hands up to your face so they are covering your eyes. You can just see through the gaps in your fingers. What would it be like if you went round like this all day? (A common response is 'exhausting' or 'frustrating'.)

iii Now slowly move your hands away from your face so you can start to see the room and everything around you. What does that feel like? (A common response is 'there's more distance', 'liberating' or 'easier'.)

After this brief exercise, further explanation can be provided about the difference between fusion and defusion – when we're fused with a thought, the thought represents reality, the truth and something important which needs to be obeyed. When we manage to put some distance between us and our thoughts, we can recognise thoughts for what they are: merely sounds, words, bits of language which may or may not be true or important and which may not necessarily be wise.

© Trudy Stewart (2020). *Stammering Resources for Adults and Teenagers: Integrating New Evidence into Clinical Practice.* **Routledge.**

The Bullseye
(reproduced with kind permission from Harris 2008)

This worksheet supports value identification and enables a client to identify to what extent he is living by his values.

YOUR VALUES: *What really matters to you, deep in your heart? What do you want to do with your time on this planet? What sort of person do you want to be? What personal strengths or qualities do you want to develop?*

1. Work/Education: includes workplace, career, education, skills development, etc.

2. Relationships: includes your partner, children, parents, relatives, friends, co-workers, and other social contacts.

3. Personal Growth/Health: may include religion, spirituality, creativity, life skills, meditation, yoga, nature; exercise, nutrition, and/or addressing health risk factors like smoking, alcohol, drugs or overeating etc

4. Leisure: how you play, relax, stimulate, or enjoy yourself; activities for rest, recreation, fun and creativity.

THE BULL'S EYE: make an X in each area of the dart board, to represent where you stand today.

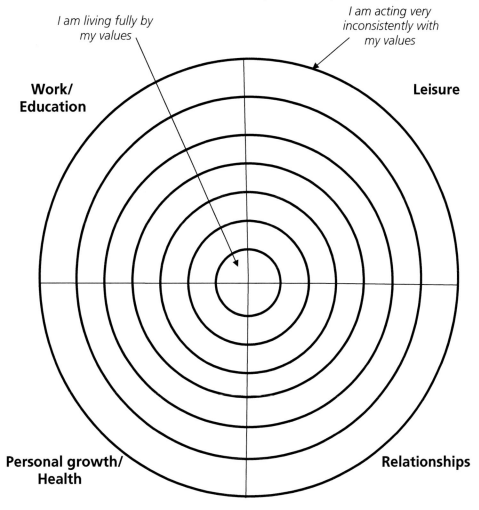

Figure 7.4 The Bullseye

Small values-based action worksheet

This worksheet enables a client to notice some small actions already completed and to identify some small future actions in the service of an important value.

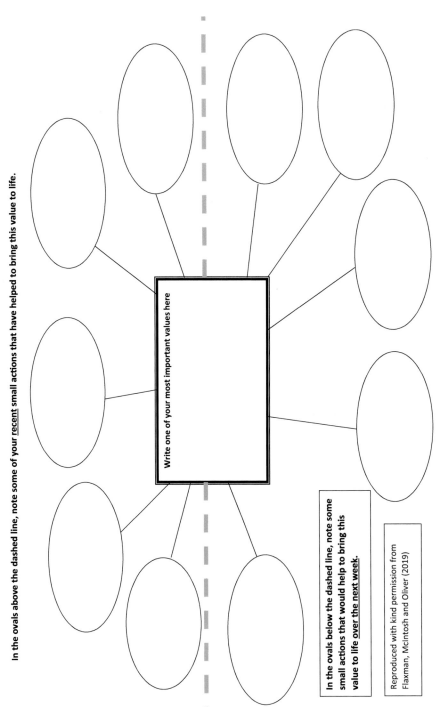

In the ovals above the dashed line, note some of your <u>recent</u> small actions that have helped to bring this value to life.

Write one of your most important values here

In the ovals below the dashed line, note some small actions that would help to bring this value to life <u>over the next week.</u>

Reproduced with kind permission from Flaxman, McIntosh and Oliver (2019)

Figure 7.5 Small values-based action worksheet

References

A-Tjak, J.G., Davis, M.L., Morina, N., Powers, M.B., Smits, J.A. and Emmelkamp, P.M. (2015). A meta-analysis of the efficacy of acceptance and commitment therapy for clinically relevant mental and physical health problems. *Psychotherapy and Psychosomatics*, 84(1), 30–36.

Beilby, J.M., Byrnes, M.L. and Yaruss, J.S. (2012). Acceptance and commitment therapy for adults who stutter. Psychosocial adjustment and speech fluency. *Journal of Fluency Disorders*, 37(4), 289–299.

Beilby, J.M. and Yaruss, J.S. (2018). Acceptance and commitment therapy for stuttering disorders. In B.J. Amster and E.R. Klein (eds.), *More than Fluency: The Social, Emotional and Cognitive Dimensions of Stuttering*. San Diego, CA: Plural Publishing.

Cheasman, C. and Everard, R. (2013). Embrace your demons and follow your heart: An Acceptance and Commitment Therapy approach to work with people who stammer. In C. Cheasman, R. Everard and S. Simpson (eds.), *Stammering Therapy from the Inside: New Perspectives on Working with Young People and Adults* (pp. 267–302). Guildford, UK: J & R Press.

Flaxman, P.E., McIntosh, R. and Oliver, J. (2019). *Acceptance and Commitment Training (ACT) For Workplace Settings: Trainer Manual*. City, University of London.

Gu, J., Strauss, C., Bond, R. and Cavanaugh, K. (2015). How do MBCT and MBSR improve mental health and wellbeing? A systematic review and meta-analysis of meditation studies. *Clinical Psychology Review*, 37, 1–12.

Harley, J. (2015). Bridging the Gap between Cognitive Therapy and Acceptance and Commitment Therapy (ACT). *Procedia – Social and Behavioral Sciences*, 193, 131–140.

Harris, R. (2008). *The Happiness Trap*. London: Constable & Robinson.

Harris, R. (2009). *ACT Made Simple*. Oakland, CA: New Harbinger Publications.

Harris, R. (2019). *ACT Made Simple* (2nd Edition). Oakland, CA: New Harbinger Publications.

Hayes, S.C., Strosahl, K.D. and Wilson, K.G. (1999). *Acceptance and Commitment Therapy: an Experiental Approach to Behaviour Change*. New York: Guilford Press.

Kabat-Zinn, J. (1996). *Full Catastrophe Living*. London: Piatkus.

Kashdan, T. and Rottenberg, J. (2010). Psychological flexibility as a fundamental aspect of health. *Clinical Psychology Review*, 30(7), 865–878.

Segal, Z.V., Williams, J.M.G. and Teasdale, J.D. (2002). Mindfulness-Based Cognitive Therapy for Depression. New York: Guilford Press.

Williams, J.M.G. and Penman, D. (2011). *Finding Peace in a Frantic World*. London: Piatkus.

List of useful resources

Useful introductory books:

- *The Happiness Trap* (Harris 2008)
- *ACT Made Simple* (Harris 2019).

The Happiness Trap on-line program by Russ Harris also includes some useful downloadable resources: www.thehappinesstrap.com

Workshops with Russ Harris; also includes useful downloadable resources: www.actmindfully. com.au

Two-day workshop ACT for SLTs, facilitated by City Lit speech and language therapists: www. citylit.ac.uk

Evolution of the Human Mind by Russ Harris (YouTube video): www.youtube.com/ watch?v=kv6HkipQcfA

The Struggle Switch by Russ Harris (YouTube video): www.youtube.com/watch?v=rCp1l16GCXI

Passengers on the Bus by Joe Oliver (YouTube video): www.youtube.com/watch?v=Z29ptSuoWRc

8 | Working together
The power of the therapeutic group

**Rachel Everard and Cathinka Guldberg,
with Sam Simpson and David Ward**

I think it is really the people who make the course in a way. It opened my eyes to a lot
of things about myself which I hadn't realised. And hearing their words and feedback
I was often surprised by what they fed back to me, stuff I wouldn't have said about
myself, so that was nice having a bit of perspective on things.
(A group attendee)

Introduction

The aim of this chapter is to describe group therapy for adults who stammer in a range of
contexts, focusing primarily on the City Lit way of working. Two different types of courses will
be described: a seven-day intensive daytime course and a ten-week public speaking evening
course. Both illustrate the powerful impact of group therapy to bring about speech and
attitudinal change.

In addition, other types of group therapy delivered by both an NHS and an independent
therapist are described, in order to demonstrate the different ways in which group therapy can
be offered and can complement individual therapy.

The chapter builds on the 'Working with groups' chapter in the *Dysfluency Resource Book* (Turnbull
and Stewart 2010), which contains useful information on the benefits of group work generally,
practical considerations when setting up a group and generic ideas when working in a group.

It is hoped the reader will take inspiration from the different models of group therapy and be
able to apply the ideas presented to their own practice.

Group work and stammering therapy

Group work for any client group brings many benefits, including:

• Reduced isolation

• Support

- Motivation

- Normalising effects

- Reduced dependency on the clinician

- Opportunities for transfer of learning.

When considering the needs of a PWS, the choice of group therapy is a natural fit. As any clinician working with this particular client group knows, a PWS is likely to experience isolation, fear, shame, social anxiety, frustration, helplessness and stigma. This clinical experience is corroborated through the many research studies exploring the impact of stammering (Boyle 2015, Butler 2013, Crichton-Smith 2002, Iverach and Rapee 2014).

A PWS will therefore benefit enormously from being with others who stammer, where he can feel less alone, share his own experiences, support and learn from others and practise challenging speaking situations in a safe, supportive environment.

Research studies evaluating the effectiveness of adult stammering therapy and adopting a qualitative approach identify time and again the significant influence of group work (Everard and Howell 2018, Irani et al. 2012, Stewart and Richardson 2004).

For these reasons, wherever possible, group work should be available as an option for an adult who stammers. This is not always possible for a range of practical considerations: sufficient number and availability of clients in a geographical area; difficulty in finding a suitable space; time and resource constraints. However, if SLTs work together as a profession, there will be ways to overcome these potential obstacles.

Stammering management

City Lit is an adult-education college in London. Its speech therapy department, a national centre of excellence in adult stammering therapy, has been offering group therapy for the past fifty years. Over time, different therapeutic approaches have been trialled, evaluated and modified. Syllable-timed speech, slow prolonged speech and vocal fold management are examples of approaches primarily focused on fluency that have at some stage been part of courses offered for a PWS. Stammering modification (also known as stammering management, stuttering modification, stammering modification or block modification) has always been on offer alongside other approaches. A few years ago the decision was made to 'nail our colours to the mast' and only offer stammering modification, as it aligns most closely with the team's philosophy around stammering as described in what follows.

Strongly influenced by the work of Van Riper (1973) and Sheehan (1970), stammering modification gives equal weight to the overt features of stammering (stammering behaviours) and covert features of stammering (thoughts and feelings associated with stammering often leading to avoidance behaviours). The iceberg analogy (Sheehan 1970), commonly used as a means to explain the holistic nature of stammering, illustrates the importance of addressing both overt and covert features using the following stages of therapy:

- **Identification** (overt and covert): the client learns how to identify in detail his own particular pattern of stammering in a curious and interested way. He also explores his thoughts, feelings and avoidance behaviours linked to stammering

- **Desensitisation:** the client becomes more open to the experience of stammering through avoidance-reduction work, voluntary stammering and self-disclosure

- **Modification:** once the client is more open to the experience of stammering and avoiding it less, he is ready to move on to learning ways to modify individual moments of stammering
- **Stabilisation:** transferring newly acquired knowledge and skills beyond the clinic room to the outside world starts early on in therapy and is key to the client consolidating and extending his skills to his individual circumstances.

Cognitive behaviour therapy, mindfulness and acceptance and commitment therapy are integrated into these four stages of therapy (see chapters 6 and 7 on mindfulness and ACT in this book). Progress is not necessarily linear, and it is possible to be working on two stages at the same time. For example, identification of overt and covert stammering is by its very nature desensitising.

This description of stammering modification is a brief overview. More detailed explanations of this approach are provided by Cheasman and Everard (2013), Manning and DiLollo (2017) and Ward (2018).

Stammering management and group work

The model of therapy described here is a seven day intensive course for a PWS. The first five days (9.30 a.m. to 5.30 p.m.) are delivered initially, followed by a four-week break to allow time for generalisation. The final two days are an integral part of the course and cover revision of learning to date, review of progress during the past four weeks, opportunity for problem solving and completion of the modification stage of therapy.

Previously the course was delivered over a longer period of time, over thirteen days altogether (split between two weeks initially and then a further three days), then reduced to eleven days altogether (split between eight days initially and then three days) before the seven-day model was introduced. The reason for reducing the length of therapy was primarily for practical reasons. Clients were finding it increasingly hard to commit to an extended period of time. Difficult decisions to reduce content had to be made, and the length of each day extended and more home practice included, to offset the decrease in clinic hours.

Table 8.1 illustrates the sequence of therapy and the different activities aligned to them.

Before joining a group, each client is offered an initial assessment. Key criteria for joining a group therapy programme are as follows:

- Readiness for therapy
- Motivation for therapy
- Response to stammering management following explanation
- Availability
- Ability to participate in a group.

The latter point is important: each member of the group needs to take an active role for the group to function properly.

Each group member needs to be aged eighteen or above and have adequate language skills to contribute and participate in the group. The speech and language therapy team will decide whether any additional learning or support needs can be met through reasonable adjustments.

Table 8.1 An overview of the City Lit seven day intensive course for adults who stammer

Day	Stage of therapy	Topics/activities
Day 1 – a.m.	Identification (overt) Desensitisation	Introductions and group gelling Assessments Group guidelines Introduction to course Hopes and fears Identification work (overt) – stammering vocabulary; video (previous student and own); tallying (Montgomery 2006)
Day 1 – p.m.	Identification (covert) Desensitisation	Introduction to mindfulness (practised daily from then on) Covert identification: iceberg Levels of avoidance Introduction to cognitive behaviour therapy
Day 2 – a.m.	Desensitisation	Home practice review Introduction to desensitisation Avoidance-reduction, aim setting and practice Eye contact SMART aims
Day 2 – p.m.	Desensitisation	Hierarchies Thought traps Avoidance-reduction work (inside and outside)
Day 3 – a.m.	Desensitisation	Voluntary stammering Group review Giving talk to whole group
Day 3 – p.m.	Desensitisation	Self-advertising Introduction to acceptance and commitment therapy Survey
Day 4 – a.m.	Desensitisation Modification	Desensitisation review Introduction to modification Post-block modification (cancellation)
Day 4 – p.m.	Modification Identification	In-block modification (pull-outs) Causes and development of stammering

Day	Stage of therapy	Topics/activities
Day 5 – a.m.	Modification Stabilisation	In-block modification practice Fears and concerns about the break Presentations
Day 5 – p.m.	Stabilisation	Toolkit Skills and qualities of being your own therapist Buddy system Aim setting for the break
Break – 4 weeks		
Day 6 – a.m.	Identification Desensitisation Modification	Review of break Revision of work covered so far Re-identification (overt) and aim setting Pre-block modification (pre-sets)
Day 6 – p.m.	Modification Stabilisation	Pre-block modification practice (inside and outside) One-to-one sessions Setting up tips and appreciations and self-report
Day 7 – a.m.	Stabilisation	Speaking circle Re-videoing Assessments
Day 7 – p.m.	Stabilisation	Tips and appreciations Support and challenge model Cycle of change Evaluation and feedback

The frequency of stammering is an important factor. If a client has more of a covert or interiorised stammer, he is advised to join an interiorised stammering course, offered as an evening weekly course to allow a more gradual pace of change. A course specifically for a PWS with interiorised stammering would be the preferred option, but this is not always possible, and other specialist centres in adult stammering therapy run 'mixed' groups successfully. A mixed group is less likely to be a problem if the therapy on offer is weekly and if it is made clear right from the start that everyone stammers differently.

What follows is a description of the elements of the therapy programme, of particular relevance to the group context.

Setting the scene

In order to create a safe and supportive environment in which each group member feels accepted and included, able to share his experiences, to learn from each other and to take risks, the following is taken into account:

Room layout: How the room is organised helps to create the right kind of atmosphere. At City Lit all tables are removed, except for one for paper, and chairs are arranged in either a circle or horse-shoe shape. Ideally, the chairs have tablets attached to them so that each person can make notes easily.

Development of the group dynamic: This is an integral part of the therapy process. As a first step, the group needs time to meet one another. It may be the first time a PWS has met another person who stammers, and for many it will be the first time they have worked in a group for people who stammer. On a practical level, name labels are provided for the first couple of days of the course so that a group member is not under pressure to say his name, and a number of ice-breakers are introduced. (See *Resource 8.1: Fun Activities for Group Therapy*.) Any anxiety in the room is acknowledged and normalised.

Group guidelines: These are 'rules' by which the group agree to abide. In an ideal world, if there is sufficient time, the group is asked to come up with their own guidelines and any important ones missing can be added, such as confidentiality and respecting one another. Alternatively, a list of guidelines is shared with the group, who have the opportunity to add further suggestions and then approve the final list. During the group review on Day 3 the guidelines are reviewed, and each individual is asked how the group is working for him and whether he wants any changes made. It can be set up as a free discussion, or each person can be asked to jot down one thing he likes about the group and one thing he would like to be different. The therapists sit outside of the group when the group review is under-way – their role is to observe, make sure everyone is invited to have his say and to provide a summary at the end.

It's okay to stammer and it's okay not to stammer: Right from the start the variabil-ity of stammering is highlighted and the point made that, although everyone in the room stammers (except perhaps for the clinician and any student speech and language therapists present), some PWS will be stammering more and some stammering less. As much time as is necessary is given to a client who stammers severely. On a few rare occasions, when a client's severity of stammering means that others have less time to contribute, strategies will be dis-cussed and put into place, such as the client indicating when he has finished or the therapist clarifying whether the person has finished speaking.

Responses to therapy: It is acknowledged early on in the therapy process that each PWS is unique and therefore his response to therapy will be different. Some individuals will find some tasks easier than others, and each group member is encouraged to focus on the indi-vidual changes he is making rather than comparing himself with anyone else.

Hopes and concerns: In the first session each person is asked to jot down on a sticky note his hopes for therapy and any concerns he has. Common themes for hopes include:

• Becoming more fluent

• Reduced anxiety around certain speaking situations (such as giving presentations, using the phone)

• Increased confidence.

If someone expresses the hope of becoming 100% fluent, this can be addressed in the whole group. The following explanation is used: for a PWS who has been stammering for some time, it is unlikely he is going to stop altogether and that it is more realistic and helpful to reframe this expectation to managing his stammer more easily. Common concerns revolve around lack of progress ('What if I'm no different after the course?'). It is useful to discuss this in the whole group, as other people might have had similar thoughts but not expressed them. This valid concern is addressed through reference to the evidence base underpinning stammering management and positive outcomes from previous clients.

Identification

To elicit a common stammering vocabulary, each PWS is asked to imagine that a Martian has landed on earth and has no vocabulary to describe stammering. Group members contribute ideas, which are supplemented if necessary. Doing this as a group exercise gives the clear message that it is okay to talk openly about stammering. The relief in the room is often palpable.

As part of overt identification, each group member is asked for his permission to be videoed (in a separate room) and for the video to be watched the same morning in a small group. It is made clear that if anyone prefers not to be videoed, his choice will be respected. (Respect for each group member's choice applies to all stages of the course so that no-one feels under undue pressure to carry out an activity he feels uncomfortable about, although he is encouraged to step out of his comfort zone.) Very few people decline to be videoed and in fact find the experience of watching their videos useful, if uncomfortable. This is an advantage of group therapy – when the majority are willing to give something a go, others are encouraged to follow. To facilitate the process of watching themselves on video, a recording of a previous client is shown so that current group members can practise the task one step removed. A subsequent video of the same previous client is also used in order to demonstrate the client's progress when attending a similar course, giving hope and encouragement at this early stage of therapy.

Giving and receiving feedback is an important skill for a client to develop and can involve giving feedback to himself and to other group members and receiving feedback from other group members and the clinician. The importance of identifying what went well and what could be done differently is emphasised.

Covert identification is particularly powerful in a group in which each person contributes his ideas to create a group iceberg. A client gains confidence from others to share what are often deeply personal feelings such as shame and fear. He begins to understand the reasons for developing avoidance behaviours, which he then explores in pairs. Sheehan's levels of avoidance are used as a basis for this discussion, described in detail by Cheasman and Everard (2013).

Desensitisation

A client is supported in this potentially challenging work by encouraging one another to step out of his comfort zone ('Well, if he can do it, so can I'). The main areas of focus are:

• Avoidance-reduction work

• Voluntary stammering

• Self-disclosure (also known as self-advertising)

• A survey with the general public.

Avoidance-reduction work is based on identification of individual PWSs' levels of avoidance, and a template of different types of aims is provided (see **Resource 8.2: Ways of Working with Avoidance in the Group**). An individual volunteers to identify his aims in front of the whole group, so the other clients can learn from the process and then carry it out for themselves.

For both voluntary stammering and self-disclosure (and indeed for any new skill), the clinician first models that particular element of therapy then asks the group what they notice and for their views on the rationale behind it. In this way each client learns from others and is encouraged to give something a go if he hears a fellow member has found something useful in the past or if he observes someone carrying out a new skill.

Modification

By this stage of therapy each client will have reduced his avoidance behaviours to some extent and will be stammering more openly and ready to work on moments of stammering. For a full explanation on how to teach the different types of modification the reader is directed to Turnbull and Stewart (2010).

The group plays an important role in the learning of the different types of modification by providing opportunities for structured practice and by giving peer feedback.

Stabilisation

From the beginning of therapy, a client is encouraged to take responsibility for his own learning by giving 100% commitment to the therapy process. The therapist's role is to teach, guide, support and facilitate, but only the PWS can make speech and attitudinal changes. Similarly, at an early stage, each client takes responsibility for setting his own aims and for carrying them out as home practice. Every morning some time is set aside for group members to report on their aims. With all new skills, outside practice, where clients go out in pairs, is scheduled with time to report back in the whole group. In this way transfer of learning is part and parcel of the therapy process, with group members offering peer support.

At the end of the first five days of the course, a 'buddy' system is set up whereby each client chooses another client to stay in regular contact with over the four-week break, ideally by phone. Regular checking in allows for a group member to:

• Talk about how the work is going

• Set daily aims to reflect on progress

• Adapt aims when necessary.

The group as a whole exchanges phone numbers and e-mail addresses so they can stay in touch with one another. In addition, establishing other types of groups (e.g. Facebook or WhatsApp groups) is actively encouraged.

Towards the end of the course, a former client is invited to share his experiences of therapy and what he has personally found helpful to keep the work going. This gives a current client an insight into what he may expect after therapy and ideas on how to maintain progress.

End of the group and what comes next

Every group dynamic is different, depending on the size of the group and the personalities involved. Generally, most groups form close bonds, and members stay in contact long after the course has finished. To mark the ending of a group an activity called 'Tips and Appreciations' is often used. Each group member is asked to think of a tip (a piece of advice, stammering-specific or more general) and an appreciation (something he particularly liked about each person) for every group member and himself. These are then shared in the whole group – each person takes it in turns to hear his tips and appreciations from the other members of the group and the therapist, and these are written down so the person has a record to take away.

Each person in the group has a one-to-one session with a clinician to reflect on his progress and to discuss options for follow-up therapy. (The necessity for follow-up therapy is made clear at initial assessment.) Follow-up therapy could include another course or one to one therapy locally, and information is also shared on self-help groups and other types of groups such as Toastmasters.

In conclusion, this type of intensive group stammering therapy enables a PWS to make significant speech and attitudinal changes as well as developing his confidence as a communicator. The group plays a key role in facilitating and accelerating these changes.

Topic-based group work

Bringing PWS together to focus on a particular skill or topic such as job interviews, assertiveness or public speaking offers a client invaluable opportunities for generalising and stabilising gains made in therapy as well as developing new skills. This type of course may encourage a client who would otherwise be reluctant to join a group to work with other PWS. For some PWS, working on a practical skill can be an easier introduction to group work than a general stammering therapy group.

This chapter will describe one such topic-based course: Public Speaking for PWS. This can be a very popular choice, and courses run several times a year to meet demand. Given that Toastmasters groups for PWS are also well attended, it is clear that public speaking is a skill that is valued by many PWS.

Benefits of public speaking groups for a PWS

A client may report a significant increase in anxiety as well as a rise in dysfluencies and secondary behaviours when speaking to groups. An individual can spend his life avoiding or attempting to avoid speaking in front of more than one or two people. Although the focus of this type of therapy group is on public speaking, its reach is far wider.

Public speaking classes can provide:

• Opportunities for generalisation of skills developed in previous therapy

• A supportive environment for a PWS to work at the higher end of his situational hierarchy

- A focus on strengthening a wide range of communication skills, thereby reducing the prominence of fluency in a client's mind
- Skills and confidence applicable to a wide range of situations such as speaking out at a work meeting or sharing an anecdote at a party.

What is public speaking?

Public speaking is said to be the "art of effective oral communication with an audience" (Merriam-Webster Dictionary). For the purposes of this chapter, public speaking is defined as speaking in a monologue format in front of a group of three or more people, whether prepared or spontaneous, formal or informal. Thus, utilising this wide definition of public speaking, the skills and confidence developed on a public speaking course are highly transferable to a wide variety of other speaking situations.

Who is this course suited to?

This type of course is most suited to a PWS who has recently attended stammering therapy. A client who has made significant progress with desensitisation and modification is likely to benefit most. The regular practice of speaking in front of a group gives excellent opportunities for generalisation and maintenance of skills developed in therapy and for developing confidence.

What resources are required?

An SLT with significant experience of working with individual PWS or groups of adults and an interest and experience in public speaking would be best placed to facilitate the course. Venue requirements are dependent on the size of the group (a maximum of ten clients is recommended), but a large meeting room or a classroom with access to the internet and a monitor to play videos from the internet is essential. Access to a video camera to play back client videos is recommended, or a client can use his mobile device to be videoed by a fellow PWS or therapist.

Structuring the sessions

These topic based groups can be offered as a two day workshop or as weekly sessions of 90 to 120 minutes of between six and ten weeks/sessions.

The session plans that follow describe a ten-week evening class. However, it could equally be delivered as a six-week course, excluding the celebratory event, or adapted to a two-day workshop. The celebratory event is a way of providing a client with an opportunity to speak to a larger audience in a supportive environment and to celebrate his achievements.

Table 8.2 contains an outline session plan. Further explanation of these topics and activities is given following this table.

Facing the fear of public speaking

The fear of public speaking, also known as glossophobia, can be powerful and debilitating. It is helpful for a client to recognise that this fear is highly prevalent among the general population. Increasing the client's understanding of what may lie behind this common fear can help him to become more tolerant of its presence. Introducing psychological explanations for why the 'fight or flight' response is often triggered in situations in which humans face a

Table 8.2 Outline session plans for public speaking course

Session/topic	Activities
Session 1: Introductory session	Introductions and ice-breaker
	Each PWS discusses a handout (see **Resource 8.3: Pre-course Assignment for Public Speaking Course**) in context of speaker known to him
	Guidelines are agreed for giving and receiving feedback and **Resource 8.5** is introduced
	Each client gives a one-minute talk in pairs followed by self-reflection and partner feedback
	Homework: clients are asked to prepare a two-minute talk for next week on a subject of their own choice (topic ideas are given in **Resource 8.4: Topic Suggestions for Talks**)
Session 2: Fear of public speaking	This session explores fear of public speaking – what and why might a person fear speaking to groups? What might be some helpful strategies?
	Client constructs his public speaking hierarchy
	Each client gives a two-minute talk to a small group (three–four group members) followed by self-reflection and feedback using a handout (see **Resource 8.5: Self Reflection and Feedback**)
	Homework: clients choose whether to do a prepared talk or speak 'off the cuff' for next week's two-minute videoed talk
Session 3: Body language and eye contact	Activities to increase awareness of body language (see suggested activities below)
	Each client gives a two-minute talk to the whole group which is recorded on the client's mobile device
	Homework: Each client watches his video at least twice and takes notes using a handout (see **Resource 8.5: Self Reflection and Feedback**)
Session 4: Rate, pausing and prosody of speech	Activities to increase awareness of rate and prosody (see suggested activities below)
	Clients share observations from watching last week's video. Each person identifies strengths and sets up to three aims to work on in coming sessions
	Homework: Clients are asked to notice people's rate and intonation in everyday life and/or radio/TV
Session 5: Self-advertising and managing stammering	Review and practise ways of self-advertising stammering to the audience
	Each person practises self-advertising in a two- to three-minute presentation to the group
	The therapist leads a group review of strategies clients are using for managing stammering. A client can choose to set aims around using, for example, in-block modification strategies in talks
	Homework: Individuals are asked to practise self-advertising and record and listen back to their attempts

Session/topic	Activities
Session 6: Speaking circle	Speaking circles concept and standards for feedback (see Turnbull and Stewart 2010)
	Time is allowed for at least two rounds of a speaking circle per client
	Each PWS reflects on his learning from experience
	Homework: Clients are required to prepare a five-minute presentation for following week
Session 7: Practice with feedback	Each client gives a longer (e.g. five- to ten-minute) presentation followed by self-reflection and feedback. The client is video recorded on his own mobile device
	Homework: Each client views his video, notes any changes, and sets further goals, using a handout (see **Resource 8.5: Self Reflection and Feedback**). He also plans a three-minute talk for the next week
Session 8: Practice and preparation	The group prepares their timed presentations and carries out planning for celebratory event followed by feedback
	Homework: The client does further preparation on his celebratory talk
Session 9: Practice of talks	The whole group practises their talks for the next week in front of everyone in the group
	Each PWS gives feedback to himself and receives feedback from others in the group
Session 10: Celebratory event with invited audience	Each person gives a prepared talk to a large invited audience consisting of clients' friends and family, other PWS in the local area (these could be invited through self-help groups, local SLT services), colleagues etc.
	A drinks reception to celebrate the group's achievements is a nice final touch.

group or an audience can enable the client to normalise his fears. For example, appreciating that the human need to be accepted by the 'tribe' can have a powerful subconscious effect on emotional states, perhaps bringing up subconscious fears of being ostracised from a group. The client can be directed to further reading e.g. Theo Tsaousides (2017) *Why Are We Scared of Public Speaking?*

Sharing and discussing other individual fears is also helpful in developing a more accepting attitude to how a client may feel when speaking in front of a group. For example, sharing memories of what may have been difficult experiences of speaking in front of his class in school can be a helpful recognition of how his feelings can also be rooted in these childhood experiences.

The therapist can facilitate a brainstorming session on 'what might help with managing anxiety' at the same time as encouraging the client to resist 'getting into a struggle against the fear'. As the client has already attended speech and language therapy, he is likely to have developed some strategies for managing anxiety. Ideas for managing anxiety that may be shared in the group and, if necessary, added to by the therapist may include:

- Mindfulness meditation and fostering a non-judgemental attitude
- CBT approach including awareness of possible 'biases' (e.g. thinking traps) in a person's thoughts
- Relaxation exercises
- Breathing exercises. Breathing exercises can be integrated into the session, whereby the therapist leads sessions that include instruction on diaphragmatic breathing and slow inhalations with slightly elongated exhalations (to prevent hyperventilation).

Resource 8.5: Self Reflection and Feedback also includes a section for the client to self-rate his level of fear. Scaling of anxiety is a helpful way of tracking progress. Additionally, evaluating how anxious he appeared (on review of video or from group feedback) can often be reassuring. Despite feeling very anxious and perhaps developing a further layer of anxiety about appearing anxious, the client may be surprised that his anxiety was not as apparent as it felt subjectively.

Focus on communication skills

The client's ability to communicate effectively and to engage the audience is the central focus of this type of class. Fostering awareness of the way in which posture, gesture, facial expression, eye contact, prosody, rate and pausing can be modified and how this can impact presentations is a central objective of these sessions. Videos of public speakers are available free of charge on the internet. For example, TED Talks and YouTube are excellent resources. Viewing and commenting on videos of speakers from the internet is a helpful first step in identifying and describing these non-verbal behaviours and also engages the client in discussion with the group about the wide range of communication styles that can be observed. For example, one speaker may use more gestures and voice and pace changes than others. Communication styles also vary in relation to context, for example formal versus informal situations. The handout *Resource 8.3: Pre-course Assignment for Public Speaking Course* can be used in the first session to hone observation skills, and then handout from *Resource 8.5: Self Reflection and Feedback* can be introduced as a way to structure feedback and self-reflection.

Suggested activities

Clients can experiment and have fun with varying their posture, gesture, facial expression and eye contact. This could initially be done in pairs or small groups, with time for reflection about how varying these behaviours impact as a speaker and a listener. Following are some suggested activities for each of these communication parameters:

- **Posture:** Clients experiment with 'power posing' and review internet videos of power posing e.g. Amy Cuddy (TED Talk 2012). They then contrast this with the effect of a less assertive or more slouched posture, both upon the speaker and listener
- **Gesture:** The SLT shows an internet video about gesture e.g. publicspeakingpower.com/public-speaking-gestures. Clients are asked to demonstrate the use of different types of gestures (such as descriptive and emphatic) in a short talk
- **Facial expression:** Clients reflect on how this affects listeners. They can experiment with this in pairs using the suggested topics in *Resource 8.4: Topic Suggestions for Talks*

- **Rate:** The SLT plays video/s of public speakers with effective speech rate and pausing e.g. Barack Obama. The group is asked a number of questions e.g. What do you notice about rate and pausing? Is it pleasant to listen to? The group is introduced to scaling of 1–10 of speech rate. Each client applies self-rating on scale of 0–10 to his own speech. He is asked: What is your usual rate? Does it rise when you're nervous? Clients then try speaking at a faster-than-normal rate on the scale and then lower by two points. Each client sets his own goal rate

- **Pausing:** The group reflect on benefits of pausing to listeners and speakers. In pairs, each PWS asks another a question and practises using a pause before responding and then practices pausing between phrases. The client may also choose to work on increasing his use of pauses in talks as part of his goal setting

- **Prosody:** Clients identify stress patterns and how these contribute to intonation. The SLT plays a video of a news presenter and asks the group to notice intonation. Each person practises varying his intonation in a variety of situations e.g. reading aloud, reciting poetry or short monologues.

Using a hierarchical approach

The client can design a public speaking hierarchy that is individual to them. For one client, speaking without notes may be top of his hierarchy; for another speaking to a small group is harder than a large group. It may be that the client wants to work towards an important public speaking event that is very high on his hierarchy, such as a wedding speech, an oral examination or a work presentation. Therefore building up to this within the group can support the client to achieve his goal. However, in the first sessions of the group, it may be helpful for the client to speak to smaller groups or pairs to start the desensitisation process and help him to feel comfortable in the group. The celebratory event provides the client with an opportunity to work at a potentially higher level of his hierarchy.

Giving and receiving feedback

Clients who attend these courses often comment that the feedback received from the group has a significant positive impact on their confidence. Agreeing on standards for giving and receiving feedback at the start of the course helps the group to work more effectively together. As well as developing skills in giving feedback to others, each client is encouraged to apply the same principles to self-reflection. Suggested guidelines could include:

- Be specific

- Be concise

- Describe behaviours rather than making judgements

- Give mainly positive as well as constructive comments to self and others.

Resource 8.5: Self Reflection and Feedback is initially used as a way of developing a common vocabulary, but with time the client relies less on using the handout and is able to focus on the salient points for feedback and self-reflection, particularly when working on goals set throughout the course.

Self-advertising of stammering

The client is encouraged to reflect on ways in which self-advertising his stammer can be helpful in the context of public speaking. Many PWS embrace the use of self-advertising at the start of presentations, stating that it helps them to react less negatively to moments of stammering and helps to prepare the audience. Sharing examples of phrases can help the client to find ways that he feels comfortable self-advertising. Some clients may wish to take an informal or humorous approach; others may wish to educate the audience a little about stammering. A client will benefit from trialling different phrases and being introduced to alternative ways of self-advertising. The therapist can introduce some examples, such as:

• Before I start, I want to let you know that I stammer, so it might take me a little longer to say what I want to, but I'm quite used to it and soon you will be too

• I stammer, so it may take me a bit of time to get my words out

• Before I start, let me just tell you that I am a PWS. It can be quite random when I stammer, I might not even stammer, but just so that it doesn't come as a surprise, I'm giving you the heads up. . . . So now, having given you the preamble, I sort of hope I do stammer.

Managing moments of stammering

In the writer's experience of running these courses, it is striking how the emphasis the client puts on his stammering diminishes as the focus of the group is on communicating authentically and effectively. Nevertheless, these sessions give the client the opportunity of working on any 'speech techniques', and he may choose to identify this as one of his aims. Additionally, a client can identify avoidance-reduction as a goal to work on during talks e.g. reducing use of fillers.

Speaking circles

Participation in a speaking circle can be a powerful experience for a client. Speaking circles were developed by stand-up comedian Lee Glickstein (1999) to help people to develop more ease when speaking in front of groups. The key rationale for speaking circles is that they help an individual experience the power of connecting with members of the audience as his authentic self. Eye contact is seen as central to connecting with the audience, and talks are unprepared, giving the speaker practice at speaking 'off the cuff'. At least two rounds are recommended, preferably three rounds. Further information about speaking circles can be found in Turnbull and Stewart (2010).

Other models of group therapy offered within the NHS

So far this chapter has described group therapy delivered by an adult-education provider. There are of course other providers of group therapy within the NHS. In what follows David Ward from Oxford NHS Foundation Trust give a useful insight into a different model of therapy.

Group therapy provided by Oxford NHS Foundation Trust

At the Apple House in Oxford, a mixed 1:1 and group approach to management of adult PWS is employed.

The approach begins with an assessment to identify client-centred goals which are appropriate, achievable and, importantly, sustainable in the longer term. Research has shown that many approaches may be effective in improving fluency in the short term. It is debateable whether this is really effective therapy, despite the often impressive-looking gains made over the therapy period, if these are not sustainable in the longer term. A further question is whether fluency itself should be considered the major outcome measure. For a PWS managing his speech-related self-perceptions, anxiety and avoidance can lead to better and more meaningful outcomes. The fact that each client brings a unique combination of challenges, both behavioural and cognitive, and that therapy should wherever possible be individualised may seem at first sight to suggest that a group perspective may not be conducive to change.

To manage this variability, a two-stage strategy is employed. A client initially attends 1:1 sessions before moving to a two-day group. The appointments – usually one hour, once weekly – help instantiate the basic concepts that have been identified for each particular individual. These may be more related to speech modification techniques, such as slide, light articulatory contact and diaphragmatic breathing, or may involve a more cognitive-based approach incorporating cognitive behavioural therapy and mindfulness techniques. Usually, there will be a combination of both behavioural and cognitive approaches, the ratio of which will vary according to individual needs. The 1:1 time period is flexible; one client can move through the process in a matter of a few weeks, while another may take up to twelve sessions.

As suggested earlier, there is much evidence to suggest that gains made in the safety and calm environment of the fluency therapy clinic do not translate easily into the client's real world. The two-day intensive programs are designed to help solidify the practices learned in 1:1 sessions in more challenging situations. The group consists usually of five to seven clients and runs from 10.00 a.m. to 4.00 p.m. across the two days. These are run at weekends to help client attendance. Clients will come with very different goals, which require different outcome measures, but the ethos is the same: to help transfer the gains made to date to a range of more challenging situations. Thus, individualised goals are adhered to within the group format. The group may also be joined by a PWS who has already undergone therapy but is now in need of a refresher. Further support is provided by two SLT students (two for each group) who in addition to their regular fluency training, also attend workshops that orientate them to the programme itself. This additional help allows better individualised feedback and some 1:1 help within the group format.

The course begins by identifying goals and a brief revision of the management strategies that each person will be building on. An individual is asked to provide his own hierarchy of difficult speaking situations, and where possible, these are incorporated into the weekend's schedule. The group then meets off-site on the Saturday afternoon in a busy town centre. Here each PWS undertakes a range of transfer exercises, the nature of which will vary depending on his needs.

In addition, most individuals will:

• Practise phone conversations
• Attend a mock interview with a stranger
• Give a presentation to the group in a novel and formal setting and to strangers.

It is important to stress that the two-day intensive group is not in addition to the therapy procedure but an integrated part of it.

There are some occasions on which this integration is not desirable, for example, a PWS with co-diagnoses such as autism or a person with very specific concerns not requiring group work. One client came for therapy fully aware of the minor blocks in his speech, but these behaviours were of no concern to him. Therapy for this PWS consisted solely of managing the big blocks he experienced when having to introduce himself on the phone. Working simply on improving fluency in this specific context was the sole focus and was achieved quickly. Neither extended 1:1 work nor group work was needed.

Group therapy offered by an independent therapist

Accessing independent speech and language therapy may be another option for an adult who stammers, particularly if it is affordable and there is no NHS local service. Here Sam Simpson, independent speech and language therapist, describes the benefits of offering a regular 'open space'.

An SLT working primarily 1:1 in the NHS or in independent practice often has to think creatively in relation to offering group opportunities. Discussing the value and complementarity of group work alongside 1:1 therapy from the outset fosters a 'no one size fits all' approach to therapy. It opens up a culture of experimentation over time and choice around therapy options and preferences. A PWS can often express an initial preference for individual therapy, as it can feel more intimate, safe and confidential. An appreciation of the value of meeting another PWS as a platform to being more open and as a means of accessing support typically emerges over time. It may mark a turning point in the therapy process and the beginnings of the development of a collective identity as someone who stammers.

In the first instance, it can be helpful to signpost online groups and communities that may be of interest and that someone can be a part of on his own terms. Examples include: the BSA Facebook group, ISAD online conference or the many communities on Twitter. A clinician can also signpost face-to-face group opportunities in her local area. This could range from a one-day topic-based workshop for an individual wanting to dip his toe into the group experience to a stammering conference (i.e. BSA conferences run every two years) for more of a weekend immersive. For a client interested in an ongoing group encounter, options such as an evening course, attending a local support group, or participation in a bespoke group, such as the King's Speakers (a Toastmasters club specifically set up for people who stammer) may be more relevant. Alternatively, the therapist may want to create a regular group opportunity as part of her stammering service.

One successful model is the Stammering Open Space, a two-hour, open drop-in group opportunity for current and past clients organised and facilitated by a therapist on a monthly or bi-monthly basis. Dates are typically scheduled a year in advance and alternate between evening and morning sessions during the week and at weekends. This allows sessions to cater for a PWS's work and personal circumstances. A client can sign up at any point of his choosing. He can choose to attend:

• One or two sessions to gain support around a particular theme or issue (e.g. starting conversations about stammering with friends and work colleagues)

• As an ongoing commitment which complements his 1:1 sessions

- As a follow-on from 1:1 therapy
- During a transitional period after therapy has ended (e.g. change of role at work).

Consequently, each group comprises a mix of newcomers and more established group members who bring experience of therapy.

Integral to every group is an initial round of introductions and hopes for the session. This provides a means of arriving and connecting and is followed by a final round of reflections on key learning and take-home messages. In between, the format varies from an informal, unstructured meet-up focusing on topics the group participants have suggested in advance through to a more structured, themed group session. The latter can be determined by the therapist or in collaboration with the group. For example, the therapist might signpost a contemporaneous blog post, podcast or news article/online ISAD article that the group might read or watch ahead of the session and use as a starting point for discussion. Materials in different formats and representing diverse viewpoints can be offered to open up more of a debate. Alternatively, a group participant may offer to read a book or research a topic of interest (e.g. the neuroscience of stammering, the Employers Stammering Network, the social model of disability, stammering pride) and present his findings to the group. The group can also offer a practice opportunity before a real-life event – ranging from facilitating a group mindfulness practice or rehearsing wedding vows through to job interview questions and advice. The flexibility of the group means the sky really is the limit in terms of its scope, format and focus.

In terms of the benefits of such an open group opportunity, PWS report on the value of meeting people at different stages in their therapy and having the opportunity to share thoughts, ideas and support with them. This can significantly reduce feelings of isolation and build confidence in a timely and meaningful way. The group also offers a platform to becoming more open in that a PWS likes the 'safeness' of the environment and feels able to share more about himself than he is able to do with others. Similarly, meeting new people and hearing their stories, pushing the boundaries and experiencing something new in a group environment are highly regarded. Finally, the collaborative nature of the group fosters mutuality, autonomy and a valuing of diversity. Such a group benefits from the skills of an experienced facilitator who is able to balance power, hold uncertainty and work with what arises as well as difference. Undoubtedly, the potential benefits outweigh the challenges.

Conclusion

This chapter has described in detail two types of courses for people who stammer, as delivered by the speech and language therapy team at a specialist centre for adults who stammer. In addition other examples of group therapy models within the NHS and within an independent setting are provided. These different models clearly demonstrate the overarching benefit of the transformative experience of group therapy.

Fun activities for group therapy

8.1.1 Icebreakers

Line-ups

Ask the group to form a line according to different criteria. Suggestions for criteria include:

- Shoe size
- distance travelled to get to the location
- Size of breakfast.

Use your imagination to think of more! Each group member talks to everyone else to find out where he should position himself on the line.

People Bingo

Each group member goes around the room, finding different people to fit each category. He may approach each person only once. He can ask that person as many questions as he wants to. After he has filled in the person's name in three appropriate boxes, he then moves on to the next person. If an individual does not fit into any of the remaining empty boxes the PWS moves on to the next person. When complete the individual shouts 'BINGO!'. If no one can complete his sheet, then the person(s) with the most number of boxes filled in wins.

Find someone who . . .

For larger groups, the number of boxes can be increased or decreased when numbers are smaller. Group motivation is always increased if there is a small prize at the end for the winner.

Table 8.3 Sample of a People Bingo matrix

Regularly downloads music from the internet	Has worked in a shop	Watches Netflix
Would like to do a bungy jump	Has seen *The King's Speech*	Is going to eat/has eaten a chocolate bar today
Likes spicy food	Has changed jobs in the last two years	Is a member of a gym
Regularly uses public transport	Reads a newspaper almost every day	Always eats breakfast

Introducing one another

Instead of having to introduce themselves, ask the group to divide into pairs. Each person then has to find out three things about the other person and vice versa. Each person then introduces the person to whom he has been talking to the whole group.

© Trudy Stewart (2020). *Stammering Resources for Adults and Teenagers: Integrating New Evidence into Clinical Practice.* Routledge.

Name game

This involves a PWS saying his own name. A clinician will gauge how appropriate this activity will be based on her knowledge of the individuals in the group. Each person thinks of an adjective which begins with the first sound of his name (for example charming Charlie, sunny Sanjay, awesome Angela). The first person says his name preceded by an associated adjective. The second PWS repeats what has been said and then says his name plus adjective, and then the next person repeats the first two names and then his name. So it might go something like this: racy Rachel, sunny Sanjay, charming Charlie and so on. This can be difficult for someone with auditory memory problems, so the therapist needs to be ready to support as required. The idea is to have fun; it's not a memory test!

8.1.2 Speaking activities

These can be used when working on any kind of speech aims (e.g. avoidance-reduction work or modification practice).

Any questions: Ask the group to divide into two. Each group thinks of some open questions they could ask the other group. Model some possible questions, for example:

- What would you do if you won a million pounds?
- If you could go anywhere in the world, with no expense spared, where would you go and why?
- If you could change one thing in the world, what would it be and why?

Once each group has around three or four questions, one group asks one of their questions, and each person in the other group answers. The other group then asks the first group one of their questions.

Time capsule: The task is for the group to decide on ten items that would go into a time capsule; a container designed to be hidden away and then re-discovered 100 years later. The ten items represent the current year, to give an idea to whoever discovers the time capsule what it was like to live at this particular time. Items can relate to any area of life:

- Politics
- Fashion
- Sport
- Film
- Books
- Music
- Technology
- Transport.

The clinician will give an example so the group gets the idea (e.g. latest type of smartphone).

Talking about your name: Each person is invited to come up to the front of the group and write his full name somewhere visible (e.g. on a whiteboard or flipchart). He then shares any information about his name that he chooses:

- Reasons for being given his name (if known)
- If his name has any particular meaning
- Any nicknames he has
- Whether he likes his name.

This is a particularly useful activity when working on modification and gives the clinician the opportunity to give some online feedback.

Who am I?: The names of well-known people are written onto labels, which are adhered to a PWS, either on his back or forehead. (The idea is the PWS cannot see the name of the individual.) Working in pairs, one person takes it in turns to ask another person questions to find out the identity written on the label. The questions must be closed questions, i.e. the other person can only answer 'yes' or 'no'. Examples of questions could include:

- Am I a man?
- Am I alive?
- Am I a sportsman or woman?

Ways of working with avoidance in the group

Instructions given to a client

Following are some examples of aims to reduce typical avoidance behaviours often used by a person who stammers. They are grouped according to some of the categories of avoidance which you have discussed. Please read through these different examples and then put together your own list of aims which are relevant to you. You may think of some aims that are not described here, and it is helpful to include them as well.

My Aims

Table 8.4 Examples of aims to reduce avoidance behaviours

Sound	Word	Speech	Feelings	Other
Reduce use of starters and fillers (e.g. ums and ers) The starters and fillers I use are . . . (and go for the word I want to say).	Reduce changing words and say the words I want to say.	At the moment I am holding back from speaking in the group: I want to work on saying things in the group when I have something to say.	At the moment I am holding back from saying some of what I'm feeling about stammering in the group. I would like to be more open about my feelings.	I want to work on keeping eye contact when I'm stammering.
Reduce backtracking (and go for the word I want to say).	Reduce using extra words and phrases (e.g. 'I went to the place where they show films 3 days ago' as opposed to 'I went to the cinema on Tuesday').			At the moment I change my rate of speech to hide my stammer (e.g. speaking very fast or very slowly). I want to work on this.
Reduce the pause I use to hold back from stammering and go straight for the word.				I find it hard to have pauses in my speech. I would like to work on this so I become more tolerant of silence.
Reduce other avoidance 'tricks' I use, e.g. coughing, swallowing, yawning etc. and go straight for the word.				At the moment I use some movement(s) to help me get words out (e.g. moving my head/foot, tapping my foot). I want to work on saying difficult words without using these 'tricks' (this is not the same as using normal gesture).
Put some sound into silent blocks so that stammering becomes more audible.				

Pre-course assignment for public speaking course

Instructions

Think of a speaker that you admire and enjoy listening to. It can be someone in the public eye whose style you find captivating, or it could be someone in your work or personal life, such as your boss or teacher, someone who speaks to large audiences or small groups. It can be someone who stammers or someone who doesn't stammer. Conjure up in your mind how he/she communicates or find a video that you can view and reflect on the following:

• What do you like about the way he/she communicates?

• How does he/she keep the audience's attention?

• How would you describe his/her communication specifically in terms of:

  • Body language

  • Eye contact with the audience

  • Rate i.e. how fast/slow he/she speaks

  • Voice loudness and variation/inflection.

Topic suggestions for talks

8.4.1 Short and spontaneous talks

My friends

My family

My school history

My job history

My current job

My hobbies

My wardrobe

My dream holiday

My dream cars/bikes in top-price, mid-price and low-price categories

My sporting hero/es

Favourite TV programmes/films

My musical taste

8.4.2 Longer prepared topics

The role of social media today

What makes a good boss at work?

A successful life is . . .

My advice to a child who stammers

Stammering in the media

Self reflection and feedback

Use the comments column to make observations of yourself, from self-reflection following a talk or from viewing your video or from feedback given by others (e.g. I used effective eye contact). Remember to recognise your strengths. The goals column can be used to set yourself goals to work towards and should be specific (e.g. to reduce rate from 8/10 to 6/10).

Table 8.5 Self reflection and feedback

Communication skill/ parameter	Comments	Goals
Eye contact		
Body posture and gesture		
Facial expression		
Rate of speech/pausing		
Volume (loudness)		
Intonation/inflection of voice		
Management of moments of stammering e.g. modification		
Avoidance behaviours e.g. fillers, word avoidance		
How anxious was I? 0–10		
How anxious did I seem?		

My overall impression of my video:

References

Boyle, M.P. (2015). Relationships between psychosocial factors and quality of life for adults who stutter. *American Journal of Speech-Language Pathology,* 24(1), 1–12.

Butler, C. (2013). Identity and stammering: Negotiating hesitation, side-stepping repetition, and sometimes avoiding deviation. *Sociology of Health & Illness,* 35(7), 1113–1127.

Cheasman, C. and Everard, R. (2013). Interiorized (covert) stammering: The therapy journey. In C. Cheasman, R. Everard and S. Simpson (eds.), *Stammering Therapy from the Inside: New Perspectives on Working with Young People and Adults* (pp. 125–160). Guildford, Surrey: J & R Press.

Crichton-Smith, I. (2002). Communicating in the real world accounts from people who stammer. *Journal of Fluency Disorders*, 27(2), 333–352.

Everard, R. and Howell, P. (2018). We have a voice: Exploring participants' experiences of stuttering modification therapy. *American Journal of Speech-Language Pathology*, 27(3), 1273–1286.

Glickstein, L. (1999). *Be Heard Now! Tap Into Your Inner Speaker and Communicate with Ease*. New York: Broadway Books.

Irani, F., Gabel, R., Daniels, D. and Hughes, S. (2012). The long term effectiveness of intensive stuttering therapy: A mixed methods study. *Journal of Fluency Disorders*, 37(3), 164–178.

Iverach, L. and Rapee, R.M. (2014). Social anxiety disorder and stuttering: Current status and future directions. *Journal of Fluency Disorders*, 40(3), 69–82.

Manning, W.H. and Dilollo, A. (2017). *Clinical Decision Making in Fluency Disorders* (4th edition). San Diego, CA: Plural Publishing, Inc.

Montgomery, C. (2006). The treatment of stuttering: From the hub to the spoke. In N. Bernstein Ratner and J. Tetnowski (eds.), *Current Issues in Stuttering Research and Practice* (pp. 159–204). Mahwah, NJ: Lawrence Erlbaum.

Sheehan, J. (1970). *Stuttering Research & Therapy*. New York: Harper & Row.

Stewart, T. and Richardson, G. (2004). A qualitative study of therapeutic effect from a user's perspective. *Journal of Fluency Disorders*, 29(2), 95–108.

Turnbull, J. and Stewart, T. (2010*). The Dysfluency Resource Book* (2nd Edition). London: Routledge.

Van Riper, C. (1973). *The Treatment of Stuttering*. Englewood Cliffs, NJ: Prentice Hall.

Ward, D. (2018). *Stuttering and Cluttering: Frameworks for Understanding and Treatment* (2nd Edition). London: Psychology Press.

9 | Working with self-help groups

Hilary Liddle and Bob Adams

Introduction

A contemporary text on therapy for adults who stammer would be incomplete without a focus on self-help groups. The following chapter provides background information about self-help groups for adults who stammer, including their historical context. It also explains the many benefits of self-help group membership, explores the role of the SLT in relation to self-help groups and discusses the differences between self-help and therapy groups. Drawing on the authors' experiences of working with a large, active self-help group in the north of England, the chapter gives advice and practical suggestions about how an SLT can work in collaboration with self-help groups in order to achieve the best possible outcomes for group participants.

What is a self-help group?

Of the many definitions of self-help groups, the one which is both recognised by the World Health Organisation and widely accepted is Katz and Bender's (1976):

> Self-help groups are voluntary, small group structures for mutual aid and the accomplishment of a special purpose. They are usually formed by peers who have come together for mutual assistance in satisfying a common need, overcoming a common handicap or life-disrupting problem and bringing about desired social and/or personal change . . . they are frequently 'cause' orientated, and promulgate an ideology or values through which members may attain an enhanced sense of personal identity. (p. 278)

Historical context

The development of self-help groups for people who stammer can be understood within the broader context of the self-help movement. The concept of self-help is generally thought to have originated with the inception of Alcoholics Anonymous in 1935 (Adamsen and Rasmussen 2001). The self-help movement, driven by the growth in consumerism, gained momentum during the mid-1960s (Ramig 1993). In the 1970s, dissatisfaction with healthcare systems, as they became less patient centred, contributed to further expansion of the self-help movement

(Trichon and Raj 2018). During this time, there were somewhat adversarial relationships between self-help and professional communities (Reeves 2006). By the end of the 20th century, self-help and professional communities were working cooperatively in a climate of mutual understanding (Reeves 2006), and there had been a dramatic increase in the number of people participating in self-help groups. In the United States, for example, 25 million people had previously participated in self-help groups (Kessler, Mickelson and Zhao 1997). Yalom and Leszcz (2005), in their discussion of the ubiquity of self-help groups, comment that it is very hard to imagine any kind of 'distress' or 'misfortune' for which there is not a corresponding group.

Two of the first national organisations for people who stammer were the British Stammering Association (BSA), a charity (formerly known as the Association for Stammerers) established in 1968, and the USA National Stuttering Association (NSA), a non-profit organisation (formerly known as the National Stuttering Project) established in 1977. There are now similar organisations worldwide supporting and promoting self-help groups for adults who stammer. An international umbrella organisation for self-help organisations, the International Stuttering Association, founded in 1995, currently links member associations in more than 40 countries. In the 21st century, advances in the internet have been instrumental in supporting the growth of the self-help movement within the field of stammering (Trichon 2010). The BSA, for example, currently lists 26 local adult self-help groups on its website, whilst the NSA website lists 124 such groups; both organisations exhort their members to establish groups in areas where groups do not already exist.

The 21st century has also seen an increased acceptance of the social model of disability in relation to stammering. The social model explains how people are disabled by the barriers created by society rather than by their impairments. In the case of stammering, barriers include society's negative attitudes, stereotyping and the stigma surrounding stammering. It is essential for an SLT to recognise the importance of engaging with the social model rather than the dominant medical model, which frames stammering in terms of the individual's 'problem' or 'deficit'. However, it is the prerogative of a PWS to redefine stammering and to challenge the negative attitudes, stereotypes and stigma surrounding it. The modern-day self-help group therefore plays a key role in helping a PWS to collectively reject the medical model's narrative in favour of an acceptance of stammering and a celebration of difference.

The benefits of working with self-help groups

It is vital to consider the role of self-help groups in the therapeutic process for the client who stammers, because, as Bloodstein and Bernstein Ratner (2008) suggest, therapists possess nothing as powerful for changing clients' attitudes as the group spirit engendered through self-help group membership. On the basis of our experiences with a flourishing self-help group, established more than 25 years ago, we can wholeheartedly attest to the power of the group spirit for effecting positive and enduring change in its membership.

Group member's insight

Thanks to the self-help group, I've learned to accept my stammering, which has given me the confidence to just get on with my life. I will always remember feeling liberated, from the very moment the group showed me that I can be open about stammering because there is no shame in it. Being with the group has helped me to realise that I am who I am, and I actually wouldn't want to be without stammering now. Since joining the group, I have grown as a person and found confidence I thought I'd never have.

There is a wealth of anecdotal evidence testifying to the benefits of self-help group participation for the individual who stammers. See, for example, some self-help group members' insights throughout this chapter. There is also a growing body of research evidence in the area. The majority of SLTs surveyed by Klassen and Kroll (2005) considered participation in a self-help group to be an important component of therapy for the adult who stammers. Plexico, Manning and DiLollo's (2005) study showed that involvement in support systems, including self-help groups, is an important factor in the 'successful management' of stammering. Research has shown that the beneficial effects of self-help group membership include:

• Anxiety reduction (Ramig 1993)

• Improved self-image (Krauss-Lehrman and Reeves 1989, Ramig 1993, Yaruss et al. 2002)

• Increased acceptance of stammering (Boyle 2013, Yaruss et al. 2002)

• Increased self-disclosure of stammering (Boyle et al. 2018)

• Decreased internalised stigma (Boyle 2013).

Trichon, Tetnowski and Rentschler's (2007) research into the experience of self-help group participation shows that what group members value most is:

  • Encouragement

  • A safe environment

  • Shared feelings

  • A sense of community

  • Exposure to other people who stammer.

An alternative to group therapy

Many of the benefits of self-help group participation outlined already can, of course, be gained through SLT-led group therapy. However, where a therapist is unable to provide group therapy, perhaps due to a lack of resources or insufficient numbers of clients, participation in a successful self-help group can be an excellent alternative. Self-help group membership may also be a useful alternative for a client who does not meet the selection criteria for a therapy group. For example, an individual who finds it difficult to access group therapy because of an attention or cognitive difficulty could find it easier to participate in a self-help group, which may be less demanding than a therapy group. In these situations, the support, encouragement and camaraderie of the group may be sufficient to meet the client's needs.

More possibilities than group therapy

As well as providing an *alternative* to group therapy, a self-help group can be a useful *adjunct* to group therapy. Because self-help groups are autonomous, voluntary organisations, they tend to be run more flexibly than professional services. This can create more opportunities for a wider range of activities and experiences and can allow groups the freedom to function in ways that benefit participants. For example, it can be helpful to have the flexibility to hold regular social events and to include a social element (e.g. beginning the meeting in a café). This can promote group cohesion (i.e. 'gelling'), which is fundamental to the successful interaction of the group and is associated with positive therapeutic outcomes (e.g. Joyce, Piper and Ogrodniczuk 2007, Ogrodniczuk and Piper 2003, Yalom and Leszcz 2005).

An important function of a self-help group can be to raise awareness of stammering. Awareness-raising events and activities provide opportunities for public speaking, which may not be available in group therapy. These events also provide the opportunity for self-disclosure of stammering, which is associated with higher quality-of-life ratings (Boyle et al. 2018). A member of self-help group may also disclose stammering and raise awareness in more informal ways. For example, our group members have 'Communication Clothing', e.g. T-shirts and jackets which promote the group and the BSA. A group member who is not ready for public-speaking challenges can choose to wear the branded clothing and even share photographs of himself on social media.

Group member's insight

> Therapy was great. It set me on the right track, but being in the group is what's really made the biggest difference to me. It's a very active group and, at times, I've felt like I was being carried along on a wave, particularly in the early days when we organised a national conference. Up to that point I hadn't really 'come out', but that changed dramatically. Since then, I've lectured to SLT students, shared my story at special events, and been on the radio to talk about stammering. My world has opened up more than I could ever have imagined.

'Giving something back'

Clients who have valued the help that they have received often feel the need to 'give something back' to others in a similar situation. Self-help group participation can offer the individual the means to do this through providing support, encouragement and inspiration to fellow group members. A self-help group member may also be invited to support the SLT service, for example, by being a good role model for another SLT client or a therapy group. A way for a self-help group member to make a wider contribution for the benefit of others is through awareness-raising activities, which serve to challenge stereotypes and reduce the stigma surrounding stammering.

Through the act of 'giving something back', the altruistic group member is able to benefit personally. Those who participate most actively in self-help groups derive the most benefit from them (Cheung and Sun 2001). Furthermore, research has shown that joining a stammering self-help group for the purpose of supporting others is associated with higher levels of psychological well-being (Boyle 2013).

Exceptional desensitisation

Long-term membership of a successful self-help group and involvement with wider stammering networks provide on-going opportunities for:

- Socialising
- Public speaking
- Disclosing stammering
- Raising awareness
- Supporting others who stammer.

As a result of these opportunities, an active self-help group member, especially one in a leadership role, may become a very confident communicator who is exceptionally desensitised to stammering and feels liberated from the negative emotions resulting from its stigmatisation.

Group member's insight

> Belonging to a self-help group is not the fruitless journey of attempting to gain fluency, but the real-life journey: to self-acceptance; to becoming a great communicator, whilst stammering; to becoming a role model; to inspiring others; to seeking new challenges that might have seemed out of reach; to becoming the person you were meant to be.

The self-help group meeting as a learning environment

Self-help groups welcome participation from non-members and often enjoy sharing their knowledge and experience with them. For the inexperienced clinician and especially the SLT student, self-help group attendance can be an excellent way to gain a greater understanding of the experience of stammering and can give insight into how to support the individual who stammers. In particular, a well-run self-help group can provide SLTs and SLT students with valuable insights into group facilitation.

A self-help group also provides an interesting environment for gathering research data. Visitors to self-help group meetings frequently include undergraduate and postgraduate researchers, as group members tend to be willing research participants, and the process for ethical approval for research with this population is less rigorous than for research with clinical populations.

The difference between self-help and therapy groups

Self-help groups often bear a close resemblance to therapy groups. However, there are several notable differences.

Access

An important distinction between the two types of groups is that self-help groups tend to be more open and accessible than therapy groups. Unlike a therapy group, self-help group membership is generally open to anyone who stammers, and there does not tend to be a formal referral and assessment process. Similarly, although a member may leave a self-help group for a variety of reasons, in contrast with a therapy group, there is no planned ending to self-help group membership. An individual is very likely to belong to a stammering self-help group for more than five years (Yaruss et al. 2002), and it is not uncommon for members to be actively engaged in a self-help group for decades. An interesting consequence of the accessible nature of self-help groups, especially large ones which attract members from far afield, is that group participants may not all be clients of the local SLT service. Some may be or may have been engaged in therapy with another SLT service; and some may have never participated in therapy and/or have no desire to do so.

Leadership

Another key difference between the two types of groups is that, unlike a therapy group, which is led by a trained therapist, a self-help group is usually self-governing and self-regulated (Lieberman 1990). A successful self-help group emphasises *internal* rather than *external* (i.e. professional) expertise. This raises questions about the SLT's role with regard to a self-help group. This will be discussed in more detail later.

Aims

The aims of self-help groups are broader than the aims of SLT led therapy groups. A main aim in both types of groups would usually be to create a supportive environment which facilitates positive change in members' experiences of stammering, for example, by reducing feelings of isolation and decreasing sensitivity to stammering. Self-help groups' aims often also include raising awareness, challenging negative stereotypes about stammering and promoting stammering charities (e.g. the BSA).

Remit

Because self-help groups are voluntary organisations run by their members rather than by professionals, they tend to have a broader remit than therapy groups. For example, as discussed, as well as directly providing support to group participants, stammering self-help groups are more likely to be actively engaged in raising awareness, challenging negative stereotypes and reducing the social stigma of stammering. A self-help group's remit is also likely to include fundraising and social events.

Process

Self-help and therapy groups function very similarly, in that the interaction between the participants is intrinsically therapeutic. According to Yalom and Leszcz (2005), a self-help group makes extensive use of most of the 'therapeutic factors', i.e. the key elements of group therapy experience which promote therapeutic change. For example, the instillation of hope, universality (i.e. recognising that experiences are shared), cohesiveness (i.e. 'gelling'), catharsis and altruism are all as important in a self-help group as they are in a therapy group. However, the therapeutic factor of interpersonal learning seems to play a less important role in a self-help group than it does in a therapy group (Yalom and Leszcz 2005).

Although the mechanisms of change in both types of groups are very similar, the conditions which promote change may vary. For example, in a therapist-led group, specific interventions with explicit theoretical underpinnings are likely to be used. As such, the sessions will be well structured, especially if the group has a limited lifespan. A self-help group uses a more eclectic approach, drawing on members' experiences, rather than utilising specific therapeutic approaches. As discussed, self-help groups tend to be open and accessible, with no limit to the length of time that a member can attend. Therefore, in a self-help group, there is usually more opportunity for activities to be delivered in a flexible and informal way, with participants continuing to make positive changes over a longer time period.

The SLT's role with a self-help group

It is very important that SLTs engage positively with self-help groups, as they are an invaluable resource. Careful consideration must be given to the SLT's role within a group as, by definition, the running of a self-help group is the responsibility of its members. As Yalom and Leszcz (2005) explain, a self-help group is more successful if 'the expertise resides with its members'. Interestingly, 50 per cent of self-help groups utilise some degree of professional involvement (Yalom and Leszcz 2005). The majority of participants in stammering self-help groups believe that SLTs should be involved in their groups but do not think that they should have a leadership role (Yaruss et al. 2002). Therefore, it is prudent for SLTs to take more of a 'back seat' in self-help groups. Alternative roles for a therapist include:

- Guide (Irwin 2007)

- Coach (Irwin 2007)

- Mentor (Irwin 2007)

- Cautious consultant (Gregory 1997)

- Supporter

- Group member.

The role a therapist adopts can partly depend on logistics. For example, she may only be able to attend meetings infrequently due to competing demands on her time and the priorities of her employing organisation. It is advisable for an SLT to consult with self-help group members about how often, if at all, they would like her to attend meetings and in what capacity. An advantage of the SLT participating in self-help group meetings on an infrequent basis is that this may enable the group to be more autonomous and self-directed. However, if a therapist is helping to launch a new self-help group, it can be beneficial for her to attend meetings more regularly, at least in the initial phase of the group's development.

The therapist's role in a self-help group will also depend on the therapist herself. Significant factors include her experience, confidence, level of expertise and general approach. For example, a therapist who is open and flexible will find it easier to work outside a clinical environment with traditional models of service delivery than a therapist who prefers more structure and predictability.

Four possible roles for the SLT are described in what follows, which, although discussed separately, are not mutually exclusive.

The therapist as an initiator

Whilst the number of self-help groups for adults who stammer is increasing, there are still areas where no groups exist. Although it is advisable for an SLT to play a secondary role in self-help groups, in areas where there are no groups, she may be ideally placed to initiate the process by encouraging clients to establish new groups. Practical suggestions about how this can be achieved are given later in this chapter.

The therapist as a consultant

The therapist who adopts an advisory or consultative role will be responsive to the group's needs, offering information and advice as requested. In this role, the therapist ideally takes an active interest in the group and ensures that she is approachable and available. A therapist may also act as confidante, especially if the group is experiencing difficulties or undergoing change. In this capacity she can help the group resolve issues by facilitating problem-solving activities specifically targeting the area of difficulty.

The therapist as a supporter

The SLT who is a supporter of a self-help group will play a more active role in the group. The level of active support should be determined by the needs of the group and the specific activities in which it is engaged. There are many ways that a therapist can support a self-help group, whilst preserving the group's autonomy. These are discussed in more detail later.

The therapist as a group member

Some self-help groups welcome participation from individuals who have an interest in stammering (e.g. professionals and friends and relatives of people who stammer). In such groups, it is possible for a therapist to take part as an ordinary group member, especially if the group is cohesive and has strong leadership. It can be a very useful learning experience for an inexperienced clinician or a student SLT to simply be part of a group. In other circumstances, where the group is smaller and less cohesive, it may be more difficult for her to be part of the group. Regardless of the exact circumstances, an SLT who attends a self-help group in a professional capacity cannot be a full group member, with the possible exception of an SLT who stammers. Such a therapist may be viewed differently to a therapist who does not stammer, as group members are likely to recognise that they have shared experiences.

The role of an SLT who stammers as (a) therapist or (b) a group member could be problematic for the person/therapist and problematic for the group. It may be potentially challenging for a group to reach a concensus on this situation. As every therapist and every group is different, any issues can be resolved according to the unique circumstances that arise. However, it is advisable for an SLT not to join a self-help group as a member in an area where she is working as an SLT.

The therapist's style of interaction

The manner in which the SLT relates to self-help group members is as important as the role (or roles) that she adopts. Excessive participation by a therapist can transform a meeting into a therapy session (Reeves 2006). Similarly, Yalom and Leszcz (2005) advise against overzealous displays of professional expertise in self-help groups. It is more useful for a therapist to discuss what has been helpful for her clients (while maintaining confidentiality) than to advise group members about what they should do (Manning 2010). When imparting information and advice, the clinician should adopt an informal manner, which reflects the equal status between her and each group member. In our experience, an attitude of mutual respect and an appreciation of our equal status enable the self-help group and the SLT service to function in partnership, working collaboratively to achieve the best possible outcomes for clients and group members.

Self-help groups and therapy: the interface

The following section, which explores the boundary between the self-help group and the SLT service, includes suggestions about how to support the individual who stammers in the following situations: therapy without a self-help group; therapy with a self-help group; and a self-help group without therapy.

Therapy without self-help group

Many SLT clients do not attend self-help groups. This is often because there is not a self-help group in the client's local area. Where a group exists, a client may be unable to attend for practical reasons and/or may simply not be interested or feel motivated to attend. This may especially be the case for a client whose need for peer support is met through group therapy.

When a client does not access a self-help group, some of the benefits of self-help group membership can be achieved in other ways. For example, it is useful for a client who is accessing individual therapy to meet others in the same situation for mutual support and encouragement. This could be in person or via a telecommunications application which specialises in video 'chat' (e.g. Skype); a client receiving therapy via tele-health would benefit from this additional activity. A client, including one who has access to group therapy, can be empowered by feeling that he is part of a larger network of individuals who stammer by joining a national organisation (e.g. BSA) and taking part in events, such as open days and conferences.

Growth in the internet has added a new dimension to self-help for people who stammer. If an SLT client is unable to attend a self-help group, open days or conferences, he can be encouraged to participate in online peer-support activity. This could be through social media, blogs, podcasts (e.g. StutterTalk) where the listener is able to post questions and comments, and websites such as The International Stuttering Association which hosts an online International Stammering Awareness Day (ISAD) conference. Trichon and Raj (2018) provide a fully comprehensive description of useful internet-based self-help activities for people who stammer (see also Linklater chapter 2 on service delivery in this book for a full discussion of this topic).

Therapy with self-help group

Whilst acknowledging that self-help group membership may not appeal to everyone, in our experience, an individual who achieves the best outcomes is one who has actively participated in both therapy and a self-help group. A client may already be attending a self-help group when he decides to begin speech and language therapy. For a client who is not a self-help group member, it is important to consider when he might join a group. If the SLT is unable to provide group therapy, it is very helpful for the client to have the support of a self-help group during the earlier stages of therapy. Conversely, if a client is attending group therapy, it may be more appropriate for him to access a self-help group once he has completed a course of group therapy or been discharged from the speech and language therapy service.

Group member's insight

> Therapy was a revelation. I gained massive insights into voice production, stammering behaviours and how they are reinforced, and different therapeutic approaches. I was also introduced to stammering group work, which I loved. Therapy was life-changing, and it seemed a natural progression to attend a self-help group.

If a client is simultaneously engaged in therapy and a self-help group, it is important for the SLT to be aware of the group's plans and activities. This will allow the clinician to use these to complement work being carried out in therapy. For example, where a client is working on public speaking in therapy, he could use a public speaking challenge carried out in a self-help group meeting to support this work. Where appropriate, a client should take responsibility for sharing relevant information about himself and his therapy with the self-help group. For example, he could be encouraged to share his therapy aims with the group or to request designated group time to role play or practise something that he is finding difficult.

Group member's insight

The self-help group and SLT sessions have worked in tandem. I used to close my eyes so tightly when I stammered that the pressure affected my vision. My world would stay dark for a few seconds after I opened my eyes. I found it really beneficial to work on my 'extras' (eye closure and facial contortions etc.) with my therapist, as it enabled me to just stammer 'naturally'. My therapist suggested that I share my aims with the self-help group. The day that they joked that they would kiss me if I shut my eyes when I stammered has gone down in the group's history as my quietest day ever!

Self-help group without therapy

There is evidence that the majority of self-help group participants receive SLT intervention at some point in their lives (Yaruss et al. 2002). However, as self-help groups tend to be more accessible than SLT services and may be better publicised, a PWS could join a self-help group without having accessed SLT support as an adult. These potential clients, if they meet referral criteria, may access the SLT service, especially if they receive encouragement from other group members. Research suggests that self-help group participation increases members' opinions of SLTs and the desire to access therapy (Yaruss et al. 2002).

It is not always possible for a self-help group member to access therapy. For example, he may not meet referral criteria, or there may not be specialist SLT provision for adults in the area. In these cases, the self-help group plays a vital role in addressing the gap in service provision, especially as therapy groups and well-run self-help groups provide similar benefits to participants. A self-help group member may have informal contact with a clinician who also attends group meetings and events. He may also benefit, indirectly, from the therapy received by other group members, especially those in leadership roles who are willing to share their knowledge and experience with others in the group.

Group member's insight

I felt desperate when I found out that there was no speech therapy in my area. Although I was nervous about joining the self-help group, I was relieved to find out that support was available. I don't know what I would have done without the group. It's been a lifeline. Everyone in the group is so welcoming, friendly, and understanding. They've seen me through my lowest points and given me the help I've needed to face difficult situations like job interviews and work presentations.

Collaborative working

It is important for self-help groups and SLT services to function in partnership, working collaboratively to achieve the best possible outcomes for clients and group members. In the following sections, we consider how therapists can work collaboratively with self-help groups in four key areas: establishing, maintaining, supporting and ending.

Establishing new self-help groups

As we stated earlier in the chapter, in areas where there is no self-help group, a therapist can play a key role in helping to establish one, although it is important to acknowledge that a self-help group could be set up independently of an SLT service.

Leadership

An important first step in establishing a new group is to identify and encourage an appropriate leader (or leaders). For an SLT service and self-help group to collaborate effectively, they should have similar approaches to stammering. It could be advantageous if the group leader is a client or ex-client of the local SLT service or of a service with shared understandings and approaches to stammering.

An ideal group leader is someone who has made significant personal change, perhaps through speech and language therapy and/or attending a self-help group and, as discussed earlier, wishes to 'give something back'. He should have an understanding of the process of change and a willingness to share personal experiences in order to motivate others in the group. Self-help group leadership is a challenging task, requiring commitment, tenacity and enthusiasm. An effective group leader will be knowledgeable, experienced, and confident. However, if a potential leader feels he lacks significant attributes, it can be helpful to share the role with another group member. Co-leadership can also enable a group to be facilitated in a more informal, flexible and non-directive manner, which is important for groups to function well (Liddle 2012). A clinician may adopt a coaching role, for a short period, until the leader feels able to assume full responsibility. Any such arrangement should be time limited. (See **Resource 9.1: Activities for Coaching a Client in Group Leadership** at the end of this chapter.)

It is important to encourage a potential group leader to develop an understanding of self-help group leadership, for example, by:

- Visiting existing self-help groups

- Interacting with existing groups via social media

- Discussing group leadership with leaders of existing groups

- Accessing written guidance regarding the setting up and running of self-help groups, e.g. resources on the BSA and NSA websites.

Sharing roles

In addition to having group members in leadership roles, it can be useful for other group members to share the burden of running the group by having assigned roles (e.g. events co-ordinator, treasurer etc.) or responsibilities (e.g. social media, technical support etc.).

Timing

As it is advantageous to have a core group of members who are committed to the successful running of a self-help group, an ideal time for them to establish a new self-help group is at the end of a course of group therapy. As the therapy sessions draw to a close, the focus can move from therapy to self-help. At the end of this chapter, there are examples of group activities that a therapist could use to facilitate this. (See **Resource 9.2: GroupActivities for Clients who are Establishing a Self-help Group**.)

Aims

As discussed earlier, the aims of a self-help group are an important consideration. It is especially important that these are considered as part of the process of establishing a new self-help group. Although determining the aims of the self-help group is the group's responsibility, it may be useful to have the SLT's input. If a self-help group and an SLT service are to work collaboratively, it is crucial that their aims are compatible. Self-help group aims typically include the following:

- To raise awareness and challenge negative stereotypes of stammering
- To provide a safe environment in which to support people who stammer
- To offer advice and guidance on issues relating to stammering
- To support the local SLT service and direct members to it
- To promote and support a national stammering charity (e.g. BSA).

Practicalities

When establishing a new self-help group, it is vital to give careful consideration to the practicalities which can affect the viability of the group.

Venue

The group venue is an important consideration when establishing a new group. A relaxed, informal, non-clinical environment works well for a self-help group. Rooms in SLT departments are less than ideal in terms of the group functioning autonomously. However, room hire can be expensive, so an SLT service may consider providing accommodation to a self-help group, especially in its early stages, whilst more suitable accommodation is sought. An advantage of meetings taking place in or near the SLT department is that clients may feel more motivated to join the self-help group. In our experience, what has worked best is a non-clinical environment with both a café and meeting rooms, close to the SLT department. The proximity to the department has made it easier to encourage clients to attend the self-help group and self-help group members to attend therapy.

Frequency

Group members need to consider how frequently to hold meetings. There are disadvantages of meeting both frequently and infrequently:

Frequent meetings:

- Difficult for members to find the time to attend
- The cost of room hire can mount up.

Infrequent meetings:

- Difficult for the group to gain momentum
- Difficult for the group to maintain cohesion.

If meetings occur at irregular intervals, members may not get into the routine of attending.

Every group is different, and experimenting with different options can be the best way to find the optimum interval between meetings.

The therapist should be aware of when the group meets and, if possible, try to avoid arranging therapy groups that coincide with self-help group meetings so that participation in both groups is possible if appropriate.

Age limit

Adult self-help group membership requires no upper age limit, but when establishing a new group, it is necessary to set a lower age limit of 18 years. Occasionally, teenaged SLT clients, under the age of 18 years, can attend an adult self-help group, either for a one-off session or more frequently. In these cases, the SLT must ensure that the young client attends each session accompanied by a parent or carer. The group leader should also be briefed so that group members are sensitive to the situation, for example, by adapting their conversational speech, language and humour etc. to ensure it is appropriate. Younger children should not attend self-help group meetings, but they and their parents/carers (and other significant individuals) may be included in some special events, such as awareness-raising activities, open events and exhibitions etc.

Maintaining self-help groups

When working collaboratively with a self-help group, an SLT can play an important role in maintaining its existence. One important factor in this is the size of the group. Recommended group size tends to be between 7 and 15 members (e.g. Conture 2001, Luterman 1991). Therapy groups are often smaller than recommended (Liddle, James and Hardman 2011) and, anecdotally, one of the challenges facing self-help groups is also low numbers. This can be problematic, as larger groups tend to be more cohesive and, consequently, more successful. A thriving self-help group may become so popular that the recommended number of members is exceeded. However, such a group can usually find creative ways of addressing any potential issues which arise as a result of this. For example, they may divide into sub-groups for some discussions and activities.

An SLT can support a small self-help group by encouraging existing members to persevere and by attending special events where additional support is required. A clinician is also well placed to direct clients to a self-help group and, thereby, help to maintain the group by increasing the size of the membership. However, Yaruss et al's (2002) study suggests that only a low proportion of self-help group participants have been encouraged to attend their groups by a therapist.

Joining a self-help group can be daunting for some clients. In such cases, it is helpful if the client can meet the group leader or another member prior to joining the group. This can sometimes be arranged as part of a therapy session. If this is not possible, a client may find it reassuring to see photographs of the group on social media. If the individual finds it difficult to initiate contact with the group, then, provided he consents, his preferred contact details can be passed to the group leader. The leader could then contact the individual to discuss group sessions and answer any queries or concerns the person may have. Alternatively, a client who is anxious about attending the group may find it easier to attend his first meeting accompanied by his SLT for support. Activities to help an anxious client to prepare for self-help group attendance are provided at the end of the chapter. (See ***Resource 9.3: Activitiesfor Preparing Clients for Self-help Group Attendance***.)

Group member's insight

> After months of angst, I finally plucked up the courage to go to a group meeting. To say I was anxious is an understatement; I felt physically sick. I'd planned in advance that I would only go to the first part of the meeting, but it was so brilliant that I decided to stay for the whole evening. I immediately felt at home. Everyone was so friendly and supportive. It was a major turning point in my life.

Supporting self-help groups

An SLT can play a key role in supporting a self-help group. It is important, however, for her to respect the group's autonomy and to ensure that group members are not disempowered by her taking the lead and/or providing too much support. In this regard, it is important to be mindful that the relationship between the self-help group and the SLT service should be a mutually beneficial partnership based on equality. For a self-help group and an SLT service to be mutually supportive, good communication is essential. As well as sharing practical information and challenges with each other, it is vital that they remember to share and celebrate the group members' many successes.

Two important areas where an SLT can provide support to a self-help group are meetings and special events/projects.

Meetings

When working collaboratively with a self-help group, an SLT may become actively involved in group meetings. When considering the level of SLT involvement in meetings, the most important consideration is the needs of the group. When a therapist attends a meeting, the group members may simply require her to participate in their usual activities. Alternatively, she may be invited to lead or co-lead a specific activity, such as a relevant game, quiz, or other activity, which might be fun and/or stimulate a discussion. Activities such as these are very important, especially at the beginning of a meeting, as fun and laughter can enhance participants' enjoyment of group meetings, help them to feel at ease, promote group cohesion and facilitate peer support. If a group is more structured, formal or lacking in spontaneity, this natural process can be inhibited. When a therapist provides such activities, it can be a good opportunity for her to model the use of an informal, non-directive approach to group facilitation. (An example of a quiz which she might use to do this can be found at the end of the chapter. See *Resource 9.4: Activities for a Therapist to Use with a Self-help Group.*)

Other activities that can be provided by an SLT at self-help group meetings include:

• Information sessions
• Workshops to develop skills in specific areas in which members are experiencing difficulty.

Appropriate topics for information sessions include:

• Specific topics which may be of interest to the group e.g. the causes of stammering or voice production etc.
• The local SLT service and how to access it and/or or other SLT services e.g. tele-health
• The latest research findings on stammering.

Appropriate topics for workshops include:

• Telephone skills
• Interview skills
• Conversational skills
• Mindfulness
• Managing difficult conversational partners (Turnbull and Stewart 2010)
• Ordering in a café/restaurant
• Public speaking/presentation skills (an example of an activity that could be used for this can be found at the end of the chapter. See *Resource 9.4: Activities for a Therapist to Use with a Self-help Group*).

Special events and projects

An excellent way for an SLT to become involved with a self-help group is to collaborate in the organisation of special events and/or projects, especially those which require time, effort and creativity to organise. Such activities can take place in addition to the self-help group meeting and include arts projects, media interviews and other awareness-raising activities for ISAD and other occasions, fundraising events, training sessions for colleagues and SLT students, open days and conferences, social events and group trips. It is usually difficult for an SLT to find the time and resources to engage in such activities, especially as they may not be considered central to her clinical role. However, sharing resources and the burden of organisation with a local self-help group can make these activities achievable. In addition, an active self-help group may be able to raise funds or access grants in a way that an SLT service is not able to do. The self-help group will appreciate the support of the SLT department and the involvement of SLT clients and students. As with self-help group meetings, it can be more appropriate for an SLT to adopt a secondary role, enabling self-help group members and clients to take the lead and assert their right to speak out.

Of all of the additional activity undertaken by self-help groups, awareness raising is arguably the most important. It is often the most challenging and the most rewarding, as it provides opportunities for openness and self-disclosure of stammering. The prospect of organising large-scale events (e.g. performances and exhibitions) can be daunting, especially for a smaller self-help group. An SLT can encourage and support a self-help group to embark on achievable, smaller-scale awareness-raising projects. These could coincide with ISAD (October 22), as this can provide a group with impetus as well as the opportunity to coordinate their activities with other organisations' activities. A good example of an achievable awareness-raising activity is Stammering Rocks, found in the Resources section at the end of the chapter.

Activities such as Stammering Rocks are useful because the process generates discussion and can help a participant to become more desensitised to stammering. They are also useful because other self-help and therapy groups can easily become involved in them. Another advantage of such activities is that they do not require the participants to engage in public speaking. However, if a participant wishes to challenge himself more, he could use the activity to provide the focus for a media interview or a presentation (e.g. in the workplace or educational setting).

When a self-help group is larger and more active, it is able to take on more ambitious projects in addition to a wide range of more easily achievable activities. Examples of activities which a self-help group and SLT service could undertake collaboratively are listed in what follows. Although they are listed under separate headings, the categories are not mutually exclusive. For example, a fundraising activity can also be used as an opportunity to raise awareness.

Awareness-raising activities:

• Art exhibitions and launch events (e.g. Art of Communication 2012)

• Media interviews

• Creating YouTube films for ISAD

• Street performances

• Information stands at festivals or community events

• Creating and displaying posters

• Presentations and after-dinner speeches (e.g. for Rotary groups)

• Sharing any of these activities on social media.

Fundraising activities:

- Themed sponsored events (e.g. Talk and Trot around a racecourse)
- Busking
- Cake sales
- Supermarket bag-packs.

Training and education:

- Hosting an evening of self-help group activities for groups of SLT students
- Lectures and presentations for students on SLT training courses
- Training events for SLTs
- Training events for staff in educational establishments
- Training events for other public-service organisations (e.g. reception staff in the NHS (Holmes and Welby 2015, Turner 2012)).

Open days and conferences for people who stammer:

- Attending open days and conferences as participants
- Facilitating workshops at open days and conferences
- Organising and hosting open days and conferences
- Taking part in on-line conferences.

Social events and group trips:

- End-of-year parties
- Meals out
- Bowling
- Barbeques and picnics
- Group trips to see stammering-related films or plays (e.g. *The King's Speech* and *Unspoken* (Rathmell and Stewart 2017)).

Ending self-help groups

Throughout this chapter there are suggestions about how an SLT can contribute to a self-help group's success. However, it is challenging to establish and run a successful self-help group. This may be due to a variety of issues, including:

- Group leadership
- Group dynamics
- Formality of the group sessions
- Lack of group cohesion
- Practical factors (e.g. venue, frequency of meetings etc.)
- Group size (i.e. low numbers of participants).

If a group is experiencing difficulties, a therapist can offer to act as a 'sounding board' for the members and support them in making a decision about the group's future. One option could be to move away from the standard format of meetings and events. For example:

• Form an informal social group and meet up, monthly, for a meal

• Form a monthly walking group.

Although such group formats may not have all the benefits of self-help group meetings, they can be easier to organise and, therefore, more sustainable. For example, there is no requirement to find a suitable meeting room, and the organiser would not need to be a skilled group facilitator.

If, despite concerted efforts, a group does not seem to be viable, it can be a more positive experience for the members if the group ends formally rather than peters out. When a group ends, it is important to acknowledge each participant's contribution and celebrate the group's accomplishments. It can also be helpful to emphasise any positive reasons for the group ending. For example, members may leave the group because they have made good progress and no longer need the group's support.

Conclusion

The growth of the self-help movement has dramatically altered the prospects of people who stammer. This chapter has highlighted some of the benefits that self-help groups bring and has underlined the need for an SLT to view groups as valuable resources for her clients. It is especially important for a clinician to recognise the potential for self-help groups to bring about fundamental changes in participants' experiences of stammering. Although self-help groups can function independently of therapy services, it is preferable for an SLT to work collaboratively with self-help groups in order to contribute to their success and improve outcomes for participants.

Despite the growth in the self-help movement and the indisputable benefits of self-help group membership, it is still only the minority of adults who stammer who participate in self-help groups. Any SLT should therefore work in conjunction with self-help groups and stammering charities, such as the BSA, to promote, develop, and ensure the sustainability of self-help groups.

Activities for coaching a client in group leadership

9.1.1 Facilitating a group discussion

- Ask the client to observe a group therapy session and to notice what strategies the speech and language therapist uses to facilitate a group discussion.

- After the session ask the client to identify and list useful strategies for facilitating a group discussion, based on his observations of the session. These might include suggestions such as:

  - Actively listening

  - Asking open questions

  - Leaving pauses

  - Giving everyone the opportunity to speak

  - Following the group's lead

  - The appropriate use of humour etc.

At the next group therapy session, invite the client to facilitate a group discussion, focussing on using one or more of the above strategies.

After the session, debrief with the client, e.g. asking 'What went well?', 'How did using the strategies help?', 'Is there anything you would do differently?' etc.

© Trudy Stewart (2020). *Stammering Resources for Adults and Teenagers: Integrating New Evidence into Clinical Practice.* **Routledge.**

9.1.2 Developing a flexible approach to leading a group session

Ask the client to write an outline of a plan for a self-help group meeting, including timings for each activity. For example:

Self-help group meeting plan

7.00 p.m.: Welcome and introductions (5 minutes)

7.05 p.m.: Warm-up game (10 minutes)

7.15 p.m.: General discussion on personal experiences of stammering (35 minutes)

7.50 p.m.: Refreshments and informal interaction (20 minutes)

8.10 p.m.: Quiz (30 minutes)

8.40 p.m.: Discussion re plans for future meetings (20 minutes)

9.00 p.m.: Meeting ends

Present the client with a scenario which requires a flexible response. For example, 'The group discussions go very well, with group members sharing personal stories. In particular, a new group member has opened up about a very difficult experience he has recently had at work'.

Client identifies a need for a possible modification to the plan (i.e. more discussion time) and revises the plan to take account of this. For example:

Self-help group meeting plan

7.00 p.m.: Welcome and introductions (5 minutes)

7.05 p.m.: Warm-up game (10 minutes)

7.15 p.m.: General discussion on personal experiences of stammering (65 minutes)

8.20 p.m.: Refreshments and informal interaction (20 minutes)

8.40 p.m.: Discussion re plans for future meetings (20 minutes)

9.00 p.m.: Meeting ends

Summary: Additional 30 minutes allowed for group discussion and quiz omitted.

Group activities for clients who are establishing a self-help group

9.2.1 Group discussion

The following questions can be used as the basis for a group discussion:

• What are the advantages and disadvantages of setting up a self-help group?

• What are the advantages and disadvantages of *not* setting up a self-help group?

9.2.2 Encouraging clients to consider how to run a successful self-help group

Divide the group into three subgroups, giving each a question to consider:

• What *activities* contribute to a successful self-help group?

• What are the *qualities* of a successful self-help group?

• What are the *practicalities* which affect the success of a self-help group?

Ask the group to reconvene and share their ideas with each other, with input from the speech and language therapist, if required.

© Trudy Stewart (2020). *Stammering Resources for Adults and Teenagers: Integrating New Evidence into Clinical Practice.* **Routledge.**

Activities for preparing clients for self-help group attendance

9.3.1 Identifying an underlying concern

This activity helps a client who is anxious about self-help group attendance to identify and articulate factors which underlie his concerns.

Ask the client to complete the following sentence by filling in the blanks:

• When I think about the self-help group, I feel concerned about _____ because _____.

Possible examples of completed sentences include:

When I think about the self-help group, I feel concerned about meeting new people because I'm worried about what they will think of me

When I think about the self-help group, I feel concerned about arriving at the group because I don't know what to expect

When I think about the self-help group, I feel concerned about being in a group situation because I find it difficult to speak in front of other people

• When I think about the self-help group, I feel comfortable about _____ because _____.

Possible examples of completed sentences include:

When I think about the self-help group, I feel comfortable about meeting new people because they are in the same situation as me

When I think about the self-help group, I feel comfortable about speaking in front of other people because I know that they will give me time to talk

The completed sentences can be used as a basis for a discussion with the client.

9.3.2 Educating the client

A client is less likely to feel anxious about self-help group attendance if he feels well informed about the self-help group.

• Discuss the benefits of self-help group participation and give the client specific information about the local self-help group

• Encourage the client to find out more about the group by asking a group member/leader questions about it or by using online resources such as the group's social media or the BSA website

© Trudy Stewart (2020). *Stammering Resources for Adults and Teenagers: Integrating New Evidence into Clinical Practice.* **Routledge.**

9.3.3 Using a client's support systems

- Encourage the client to think about *who* could support him attending a group, e.g. partner, friend, speech and language therapist

- Encourage the client to think about *how* someone might support his attendance, e.g. encouraging him to attend, attending a group meeting with him or meeting him for coffee after a meeting.

9.3.4 Taking small steps

If a client is very anxious about attending a group, it can be helpful to take small steps towards the goal of full participation in the group.

Ask the client to commit to one of the following (or an alternative suggestion of his own):

- Meeting the group leader prior to attending the group

- Attending part of the meeting, e.g. the first 10 minutes

- Attending a self-help group awareness-raising event as an observer rather than as a group member.

Encourage the client to think about what steps he would take after achieving any of these things. A client may find that once he has taken the initial step of meeting the group members, he will feel more comfortable about participating fully in the group's activities.

Activities for a therapist to use with a self-help group

9.4.1 True/false quiz

Divide the group members into two teams. Give each team a set of eight cards, with a different statement about stammering printed on each card:

- The average age that children start stammering is 3½ years

- Stammering is more common in women than in men

- Stammering can run in families

- 1% of the world's population stammers

- People stammer more when they are tired

- When someone is stammering, it is helpful to remind them to speak slowly

- People who stammer can be excellent communicators

- People who stammer cannot become speech and language therapists.

Ask the teams to discuss the statements and sort the cards into piles depending on whether they believe the statements to be true or false. When the teams have completed the task, ask them to reconvene and share their responses.

9.4.2 Presentation skills: gaining confidence through table-top talks

Place a random assortment of readily available items on a table. Invite group members to take turns to select an item and talk to the group about it for one minute. The group members can present information that is factually correct or tell a fictional story about the chosen item. After each presentation, group members give feedback to the speaker about what they valued about the presentation. The focus of the feedback should be about the speaker's communication skills rather than the level of fluency.

© Trudy Stewart (2020). *Stammering Resources for Adults and Teenagers: Integrating New Evidence into Clinical Practice.* Routledge.

9.4.3 Awareness-raising activity

Stammering Rocks

Group members use the question 'What would you like the world to know about stammering?' as the basis for a discussion. They then use their ideas to generate informative, thought-provoking, assertive or humorous messages about stammering. Examples of messages include:

• Proud to be d-d-different

• Listen

• What we say is worth repeating.

• We block! We rock!

Group members decorate the upper surfaces of small rocks with the messages; on the underside of the rocks, they write brief information about social media and websites linked to the activity (e.g. #StammeringRocks or Facebook Stammering Rocks).

After the rocks have been decorated, group members hide them or place them in prominent positions around the neighbourhood or elsewhere, such as at tourist attractions. Members of the public find the rocks and take photographs, which they upload to the internet, using the information provided on the underside of the rock.

References

Adamsen, L. and Rasmussen, J.M. (2001). Sociological perspectives on self-help groups: Reflections on conceptualization and social processes. *Journal of Advanced Nursing*, 35(6), 909–917. doi: 10.1046/j.1365–2648.2001.01928.x

Art of Communication [Exhibition] (2012). Gallery at The Point, Doncaster; October 2012-January 2013.

Bloodstein, O. and Bernstein Ratner, N. (2008). *A Handbook on Stuttering* (6th Edition). New York: Delmar.

Boyle, M.P. (2013). Psychological characteristics and perceptions of stuttering of adults who stutter with and without support group experience. *Journal of Fluency Disorders*, 38(4), 368–381.

Boyle, M.P., Beita-Ell, C., Milewski, K.M. and Fearon, A.N. (2018). Self-esteem, self-efficacy, and social support as predictors of communicative participation in adults who stutter. *Journal of Speech, Language, and Hearing Research*, 61(8), 1893–1906.

Cheung, S.-K. and Sun, S.Y.K. (2001). Helping processes in a mutual aid organization for persons with emotional disturbance. *International Journal of Group Psychotherapy*, 51(3), 295–308.

Conture, E.G. (2001). *Stuttering: Its Nature, Diagnosis and Treatment*. Boston: Allyn & Bacon.

Gregory, H. (1997). The speech-language pathologist's role in stuttering self-help groups. *Seminars in Speech and Language*, 18(4), 401–410.

Holmes, J.L. and Welby, J. (2015). A qualitative evaluation of participants' experience of stammering awareness training. *Proceedings of 10th Oxford Dysfluency Conference 17–20th July 2014*, 193, 306–307. https://doi.org/10.1016/j.sbspro.2015.03.284

Irwin, M. (2007). SLPs and self-help groups-why a close relationship is vital. *Perspectives on Fluency and Fluency Disorders*, 17(1), 13–15.

Joyce, A.S., Piper, W.E. and Ogrodniczuk, J.S. (2007). Therapeutic alliance and cohesion variables as predictors of outcome in short-term group psychotherapy. *International Journal of Group Psychotherapy*, 57(3), 269–296.

Katz, A.H. and Bender, E.I. (1976). Self-help groups in western society: History and prospects. *Journal of Applied Behavioral Science*, 12(3), 265–282.

Kessler, R.C., Mickelson, K.D. and Zhao, S. (1997). Patterns and correlates of self-help group membership in the United States. *Social Policy*, 27(3), 27–46.

Klassen, T.R. and Kroll, R.M. (2005). Opinions on stuttering and its treatment: A follow-up survey and cross-cultural comparison. *Journal of Speech-Language Pathology & Audiology*, 29(2), 73–82.

Krauss-Lehrman, T. and Reeves, L. (1989). Attitudes toward speech-language pathology and support groups: Results of a survey of members of the National Stuttering Project. *Texas Journal of Audiology and Speech Pathology*, 15(1), 22–25.

Liddle, H. (2012). *An Exploration of Group Therapy for School-aged Children Who Stammer: Practice and Process* (Unpublished doctoral thesis). Leeds Metropolitan University, UK.

Liddle, H., James, S. and Hardman, M. (2011). Group therapy for school-aged children who stutter: A survey of current practices. *Journal of Fluency Disorders*, 36(4), 274–279.

Lieberman, M. (1990). A group therapist perspective on self-help groups. *International Journal of Group Psychotherapy*, 40, 251–278.

Luterman, D. (1991). *Counselling the Communicatively Disordered and Their Families* (2nd Edition). Austin, TX: Pro-Ed.

Manning, W.H. (2010). *Clinical Decision Making in Fluency Disorders* (3rd Edition). New York: Delmar.

Ogrodniczuk, J.S. and Piper, W.E. (2003). The effect of group climate on outcome in two forms of short-term group therapy. *Group Dynamics: Theory, Research, and Practice*, 7(1), 64–76.

Plexico, L., Manning, W.H. and Dilollo, A. (2005). A phenomenological understanding of successful stuttering management. *Journal of Fluency Disorders*, 30(1), 1–22.

Ramig, P.R. (1993). The impact of self-help groups on persons who stutter: A call for research. *Journal of Fluency Disorders*, 18(2–3), 351–361.

Rathmell, N. and Stewart, T. (2017). *Unspoken: A Short Play about a Man and His Stammer*. UK: Southernwood Press.

Reeves, L. (2006). The role of self-help/mutual aid in addressing the needs of individuals who stutter. In N.B. Ratner and J.A. Tetnowski (eds.), *Current Issues in Stuttering Research and Practice* (pp. 255–278). Mahwah, NJ: Erlbaum.

Trichon, M. (2010). *Self-help Conferences for People Who Stutter: An Interpretive Phenomenological Analysis* (Doctoral dissertation). Retrieved from ProQuest Dissertations and Theses Open – http://pqdtopen.proquest.com (#3446333).

Trichon, M. and Raj, E.X. (2018). Peer support for people who stutter: History, benefits, and accessibility. In B.J. Amster and E.R. Klein (eds.), *More than Fluency*. San Diego: Plural.

Trichon, M., Tetnowski, J. and Rentschler, G. (2007). *Perspectives of Participants of Self-help Groups for People Who Stutter*. Paper presented at the Fifth World Congress on Fluency Disorders, Dublin.

Turnbull, J. and Stewart, T. (2010). *Dysfluency Resource Book* (2nd Edition). London: Routledge.

Turner, M. (2012). NHS reception staff training: A personal reflection. *Getting the Word Out*. Stammering Support Centre magazine. November 2012.

Yalom, I.D. and Leszcz, M. (2005). *The Theory and Practice of Group Psychotherapy* (5th Edition). New York: Basic Books.

Yaruss, S., Quesal, R.W., Reeves, L., Molt, L.F., Kluetz, B. and Caruso, A.J. (2002). Speech treatment and support group experiences of people who participate in the National Stuttering Association. *Journal of Fluency Disorders*, 27(2), 115–134.

Index

Note: Page numbers in *italics* indicate a figure and page numbers in **bold** indicate a table on the corresponding page.